The Princess Bride
and Philosophy

Popular Culture and Philosophy® Series Editor: George A. Reisch

For full details of all Popular Culture and Philosophy® books, visit www.opencourtbooks.com.

Popular Culture and Philosophy®

The Princess Bride and Philosophy

Inconceivable!

Edited by

RICHARD GREENE AND
RACHEL ROBISON-GREENE

OPEN COURT
Chicago, Illinois

Volume 98 in the series, Popular Culture and Philosophy®, edited by George A. Reisch

To find out more about Open Court books, call toll-free 1-800-815-2280, or visit our website at www.opencourtbooks.com.

Open Court Publishing Company is a division of Carus Publishing Company, dba Cricket Media.

Copyright © 2016 by Carus Publishing Company, dba Cricket Media

First printing 2016

Printed and bound in the United States of America.

ISBN: 978-0-8126-9914-2

Library of Congress Control Number: 2015947718

For Henry

Contents

Thanks

Working on this project has been a pleasure, in no small part because of the many fine folks who have assisted us along the way. In particular a debt of gratitude is owed to David Ramsay Steele and George Reisch at Open Court, S. Morgenstern (of course!), the contributors to this volume, and our respective academic departments at UMass Amherst and Weber State University. Finally, we'd like to thank those family members, students, friends, and colleagues with whom we've had fruitful and rewarding conversations on various aspects of all things *Princess Bride* as it relates to philosophical themes.

Hello. My Name Is Inigo Montoya. You Bought This Book. Prepare to Enjoy!

Grandpa, what kind of book is this? Is this going to be one of those kissing books?

No! This is going to be a philosophy book. It's a very special book with tales of the philosophers my grandfather read to me. Now pay attention! Here's what it says:

We first came across this collection of essays on *The Princess Bride* whilst traveling a road on the westernmost banks of Florin. A man sailing from Guilder, claiming to be both the sixteenth Dread Pirate Roberts and a direct descendant of Simon Morgenstern, recounted tales of a Man in Black, a Giant, a Master Swordsman, an Evil Sicilian, a Princess, a Prince, a Miracle Worker, and a man with Six Fingers on one hand.

He also told us of a group of scholars who knew these tales of true love and high adventure, and were also well versed in philosophy. We listened for several days to stories about how the adventures of the Princess and the Man in Black and the Master Swordsman, and the Six-Fingered Man can teach us great philosophical lessons in logic, metaphysics, ethics, philosophy of language, political philosophy and many other branches of occult learning. He said that it was all "inconceivable!" He kept using that word. I do not think it means what he thinks it means. He also said that Plato, Aristotle, and Socrates were morons, but the philosophers weren't buying it.

Not everything this Mr. Morgenstern reported was good or interesting, but much of it was. So we've thrown out the bad bits and here, for the first time, we endeavor to repeat the good parts of his tales to you.

Would you like me to read on?

As you wish!

I

Deceptive Words

I do not think it means what you think it means.

1
True Love and False Fronts

DON FALLIS

Most people think that *The Princess Bride* is about *true love*. The deep and abiding love that Westley and Buttercup share is what ultimately allows them to live happily ever after. It is what convinces the Dread Pirate Roberts, who (usually) takes no prisoners, to spare Westley's life. According to the old hag in Buttercup's nightmare, true love is how the two of them survive the Fire Swamp. And it is what convinces Miracle Max, despite his retirement, to bring Westley back from being (mostly) dead.

Admittedly, true love is a very important topic. As Miracle Max explains, "true love is the greatest thing in the world. Except for a nice MLT, a mutton, lettuce and tomato sandwich, where the mutton is nice and lean and the tomato is ripe." But it's not what *The Princess Bride* is really about. The movie is about lying and duplicity. The most obvious example is when the Dread Pirate Roberts and Vizzini the Sicilian compete to see who can outwit the other. While he is focused on trying to fool and distract the pirate, Vizzini fails to recognize that Roberts has rigged the game by putting poison in both goblets. But deception is actually woven throughout the entire movie.

People in Masks Can't Be Trusted

The whole plot is driven by Prince Humperdinck's attempt to start a war with Guilder by framing that country's rulers for kidnapping and murdering Princess Buttercup, his bride-to-be.

Humperdinck hires Vizzini to carry out this task. After kidnapping her, Vizzini places some "fabric from the uniform of an Army Officer of Guilder" under the saddle of her abandoned horse to make it look like it's the Guilderians who have abducted her. He intends to complete the frame by leaving "her body dead on the frontier of Guilder." After Vizzini himself unexpectedly dies of iocane poisoning, Humperdinck has to modify the plan. But actually, "it's going to be so much more moving when I strangle her on our wedding night. Once Guilder is blamed, the nation will be truly outraged. They'll demand we go to war."

Then there is the Dread Pirate Roberts. As Humperdinck tells Buttercup, "Pirates are not known to be men of their word." But the deceptiveness of the Dread Pirate Roberts goes well beyond the piratical norm. The Dread Pirate Roberts is not even a real person (anymore). It's only a role that several pirates (most recently, Westley) have played over the years. (The original Dread Pirate Roberts has been retired for years and is "living like a king in Patagonia.") At intervals, the current Dread Pirate Roberts identifies a replacement. The two of them then proceed to fool the new crew of the *Revenge* and the rest of the world into thinking that this replacement is the *real* Dread Pirate Roberts. After all, "no one would surrender to the Dread Pirate *Westley*."

And it's not just the bad guys in *The Princess Bride* who engage in such trickery. Our heroes have to use several bluffs and ruses in order to rescue Buttercup from the castle. Fezzik puts on a burning "holocaust cloak" and pretends to be the murderous Dread Pirate Roberts in order to frighten away the sixty men guarding the gate. While pretending that he is simply lying comfortably on the bed, Westley tricks Humperdinck into throwing down his sword. Humperdinck does think that Westley might be bluffing, but he is too cowardly to take the chance. ("I might be bluffing—it's conceivable, you miserable vomitous mass, that I'm only lying here because I lack the strength to stand—then again, perhaps I have the strength after all.")

In fact, even the storybook itself (as read by the grandfather) is deceptive. At various points, it gives a false impression about what is going on, such as that Humperdinck has married Buttercup or that Count Rugen has killed Westley.

We Are Men of Action—Lies Do Not Become Us

Bad guys like Vizzini and Humperdinck often do great harm with their deceits. But even when the good guys engage in deception, there's a significant cost (and not just to the bad guys). In a world full of deceivers, people have to go around worrying about potentially being deceived. And it becomes very difficult for us to work together to get things done if we can't trust each other. As Ralph Waldo Emerson (1803–1882) noted in his *Essays*, "every violation of truth is not only a sort of suicide in the liar, but is a stab at the health of human society."

Here's just one example. When Inigo is waiting for the Dread Pirate Roberts to climb to the top of the Cliffs of Insanity, he offers to speed things up by pulling Roberts up with a rope. Although it would certainly be in the pirate's interest to be able to avoid the arduous and dangerous climb to the top, he just can't trust that Inigo will actually pull him up. Since Inigo is clearly planning to kill Roberts in a duel when he gets to the top anyway, he might simply release the rope and send Roberts plummeting to his death. So, even though Inigo promises that he will not kill Roberts until he reaches the top and gives his "word as a Spaniard," Roberts has to keep climbing. ("I've known too many Spaniards.") It is only when Inigo solemnly says, "I swear on the soul of my father, Domingo Montoya, you will reach the top alive" that Roberts finally decides to trust him.

Adversarial Epistemology in Storybook Form

Like any good children's story, *The Princess Bride* uses adventure and romance to teach us about life. In particular, we can learn from this story how to navigate a world full of *epistemic* adversaries like Humperdinck, Vizzini, and the Dread Pirate Roberts.

Epistemology is the study of what knowledge is and how we can acquire it. Toward this end, epistemologists have thought a lot about the various *threats* to knowledge. In this regard though, most epistemologists focus on how we may be misled *inadvertently* by perceptual and cognitive illusions. In other words, they worry about things like the Lightening Sand in the Fire Swamp that appears to be solid ground. However, a few prominent epistemologists (including Descartes, Kant, and Hume) have investigated how we may be misled *intentionally* and what we can do about it.

Malicious Demons of Unusual Size

The most notable example of Adversarial Epistemology in the history of philosophy comes in René Descartes's seventeenth-century *Meditations on First Philosophy*. Descartes wanted to see if there was anything that he could know for certain. He concluded that, unfortunately, most of his beliefs were open to doubt. For instance, Descartes realized that he might only be dreaming "that I am here in my dressing-gown, sitting by the fire—when in fact I am lying undressed in bed!" But in addition, there could even be "some malicious demon of the utmost power and cunning who has employed all his energies in order to deceive me." It's possible that "the sky, the air, the earth, colors, shapes, sounds and all external things are merely the delusions of dreams which the demon has devised to ensnare my judgment."

This is the kind of thing that epistemic adversaries always try to do. They try to make the world look some way that it is not. For instance, Vizzini and Humperdinck fabricate evidence in order to make it appear that Guilder has abducted and killed Buttercup.

Nevertheless, Vizzini would certainly say that the existence of Descartes's malicious demon is "Inconceivable!" And while it actually is conceivable ("You keep using that word—I do not think it means what you think it means."), it *is* exceedingly unlikely. It's a crazy idea. Not even Descartes thought that there really was a malicious demon using "all his energies in order to deceive me." He was just using this imaginative exercise to test the certainty of what he believed.

Now, *The Matrix* does depict a science-fiction scenario that's pretty close to what Descartes had in mind. But that is not the movie that we are concerned with here. Admittedly, *The Princess Bride* is a fantasy. In addition to princes and princesses, there are giants, and pirates, and Shrieking Eels, and Rodents of Unusual Size. But there isn't really anything that you couldn't find in the real world if you looked hard enough. Fezzik is just an exceptionally big guy, and there is a species of guinea pig from South America that typically weighs well over a hundred pounds.

In any event, Descartes's solution to the problem of the malicious demon will not help us deal with epistemic adversaries in the real world. Descartes famously identified one fact (that he himself exists) that not even the demon could deceive him about. (He cannot doubt his own existence because he must exist in order to do all of this doubting.) But in order to secure his knowledge of any other facts, he had to argue that there is an all-powerful and benevolent being who is concerned that we not be misled. As Descartes put it, "since God does not wish to deceive me, he surely did not give me the kind of faculty which would ever enable me to go wrong while using it correctly." But even if his arguments for the existence of (a benevolent rather than a deceitful) God are correct, they only rule out the possibility of an *all-powerful* epistemic adversary such as Descartes's malicious demon. They don't rule out the possibility of more mundane epistemic adversaries such as Vizzini and Humperdinck.

I Want You to Be Totally Honest with Me

We learn a lot about the world from what other people tell us. As David Hume (1711–1776) put it, "there is no species of reasoning more common, more useful, and even necessary to human life, than that which is derived from the testimony of men, and the reports of eye-witnesses and spectators." But epistemic adversaries such as Vizzini and Humperdinck are quite willing to lie whenever it's to their advantage. Thus, *epistemologists of testimony*, who study how we can acquire knowledge from what other people say, have to worry about this possibility.

Immanuel Kant (1724–1804) is best known for his work in metaphysics and in ethics. But in his *Foundations of the Metaphysics of Morals*, Kant actually did some Adversarial Epistemology of testimony. On the way to explaining why it's wrong to lie, he famously argued that it is not possible for everyone to lie whenever it is to her advantage. According to Kant, if everyone did that, we would not trust what anybody said and there would be no point in anybody lying. Thus, it is not possible for *everyone* to be an epistemic adversary.

Unfortunately though, this bit of Adversarial Epistemology does not help us very much. As with Descartes's solution to the problem of the malicious demon, Kant's argument only rules out a very extreme scenario that we just don't confront in *The Princess Bride* or in real life. Although there are certainly a lot of liars in *The Princess Bride*, not *everyone* is an epistemic adversary who lies whenever it is to their advantage. It's not as if the movie takes place in Australia, which as Vizzini reminds us, *is* "entirely peopled by criminals."

Moreover, it doesn't even look as if Kant's argument is correct. As philosopher Derek Parfit points out in his *On What Matters*, even if everyone lies whenever it is to their advantage, it will sometimes be most advantageous for people to simply tell the truth. Indeed, Humperdinck is often quite accurate in his pronouncements, as when he tells Rugen at the top of the Cliffs of Insanity, "there was a mighty duel—it ranged all over. They were both masters." But if people sometimes tell the truth, we can't be sure that they are lying on any given occasion. So, they can still potentially deceive us with a lie. Thus, contrary to Kant's claim, even if the world were full of epistemic adversaries, there would still be a point to their lying to us.

Of Miracle Max

In the chapter "Of Miracles" in his *An Enquiry Concerning Human Understanding*, Hume also did some Adversarial Epistemology. According to Hume, "when any one tells me, that he saw a dead man restored to life, I immediately consider with myself, whether it be more probable, that this person should either deceive or be deceived, or that the fact, which he relates, should really have happened." With this, Hume certainly leads us to ask the right sort of question for our purposes here. For instance, if Humperdinck says that Guilder has kidnapped his fiancée, I should "consider with myself, whether it be more probable, that this person should either deceive or be deceived" or that Guilder really has kidnapped his fiancée.

When it comes to reports of miracles, Hume quite reasonably recommends that we not believe such extremely implausible claims because deception is more likely than a violation of well-established laws of nature. For instance, despite his name, we should not believe that Miracle Max raised Westley from the dead with a chocolate-covered miracle pill. The pill does revive Westley. But Westley is "only mostly dead. There's a big difference between mostly dead and all dead . . . mostly dead is slightly alive." Max even admits that he can't actually raise someone from the dead. ("With all dead, there's usually only one thing that you can do . . . Go through his clothes and look for loose change.")

Unfortunately though, just as Descartes's solution to the problem of the malicious demon does not provide much assistance in dealing with real-life epistemic adversaries, Hume's suggestion for how to deal with reports of miracles does not help us much either. The statements made by the epistemic adversaries in *The Princess Bride* are typically quite plausible. No one ever claims that anything truly miraculous occurs (with the possible exception of true love, of course). For instance, it would not violate any laws of nature for *Guilderians* to have kidnapped Buttercup.

You Were Clever Enough to Discover What That Looks Like

Even so, Hume did give some additional suggestions for evaluating testimony that are applicable to more than just reports of miracles. In particular, he proposed that

> we entertain a suspicion concerning any matter of fact, when the witnesses contradict each other; when they are but few, or of a doubtful character; when they have an interest in what they affirm; when they deliver their testimony with hesitation, or on the contrary, with too violent asseverations.

The most obvious suggestion here for detecting deception is that we pay attention to how someone delivers her testimony. Is there a quiver in her voice? Does her heart rate go up? Is she sweating? Does she avoid eye contact? But even though these are the sorts of things that come to mind when we think about *lie detection*, they are not very helpful when it comes to identifying epistemic adversaries in *The Princess Bride*. With the exception of Inigo, who is a "rotten liar" as Max points out, the epistemic adversaries in *The Princess Bride* deliver their lies with confidence. Even in the real world, how someone delivers her testimony is not a very reliable indication of deception. Indeed, as we're told in a 2002 article by Park et al., it's not how people usually catch liars.

These days, unfortunately, we also think about torturing people in order to get them to reveal the truth. In addition to being morally repugnant, these techniques are not particularly effective at eliciting reliable information. The victims of these techniques often just say what they think that the torturer wants to hear. There is one potential exception to this rule, however. As Rugen tries to do when he hooks Westley up to "The Machine," it may be possible to get people to be honest about how much pain the torture is causing.

A more helpful suggestion from Hume is that we consider whether witnesses "have an interest in what they affirm." Miracle Max's wife Valerie uses this technique of paying attention to potential bias in order to catch Max in a lie.

After Max pumps his lungs full of air and asks him, "What's so important? What you got here that's worth living for?," Westley softly replies, "true love." But Max tells everyone, "he distinctly said 'to blave.' And, as we all know, 'to blave' means 'to bluff.' So you're probably playing cards, and he cheated." Valerie immediately calls him out as a liar, however. How does she know? For one thing, she heard for herself what Westley really said. But how does she know that Max is lying and is not just mistaken? She knows that Max has a motive to lie. ("He's afraid. Ever since Prince Humperdinck fired him, his confidence is shattered.") More precisely, she knows that Max has an interest in *not* affirming that Westley has a good reason to be brought back to life.

Another good strategy that Hume recommends is that we consider whether "the witnesses contradict each other." The basic idea here is that we can identify liars by looking for *inconsistencies*. As Sherlock Holmes once put it, "we must look for consistency; where there is a want of it we must suspect deception." *The Princess Bride* actually provides several examples of people using this technique.

When Westley and Buttercup emerge from the Fire Swamp and are surrounded, Buttercup agrees to surrender in exchange for Humperdinck's promise to return Westley to his ship and release him. Then when Buttercup decides that she must kill herself rather than marry the Prince, Humperdinck promises to send his "four fastest ships" after Westley to see if he still wants her. But then, just before the wedding, Humperdinck says, "tonight we marry. Tomorrow morning, your men will escort us to Florin Channel where every ship in my armada waits to accompany us on our honeymoon." Of course, it would not be possible for *every* ship in the Prince's armada to accompany them if he had actually sent his four fastest ships after Westley as he had promised to do. As a result of this inconsistency, Buttercup finally realizes that Humperdinck is not being honest with her. ("You never sent ships. Don't bother lying.") In a similar vein, the grandson catches most of the book's deceptions (and gets quite upset) because things don't fit with what he knows about what happens in storybooks. ("You read that wrong. She doesn't marry Humperdinck, she marries Westley.")

Of course, we do have to be very careful about how we apply this principle of deception detection. True love is almost lost when Westley mistakenly accuses Buttercup of deceit because it doesn't make sense to him why she would agree to marry the Prince. ("Where I come from, there are penalties when a woman lies.") Also, even if someone's story *is* consistent, he still could be trying to deceive you. Malicious demons and Sicilians both strive for consistency.

Final Fade Out

Fezzik gives Inigo some good advice when he says, "People in masks cannot be trusted." However, his advice does not go nearly far enough. In *The Princess Bride*, and in real life, epistemic adversaries do not always wear masks, at least physical ones. How do we know when we're dealing with one of these more subtle deceivers? Fortunately, *The Princess Bride* provides an answer by teaching us many of the important lessons from David Hume's work on *Adversarial Epistemology*.[1]

[1] I would like to thank Tony Doyle, James Mahon, Kay Mathiesen, and Dan Zelinski for extremely helpful feedback. This chapter was written while I was a visiting fellow at the Tanner Humanities Center at the University of Utah.

2
Why Men of Action Don't Lie

James Edwin Mahon

The Princess Bride is about romantic love. But it's also about non-romantic love. In fact it's just as much about what the Greek philosopher Aristotle calls *philia*, or *brotherly love*, as it is about *eros*, or romantic or intimate love.

Philia does not mean just bromance. *Philia* includes the love that a doting grandfather has for his recovering sick grandson, and the love that a devoted son has for his murdered father. And *philia* is not just about male bonding, either. It includes the love that a princess has for her rescuers, who were originally her kidnappers (inconceivable!), as well as the love that she has for her kind father-in-law-to-be.

Nevertheless, *The Princess Bride* says at least two things that apply specifically to relationships between men. The first is that deception does not occur between men when there is *philia*, or brotherly love, between them. Male *friends* do not lie to male *friends*. (Bros before everyone else.) The second is that men's deception of other men is dishonorable and cowardly. That is, *real* men don't lie to other *real* men, whether they are friends or enemies. To quote Westley—a.k.a. the Man in Black, a.k.a. the Dread Pirate Roberts—after Prince Humperdinck has promised Princess Buttercup that he will spare Westley and return him safely to his ship if she will agree to marry him, and Count Rugen says to Westley that they must get him to his ship: "We are men of action. Lies do not become us."

The Circle of Friends

Although *The Princess Bride* is obviously about one relationship—the romantic relationship between Westley and Buttercup—it's less obviously about several other relationships. These include the relationship between the unnamed grandfather, played by Peter Falk, and the unnamed grandson, played by Fred Savage; Inigo Montoya's relationship to his murdered father; and Buttercup's relationship to her future father-in-law, the King. By far the most important other relationship, however, is the friendship between Inigo and Fezzik.

Vizzini has hired Inigo and Fezzik for the job of kidnapping Princess Buttercup of Florin and making it look like it is the work of the neighboring kingdom, Guilder. But Inigo and Fezzik are more than merely co-workers. They are friends. They are unwaveringly loyal to each other, and they support each other. As Aristotle would say, they have *philia*—love, of a brotherly kind—for each other.

Vizzini constantly mocks and verbally abuses them. When Fezzik discovers that Vizzini—who, it is later revealed, was actually hired by Prince Humperdinck to kidnap his own bride-to-be—plans for them to kill Buttercup and leave her body on the border between the two kingdoms, he says "I just don't think it's right, killing an innocent girl." Vizzini replies "Am I going mad, or did the word "THINK" escape your lips? YOU WERE NOT HIRED FOR YOUR BRAINS, YOU HIPPOPOTAMIC LAND MASS!" (emphasis in the original). When Inigo says he agrees with Fezzik, Vizzini replies, "OH! THE SOT HAS SPOKEN," and adds, "REMEMBER THIS, NEVER FORGET THIS: WHEN I FOUND YOU, YOU WERE SO SLOBBERING DRUNK, YOU COULDN'T BUY BRANDY!" Afterwards, Inigo makes a point of cheering Fezzik up, by playing a rhyming game with him, and by telling Fezzik that "You have a great gift for rhyme"—an intellectual gift rather than a physical gift.

It's not an exaggeration to say that the friendship between Inigo and Fezzik forms the emotional core of the movie. The real breakthrough in the plot occurs when they decide to include Westley in this friendship, after Westley has defeated both of them. This happens after Fezzik rescues a depressed and drunken Inigo from the Brute Squad, who are clearing out the Thieves' Forest (Fezzik is on the Brute Squad, but defects to help Inigo instead), and nurses him back to health, telling him about the death of Vizzini and the existence of Count Rugen, the man who murdered Inigo's father. Vengeance finally within his grasp, Inigo realizes that he needs Westley's help in order to strategize storming the castle and killing Count Rugen: "I need the man in black. . . . Look, he bested you with strength, your greatness. He bested me with steel. He must have out-thought Vizzini. And a man who can do that can plan my castle onslaught any day."

The difference is that Westley will help Inigo and Fezzik as their *friend*, and not as their abusive boss. Their tight circle of friends will be expanded to include Westley, the man who defeated both of them, but who also treated them with respect. Before they commenced their great sword fight, Inigo told Westley "You seem a decent fellow. I hate to kill you." To which Westley replied, "You seem a decent fellow. I hate to die." After he has defeated him but spared his life, knocking him out cold, Westley says over the unconscious Inigo, "Please understand that I hold you in the highest respect."

Fezzik and Inigo, helped by the spirit of Inigo's dead father, rescue a "mostly dead" Westley from The Machine in the Pit of Despair. Pooling their little money, they bring Westley to Miracle Max and buy a miracle pill to revive him. When he revives, he thinks that Inigo and Fezzik are out to kill him. But as soon as Westley realizes that they have brought him *back* from death, he asks, "Are we enemies?" From the response of Inigo he deduces that, to the contrary, they are now working together. They are no longer enemies.

In storming the castle, rescuing Buttercup, and avenging Inigo's father, the three of them become friends. Indeed, afterwards Westley asks Inigo if he would like to take over his job as the Dread Pirate Roberts, commanding the pirate ship named— appropriately enough—*Revenge*. At the end of the movie, the four of them—Inigo, Fezzik, Westley, and Buttercup—ride off together, firm friends for life. The feeling between the 'family' of Inigo, Fezzik, Westley, and Buttercup is a form of *philia*.

Friends Don't Lie to Friends

We know that *The Princess Bride* "is about lying and duplicity" (see the previous chapter). But the lies and deceptions of the movie occur between people who lack *philia* for one another. There is no deception between people after they develop *philia* for each other—with one important exception, which we'll look at soon.

Prince Humperdinck and Count Rugen (or Tyrone, as he calls him) have something like a relationship of friendship with each other. Although they deceive and lie to others, they do not lie to *each other*. When the two of them see Buttercup looking miserable, after she has agreed to stay and marry Humperdinck if he will spare Westley's life and return him to his ship, Humperdinck says to Count Rugen, "She's been like that ever since the Fire Swamp. It's my father's failing health that's upsetting her." This is false, but he doesn't mean for Count Rugen to believe what he says. Count Rugen replies, "Of course." But he doesn't mean for Humperdinck to believe what he says, either. These are knowing falsehoods. Count Rugen is the only other person who knows about Humperdinck's plot to have his own fiancée kidnapped and murdered.

Nevertheless, theirs is not a relationship of *philia*. When Count Rugen promises to give Inigo anything he wants in return for sparing his life, it may be assumed that he would help kill Humperdinck, if that is what it would take. Prince Humperdinck, meanwhile, in a fit of jealousy after Buttercup tells him that he is "nothing but a coward with a heart full of fear" and that she and Westley "are joined by the bonds of love," turns The Machine up the maximum amount, fifty years, in order to kill Westley, contrary to Count Rugen's wishes and ruining his chance for making scientific observations of Westley's suffering.

Meanwhile, Fezzik never lies to Inigo, and Inigo never lies to Fezzik. They never will, either. They have *philia* for each other. They look out for each other.

Fezzik does not attempt to deceive the man in black, a.k.a. Westley, when they first meet and fight. From his hiding place, Fezzik deliberately misses Westley's head with a rock, even though he has been told by Vizzini to kill Westley. He says that, "We should face each other as God intended . . . sportsmanlike. No tricks, no weapons, skill against skill alone." (Westley defeats him by jumping on to his back and putting him in a chokehold until he passes out). As soon as Westley becomes his friend, however, Fezzik would not dream of deceiving him. Now they have *philia* for each other.

It is at the insistence of his friend Westley that Fezzik later participates in a deception, when he wears a holocaust cloak and is set on fire (the cloak protects him) and is wheeled towards the soldiers guarding the castle, saying "I am the Dread Pirate Roberts! There will be no survivors!" Of course, the soldiers are no friends of Fezzik, and there is no *philia* between them. There is just no other way for them to rescue Buttercup and avenge Inigo's father.

Before Inigo and Westley become friends, Inigo practices a certain kind of deception on Westley. Nevertheless, Inigo does not *lie* to Westley, ever. He does have the opportunity to lie to him. When Westley is climbing up the Cliffs of Insanity, Inigo offers to help him up by throwing him a rope, and promises not to kill him before he reaches the top (presumably by throwing the rope off the cliffs, or pushing him off when he got to the top.) Westley doesn't trust his promise. "Is there not any way you'll trust me?" he asks Westley. Westley replies "Nothing comes to mind." And then Inigo looks him in the eye and says, "I swear, on the soul of my father, Domingo Montoya, you will reach the top alive." Although they are not yet friends, Westley trusts Inigo, and accepts the offer of help. Inigo could have lied, and could have killed Westley. But he did not.

The deception that Inigo practices on Westley is that of fighting Westley with his sword in his weaker left hand, so that the swordfight will be more fun for him. What he doesn't know is that Westley is practicing the same deception on him. However, it may be said that this deception is the kind of deception that is *allowed* in such sword fighting, in the same way that feinting is allowed in sword fighting. It is not *cheating* at sword fighting to pretend to be left-handed and to lull your opponent into a false sense of security. In that sense, Inigo is not doing something disreputable or cowardly by fighting him with his left hand, at first.

There is one occasion when Inigo, in complete desperation, and in an effort to save Westley, lies to someone who is not (yet) a friend of his. In trying to convince Miracle Max to make a miracle pill to revive Westley, he tells Max that it is for a noble cause, that "His wife . . . is crippled. The children are on the brink of starvation." To which Max replies, "Are you a rotten liar!" This happens before Max becomes a friend of theirs. Knowing that Max is right, Inigo immediately tells him the truth: "I need him to help avenge my father, murdered these twenty years."

Max does lie to Inigo and Fezzik. He says that Westley did not say, when he put the bellows to Westley's lips to find out what is so important that he must live for, "True love," but in fact: "He distinctly said "To blave," and as we all know, to blave means to bluff, heh? So you were probably playing cards, and he cheated." However, Max's wife Valerie immediately calls Max a liar, and starts telling them that he has lost his confidence in his abilities since Prince Humperdinck fired him. This is the beginning of a change in their relationship, from non-friends to friends. Max comes to realize that by helping Westley, he can make Prince Humperdinck suffer. "That is a noble cause," he says. Once they become friends, there is no more lying or deceiving between them. (Although Valerie asks Max, when Inigo and Fezzik are leaving with Westley, if he thinks the pill will actually work, and Max replies, "It would take a miracle!", this is a joke. The pill does indeed work.)

Bad People Have No Friends and Lie to Anyone

Humperdinck, Count Rugen, and Vizzini practice the very worst kind of deception in *The Princess Bride*. More often than not, the innocent Princess Buttercup is the target of their lies. Humperdinck deceives Buttercup—and the people of Florin—into thinking that he wishes to marry her, when in fact he plans to have her murdered before the wedding by Vizzini, and have Guilder framed for it, in order to get the people to support a war with Guilder, the neighboring kingdom he plans to conquer. Count Rugen is in on this deception.

Humperdinck later lies to Buttercup that he will return Westley safely to his ship if she will agree to stay and marry him. Meanwhile he whispers to Count Rugen, "Once we're out of sight, take him back to Florin and throw him in the Pit of Despair." Later again, he lies to Buttercup that he will send his four fastest ships in all four directions to search for Westley and see if he still wishes to be with her. Count Rugen is in on this deception also. Only when the prince slips up, and tells Buttercup that "every ship in my armada waits to accompany us on our honeymoon," does she realize what he truly is: "I am a silly girl, for not having seen sooner that you are nothing but a coward with a heart full of fear."

The first words out of Vizzini's mouth are a lie to Princess Buttercup: "We are but poor, lost circus performers. Is there a village nearby?" When she tells them that "There is nothing nearby . . . not for miles," Vizzini, helped by Inigo and Fezzik, promptly kidnaps her. He also misleads Inigo and Fezzik about the job he has hired them to do—he has not told them that Buttercup is to be murdered. He even lies to them about the job. He tells them, "Once the horse [Buttercup's horse, with fabric taken from the uniform of a Guilderian officer] reaches the castle, the fabric will make the prince suspect the Guilderians have abducted his love. When he finds her body dead on the Guilder frontier, his suspicions will be totally confirmed." In fact, the prince has hired Vizzini to kidnap the princess.

All of these lies are lies told by bad men for an evil end. There is no prospect of *philia* between these bad men and the 'family' of Inigo, Fezzik, Westley, and Buttercup. Indeed, these bad men can't even have *philia* for each other. All of this is also consistent with what Aristotle says about *philia*: *philia* can only exist between *good* people, and never between *bad* people.

Good People Lie to Bad People Only for Good Ends

The evil trio of Humperdinck, Count Rugen, and Vizzini are not the only people who lie and deceive in *The Princess Bride*, however. Westley, the hero of the film, also engages in lies and deception. Indeed, he proves to be a master of deception, defeating even the formidable Vizzini. Nevertheless, Westley's deception is only practiced on bad men and those who would support them, and only for the good end of protecting himself or those for whom he has *philia*—again, with one important exception, which we'll get to in a minute.

Westley deceives Vizzini in the Battle of Wits, but does so in order to save his true love, Princess Buttercup, from being murdered by Vizzini. He organizes the deception of the soldiers guarding the castle, but again, only in order to save Buttercup, and help Inigo avenge his father. And he deceives Prince Humperdinck into thinking that he is fully recovered and will kill him unless he surrenders, but again, only in order to save Buttercup from being murdered by the prince.

It's true that Westley also lies to Princess Buttercup. He tells her that he, the Dread Pirate Roberts, killed Westley. This might be harder to justify than his other lies. However, he only does this because he thinks that she has betrayed him in getting engaged to Prince Humperdinck. That is, he thinks of her as being bad, like Vizzini and the others.

It is actually Westley who places a high value upon honesty. Before he reveals his true identity to the kidnapped princess, he mocks her promise of a ransom if he releases her: "And what is that worth, the promise of a woman? You're very funny, Highness." When she tells him that "I have loved more deeply than a killer like you could ever dream," he—in a moment that truly tests our willingness to be sympathetic to his character, as well as his claim to be a chivalrous rescuer—nearly strikes her in the face with the back of his hand, and tells her: "Where I come from, there are penalties when a woman lies." (One wonders about the fate of women where he comes from). He also says that before he killed Westley, Westley spoke to him of his true love, "a girl of surpassing beauty and faithfulness," and he tells her that, "You should bless me for destroying him before he found out what you really are. . . . Now tell me truly, when you found out he was gone, did you get engaged to your prince that same hour, or did you wait a whole week out of respect for the dead?"

As soon as Buttercup discovers his true identity, and promises her true love that "I will never doubt again," Westley forgives her, and from that point on, he is honest with her— with the one important exception, which we can now finally talk about. When Westley knows that Humperdinck is lying to Buttercup about sparing his life and returning him safely to his pirate ship in return for her hand in marriage, he does not say anything to her about it. He allows her to continue to be deceived, because he believes, paternalistically, and chauvinistically, that it would be better for her to mistakenly believe that he is alive than for her to think, once again, only for real this time, that he was dead. It is a deception of omission, but it is a deception, because of his *philia* for her (not his romantic love, because he will never see her again, he thinks). But Westley's deception of Buttercup out of *philia* raises an important question that needs to be answered.

Male Friends Don't Lie to Male Friends

In *The Princess Bride*, the bad men who are incapable of being friends—who are incapable of having *philia* for anyone—and who are truly alone in the world, lie to good people. In principle, they will even lie to their 'friends,' if needs be. Meanwhile, good men who have friends, who have *philia* for other people, only lie to bad people, and do so only when it is necessary to protect themselves or their friends from harm. They do not lie to their friends. The important exception to this rule is that of Westley's deception of Buttercup, even after they have been reunited. This needs further discussion.

Buttercup is a woman. Although not perhaps a damsel in distress, she spends most of the movie either kidnapped or a prisoner, and is in constant need of being rescued by men. More relevantly, she spends most of the film being lied to by men. Even her true love, Westley, lies to her about his own death, because he believes her to be unfaithful. Later, after they have made up, Westley still allows her to remain deceived about Prince Humperdinck's plans for killing him, because he wishes to protect her from any more suffering. It is a deception of Buttercup that he practices out of his *philia* for her. This is the exception to the rule about friends not lying to friends: although there can be no lying to other *male* friends, even out of *philia*, there *can* be lying to *women* 'friends' (and presumably, *children* 'friends'), out of *philia*, in order to protect them from harm.

This is, unfortunately, also in keeping with what Aristotle says: the *philia* that exists between men is different from the *philia* that exists between men and women, and between parents and children. *Philia* in its purest form can only exist between equals, and, according to Aristotle, men and women can *never* be equal. Men are above women, just as parents are above children (and masters above slaves). Hence, according to him, only men can be *friends*. *Philia* in its purest form can *only* exist between men.

This is the real meaning of Westley's line to Count Rugen that "We are men of action. Lies do not become us." Really what Westley is saying is: "Men lying to women is one thing. I can condone that, when it protects them from harm, as is the case now. But men lying to men is another thing entirely. Real men don't lie to real men. Real men confront each other. Lying is beneath real men." Count Rugen's reply to Westley is: "Well spoken, sir." It is clear that Count Rugen understands this chivalrous, and chauvinistic, code of male honor. He understands it, even if he is a coward and a sadist.

Once the exception to the rule about not lying to those for whom one has *philia* is understood, it is possible to reformulate the rule, such that it is now an exceptionless code of male honor about friendship: *male friends don't lie to male friends*.

This reformulation helps us to explain what the movie says about the relationship between *philia* and deception. Deception occurs where there is lack of *philia* between people. Evil men lack the capability of having *philia* altogether, and practice lies and deception on anyone they wish to deceive, for whatever reason. Good men, or real men, however, who have *philia* for their male friends, do not practice lies and deception on their male friends.

Real Men Don't Lie to Other Real Men

This is still not all that the film says about deception and male honor, however. The rendering of Westley's line to Count Rugen, "We are men of action. Lies do not become us" as "Real men don't lie to real men" is broader than the rule that male friends do not lie to male friends. What the film says, in the end, is that real men do not lie to other men at all, if they don't believe them to be bad men. That is, *real men do not lie to other real men at all, even if these other real men are their enemies*. More succinctly: *It is dishonorable and cowardly to lie to another real man, even if he is your enemy*. This is the exceptionless code of male honor about deception in *The Princess Bride*.

The three early battles in the film embody this code. The first battle is the battle between Inigo and Westley, the sword fight, which is a test of his skill. Inigo is a real man, and he considers Westley to be another real man. (By contrast, he does not consider Miracle Max to be a real man, when they first encounter him, since Max appears to be unwilling to help them, and lies to him.) Since Westley is another real man like himself, he does not lie to Westley about helping him up the cliffs. That would be dishonorable and cowardly. He is truthful with Westley throughout their encounter. He only deceives him about being left-handed, and that is the sort of deception that is allowed in a sword fight. It is part of the sport. Westley, likewise, is a real man, and considers Inigo to be another real man. Since Inigo is another real man like himself, he does not lie to Inigo during their encounter. That would be dishonorable and cowardly. He also only deceives Inigo about being left-handed, a deception that is par for the course in sword fighting.

The second battle is the battle between Fezzik and Westley, a test of his strength. Again, Fezzik is a real man, and he considers Westley to be another real man. Since Westley is another real man, he does not kill Westley with a cowardly, deceptive attack from his hiding place (by contrast, he does not consider the soldiers guarding the castle to be real men, and participates in a deception of them). Instead, he practically states the movie's chivalrous message to him: "We should face each other as God intended . . . sportsmanlike. No tricks, no weapons, skill against skill alone." Likewise, Westley considers Fezzik to be another real man like himself, and does not deceive him. That would be dishonorable and cowardly. (When, during the fight, he falsely tells him that he wears a mask "because they're terribly comfortable. I think everyone'll be wearing them in the future," he is, of course, only joking).

The third battle, however, is a very different battle. Indeed, it is the very opposite of the previous two battles. Westley challenges Vizzini to a "Battle of Wits" for the life of Buttercup, and Vizzini accepts. But whereas the first two battles were sportsmanlike and free of deception, this third battle is won by means of a deception—a lie—practiced by Westley on Vizzini. Westley puts the deadly, undetectable poison Iocaine into two goblets of wine. But he tells Vizzini that he has put it only into one goblet of wine, and asks Vizzini to chose a goblet; they will then drink their goblets at the same time. Vizzini himself lies to Westley, telling him that he sees something in the bushes, in order to distract Westley, and change the goblets without him knowing, so that Westley will be mistaken about which goblet Vizzini has chosen. But Vizzini's deception is of no use. Vizzini drinks the poison and dies, thinking that he has won. Westley drinks poisoned wine also, but, as he tells Buttercup over Vizzini's dead body, "They were both poisoned. I spent the last few years building up an immunity to Iocaine powder."

Importantly, Vizzini is *not* a real man. Vizzini is a liar and a murderer, and he is holding a knife to innocent, defenseless Buttercup's throat. Because he's not a real man, there is no question about him not lying to Westley. Of course he will lie to Westley, and he does. True to form, Vizzini 'breaks the rules' of the Battle of Wits. He cheats. He distracts Westley with a lie about seeing something in the trees, long enough for him to switch the goblets, so that Wesley will be deceived about Vizzini's choice. Westley, by contrast, is a real man. But he does not consider Vizzini to be a real man.

Because Westley does not believe Vizzini to be a real man, he has no compunction about lying to him, and he does. Westley *also* 'breaks the rules' of the Battle of Wits. In contrast to his honorable contests with Inigo and Fezzik, Westley *cheats* against Vizzini. He lies about having putting poison in just one of the goblets. As a result, whichever goblet Vizzini chooses, he will be poisoned, and Westley will live.

Vizzini, however, can hardly complain about Westley's 'breaking the rules' and cheating at the Battle of Wits, since he does it himself. (He might even think, to paraphrase another William Goldman movie, "Rules? In a Battle of Wits? No rules!"[1]) His mistake is to *fail* to detect Westley's lie. Westley is simply the better deceiver of the two. Vizzini makes the same mistake that Inigo and Fezzik make—that of being overconfident, and underestimating Westley as an opponent. Inigo underestimates Westley's skill, and fights him first with his left hand. Fezzik underestimates Westely's strength and agility, and fights him out in the open without weapons. In Vizzini's case, he underestimates Westley's cunning intelligence.

Triple Bluffs, Quadruple Bluffs, and Quintuple Bluffs

The Battle of Wits in *The Princess Bride* sheds light on an important problem in the philosophy of deception: the problem of how to deceive in the context of open distrust.

---

[1] I am, of course, alluding to what Logan says to Butch in *Butch Cassidy and the Sundance Kid*: "Rules? In a knife fight? No rules!" (In Goldman's *Four Screenplays and Essays*).

How do you lie, or even simply deceive, in a situation of open distrust? The answer, at least according to a number of contemporary philosophers, is that you cannot lie in such a situation. This is because lying involves a breach of trust between two people; if there is open distrust, there is no trust, and if there is no trust, then there can be no breach of trust, and hence, no lie. The best that Vizzini, or Westley, can do in the Battle of Wits is to pull off that most difficult of deceptions, namely, a *triple bluff*. This would not be a lie. But it is not even clear that either of them can pull off a triple bluff. And hence, it's not clear that either of them can deceive the other.

First-order deception, or ordinary deception, is where your victim trusts you, and you deceive him, with a lie, or some other deceptive act. Prince Humperdinck deceives gullible Princess Buttercup ("silly," she later calls herself) in this way with his many lies to her. Ordinary deception is precluded in a Battle-of-the-Wits situation, since there is no trust in this situation, but in a non-Battle-of-the-Wits situation, this would be a case of secretly putting poison into your unsuspecting victim's goblet of wine, and asking him to drink. Second-order deception, or *double bluffing*, is when your victim distrusts you, you know that he distrusts you, but, importantly, *he* does not know that *you* know this, and you deceive him by saying, or doing, the opposite of what you want him to believe. You tell him the truth, in order to get him to believe what is false. Or, to give the example that Vizzini gives in the Battle of Wits, if you have two goblets of wine, one of which contains poison, and you ask the person whom you know distrusts you (although he does not know that) to choose a goblet, "a clever man would put the poison in his own goblet." That is, you give yourself the poisoned goblet, in order to deceive your victim. The secretly distrustful person will ignore the goblet in front of him, and choose the goblet in front of you, and die from drinking the poison.

Double bluffing only works, however, when the victim's distrust is *secretly known to you*. When the victim's distrust is *openly known to you*, it does not work. Third-order deception, or *triple bluffing*, is when your victim distrusts you, and you know that he distrusts you, and he knows that you know that he distrusts you. Hence, you *pretend* to *double bluff*, but you actually do what you do in first-order deception. You say, or do, what you want him to believe, in order to deceive him. Since he expects you to tell the truth, or give yourself the poisoned goblet, to deceive him, you tell him a falsehood, or give him the poisoned goblet, in order to deceive him. As Vizzini describes the triple bluff, "But you must have known that I was not a great fool [and so, would not take the goblet in front of me], you would have counted on it [and so, would have put the poison in the goblet in front of me], so I can clearly not choose the wine in front of me."

The problem with triple bluffing is obvious. In a triple bluff, your victim knows that you know that he distrusts you. It follows that your victim is aware that you are trying to deceive him. Therefore, your victim will anticipate that you will try to triple bluff him, exactly as Vizzini anticipates. But you will know that your victim will anticipate this. Hence, you will *pretend* to *triple bluff*, and in fact *quadruple bluff* (tell the truth, or put the poisoned goblet in front of yourself). However, your victim will anticipate this also. And you will know that your victim will anticipate this also. Hence, you will *pretend* to *quadruple bluff*, and in fact *quintuple bluff* (tell a falsehood, or put the poisoned goblet in front of him). And so on, and so on, *ad infinitum*. This is the import of what Vizzini says in the Battle of Wits:

> Now, a clever man would put the poison into his own goblet, because he would know that only a great fool would reach for what he was given. I am not a great fool, so I can clearly not choose the wine in front of you. But you must have known that I was not a great fool, you would have counted on it, so I can clearly not choose the wine in front of me.

There is no end to this kind of reasoning. Vizzini could keep going. Indeed, in way he does, because he never finishes—he is simply interrupted.

What *The Princess Bride* demonstrates is that there is no *reliable* deceptive strategy once there is open distrust between people. It's just as likely you will fail to deceive your victim as that you will deceive your victim. This is what the Battle of Wits proves. If you 'play by the rules' of the Battle of Wits, there is no way to guarantee victory. The only way to guarantee victory is to cheat, and hence, to deceive. And that's exactly what both of them do.

3
The Magic of a Promise

DANIEL MALLOY

> To breed an animal *with the right to make promises*—is not this the
> paradoxical task that nature has set itself in the case of man?
>
> —FRIEDRICH NIETZSCHE, *On the Genealogy of Morals*

The Princess Bride is a story about promises. It's the story of
how Westley defied death itself to keep a promise to Buttercup,
and to stop her from making a promise to Humperdinck. But
there are far more promises at play in *The Princess Bride*.
Virtually all of the relations among the characters are defined
by the promises they make. The lines between good and evil are
drawn by those who keep their promises and those who don't.
Kidnappers Inigo and Fezzik are good people because they
keep their promises. Humperdinck, Vizzini, and Rugen manifest their villainy by their willingness to break their promises.

It's appropriate that a fairytale like *The Princess Bride*
should be about promises, because promises are the closest
thing to magic in everyday life. Like an incantation from
Miracle Max, a promise changes the world around it. What was
just a possibility before the promise becomes an obligation once
it's made.

For all their magical power, we don't think much about
promises. They're just too common—they surround us every
day. That's actually a testament to their magic. Promises surround us all the time because they're powerful: our ability to
live together in communities, to work for common goals, and to
rely on one another, all depend on the existence of promises.

What is a promise? Why should we keep our promises? Perhaps the concept of a promise is broad, and covers a wide variety of actions beyond explicit promises and contracts; what makes promises binding is their ties to our self-respect.

How to Make a Promise

Not all promises look like promises. Some look similar, like vows and oaths and contracts, but others hardly resemble standard promises. Westley's last declaration to Buttercup before he sets off to find his fortune, "I will always come for you," doesn't look much like a promise. It doesn't include any of the standard promise words. Westley doesn't say "I swear . . ." or "I vow . . ." or "Upon my oath . . ." or "I give you my word . . .". He just says that he will, and there are several ways we could take that.

"I will always come for you" could be a prediction. Westley could mean that he will always come for Buttercup in the same way that we say "It always rains in April" or "I always have coffee with breakfast." Taken like this, "I will always come for you" doesn't tell us much about Westley. If "I will always come for you" is a prediction, then it's an impersonal statement of fact. It communicates nothing more about Westley than similar statements of fact, like "Westley has eyes" or "Westley is a man."

But Westley might be expressing a desire. "I will always come for you" could be a statement of what Westley's hopes. This makes it more personal, but not quite personal enough. But if "I will always come for you" states a desire, then it seems to lack commitment. It's a wish about the way the world will be, and not much more.

More personally, "I will always come for you" could be a statement of intent. Westley might be communicating what he plans to do. All promises are statements of intent, but not all statements of intent are promises. Threats are also statements of intent. When Humperdinck begs off joining Rugen in the Pit of Despair by explaining all the things he has to do, he makes a statement of intent: "I've got my country's five-hundredth anniversary to plan, my wedding to arrange, my wife to murder, and Guilder to frame for it." But while he intends to do all of this, he hasn't promised to do any of it.

Each of these possibilities misses something that is plainly expressed in Westley's statement. "I will always come for you" isn't just a prediction or a wish or even a statement of intent. In spite of appearances, it's a promise. What it has that these possibilities lack is an element of obligation. Westley would be wrong not to come for Buttercup.

You Keep Using That Word

Just as some promises don't look like promises, some things that appear to be promises plainly are not. If I tell someone, "If you touch my stuff, I promise you'll regret it," I haven't made a promise. I've made a prediction or a threat, but not a promise. There are two reasons that isn't a promise. First, promises are first-person affairs. You can only make promises for yourself. Good friends though they may be, Inigo can't make promises for Fezzik. Also, promises must be promising. You can't promise something to someone that they don't want. When Vizzini asks Fezzik, "Do you want me to send you back where you were? Unemployed, in Greenland?", he's not making a promise, because plainly Fezzik doesn't want to go back to being unemployed in Greenland.

There are also statements that look like promises, but are made without the intention of carrying them out. Most of the promises made by Vizzini, Humperdinck, and Rugen are like this. When Vizzini promises Buttercup that if she returns to the ship no harm will come to her, he has no intention of keeping his promise. He plans to kill her, after all. But even though this promise is made insincerely, it may still be a promise. Ethically, it makes little difference—whether an insincere promise is a promise or not, it's wrong. If it's a promise, then that promise is binding and will, in the fullness of time, be broken. If it isn't a promise, then the person is lying.

We shouldn't require promises to be sincere, though, because promises are about the future. This gives the insincere promiser a grace period. If we consider an insincere promise a promise rather than a lie, then there's still the chance that it will be fulfilled. If Count Rugen's promised price for the sword Domingo Montoya made him was offered insincerely, then he lied about his intent. But if he decided to pay the promised price, then he would have lived up to the promise. He still lied, but he didn't break his promise. An insincere promise can still be kept, just like a sincere one.

So sincerity of intent isn't part of what makes a promise a promise. As John Searle refines this particular aspect of promising, it's the responsibility for the intent that makes a promise a promise. An insincere promise may be kept or broken, just like a sincere promise. The difference is that the insincere promiser lies in making the promise and the sincere promiser doesn't; both are equally bound by their word, and would be equally wrong to break it.

Where Is the Poison?

The core puzzle of promises is how they do what they do. How do promises create obligations? One answer, called *conventionalism*, is well illustrated by the challenges Westley faces in pursuing Buttercup. Westley crosses swords with Inigo, fights Fezzik hand-to-hand, and matches wits with Vizzini. In each case, he enters into a game defined by rules. Obeying the rules involves giving up a possible advantage, but once the game is entered there is no way of backing out or breaking the rules without incurring penalties.

Inigo helps Westley complete the final phase of his climb up the Cliffs of Insanity and then gives him a chance to rest before they duel. Westley notes that he's been more than fair about the whole thing. If Inigo's goal is to kill Westley, he could have done that. He could have dropped rocks on him during his climb, or attacked him the instant he reached the top. Instead Inigo assists Westley, and then handicaps himself by fighting left handed. Inigo wants to kill Westley, but only in accordance with the rules.

Conventionalism holds that promises are similar to these sorts of games—they are rule-bound practices. Just as Inigo could have avoided facing Westley in a fair fight, we can avoid making promises. Just as Inigo had to limit his options to make the duel with Westley fair, in making promises we limit our options.

But while we lose options when we make promises, we also gain when others promise. Fighting Fezzik hand-to-hand, Westley was severely outmatched. He would have been better off with his sword. But if he kept his sword, Fezzik would have used his rock—and Westley would have stood no chance at all. By laying down his sword, and, in turn, getting Fezzik to put down his rock, Westley improved his odds of surviving the encounter.

The convention of promises is thus useful and fair. It's useful because it allows us to coordinate our actions with others and thus to make plans for the future. It's fair because each person is equally bound by the promises she makes.

John Rawls (1921–2002) argued that fairness makes promise-keeping obligatory. In making a promise, one takes advantage of the benefits that come from the convention of promises, such as being trusted. It's cheating to make a promise and then break it. The promise-breaker fails to live up to her part of the convention, while still getting the benefits of it.

In the Battle of Wits, nobody plays by the rules. Westley falsely implies that the rules are fair—meaning that Vizzini has at least a chance of winning. Vizzini distracts Westley and switches the goblets, thus changing the initial conditions of the game. He cheated by seeking to alter the conditions of play to give himself an advantage. The fact that Westley had already cheated changes nothing. Vizzini and Westley both broke the conventions of the game and sought an unfair advantage over the other—Westley was just better at it.

As You Wish

"As you wish" really means "I love you." On at least one interpretation, "I love you" includes an implicit promise. Westley is promising not only to do as Buttercup has commanded, but also to treat her in certain ways. If "I love you" is a promise, then "As you wish" raises a couple of problems for conventionalism.

First, Buttercup does not understand the promise. She understands Westley's agreement to do her bidding, but not the further implications of the phrase. Her failure in this case isn't her fault, because no convention existed between Buttercup and Westley that made the rules of "As you wish" explicit. If conventionalism is right, then this lack of convention means that there's no promise.

Thomas Scanlon argues that in the absence of convention, there is still a promise, and one that Westley would be wrong to break. Buttercup's failure to understand doesn't erase the promise. Neither does Westley's failure to express himself clearly. He made a promise, and he's bound by it. Conventions don't make promises obligating: they set some conditions on them. When Westley apparently broke his promise to Buttercup by dying, she doesn't blame him for it. By convention, she understands that certain promises are invalidated by death.

There is also the harm of breaking a promise. For conventionalism, the harm of broken promises is done to the convention of promising itself. Breaking a promise is wrong because it makes the convention of promising less stable and reliable. When Vizzini and Humperdinck break their promises, they make it harder for everyone to rely on promises. But this underplays the harm done to the promisee. According to conventionalism, the primary harm in promise breaking isn't done to the promisee, but to the convention itself. Everyone who participates in it finds life just a bit harder because one free-rider cheated. But this doesn't seem right. Surely the wrong of promise breaking has something to do with the harm done to the promisee. After all, Vizzini and Humperdinck don't make promises to all other promise makers or to the idea of a promise. The both make promises to Buttercup, and she's the person harmed by their failure to keep them.

I Will Never Doubt Again

Another theory about promises is called *expectationalism*. Expectationalism maintains that the source of a promisor's obligation is in the expectation she creates in the promisee. The pair of promises Prince Humperdinck makes to Buttercup give her expectations about what he will do. He promises that Westley will be returned to his ship and no harm will come to him; then Humperdinck promises to send his four fastest ships to intercept the *Revenge* and deliver Buttercup's message to Westley.

The second promise is only possible because Buttercup believed the first one. Humperdinck gave his word that Westley would be returned to the *Revenge*, and Buttercup expected him to fulfill it. When he makes the second promise, he implies that he has, in fact, returned Westley to his ship. In both cases, Humperdinck relies on Buttercup's trust that he will do as he promises in order to manipulate her.

For expectationalism, it's this manipulative aspect that makes breaking promises wrong. The obligation to keep promises is based on the trust that they display. Whenever one person trusts another, they make themselves vulnerable to an extent. To trust someone means to give them the opportunity to hurt you.

So, in making promises, promisors ask promisees for their trust. In the conversation between Westley and Inigo while Westley is climbing the Cliffs of Insanity, Inigo offers his help, but since he's planning on killing Westley at the top, he knows that Westley has little reason to trust him. Only when he swears on the soul of his father does Westley relent and accept the Spaniard's help—thus making himself vulnerable to a betrayal that would have cost him his life.

Happily, Inigo's promise was sincere and unbroken. But the same thing happens whenever someone makes a promise. The promisee is led to expect something from the promisor. And, if the promisor fails to deliver, the promisee is hurt. Recall the argument between Miracle Max and his wife Valerie: after trying to send Fezzik and Inigo on their merry way without even attempting a miracle, Valerie explains that his confidence has been shot ever since Humperdinck fired him. Max gets upset, demanding, "Why'd you say that name? You promised me you would never say that name!" Valerie broke her promise and frustrated Max's expectation, violating his trust and damaging their relationship.

Get Used to Disappointment

The primary trouble with expectationalism is that it makes the obligation of promises depend entirely on the promisee's feelings. If the response to your promise is "Yeah, right, we'll see," then breaking your word isn't so bad, because you're not trusted to begin with. If you cultivate a reputation for being unreliable, your promises aren't as binding as someone with a reputation for dependability. As Humperdinck tells Buttercup, "Pirates are not known to be men of their words," so she shouldn't pin her hopes on the Dread Pirate Westley.

Also, there's sometimes a disconnect between what the promisor promises and what the promisee expects. Westley's "As you wish" promised far more than his mere obedience, but that was all Buttercup expected. On the other hand, Vizzini's expectation in the battle of wits was that only one of the goblets was poisoned; but Westley never promised that. He only said that after they both drank they would "find out who is right . . . and who is dead."

And there are other ways than promising of deliberately raising expectations. When the Dread Pirate Roberts tells Westley, "I'll most likely kill you in the morning," he creates an expectation, but certainly not by making a promise, and certainly not one that he's obliged to live up to. At least, Westley doesn't complain that he never fulfilled it. But of course, this isn't a promise. It's a threat. The trouble is that expectationalism doesn't give us a good explanation of why promises create obligations, but other forms of intentionally raising expectations don't.

Father, I Have Failed You for Twenty Years

Inigo never states that his mission of revenge is based on a promise, but it seems likely that it is. But who is the promisee? Certainly not Rugen; what Inigo promises, Rugen doesn't want. Based on some of his expressions, the promise was probably made to his father; that presents problems for both conventionalism and expectationalism.

Inigo's father, Domingo, was probably already dead when he made his promise. His death, after all, was the reason for the promise. But, being all dead, he couldn't have his expectations raised by Inigo's promise. So, Inigo's failure to fulfill the promise couldn't have dashed his hopes or interfered with his plans. The all dead have neither.

Conventionalists have an easier time accounting for the obligation of Inigo's promise. His promise is binding because it calls on the convention of promising. Admittedly, Inigo gets no apparent advantages from his promise—his father isn't trusting him with anything. But he does draw some advantages. Imagine, for instance, that the entire story about the six-fingered man is a lie. Does Inigo derive any benefits from telling people the story? A son who has dedicated his life to getting justice for his father, at the cost of every other pursuit makes for a sympathetic, trustworthy character. So, although Inigo gets no benefit from Domingo through his promise, he does derive a benefit from every sympathetic ear he tells the tale to.

Even Westley tells him, just before their duel, "I certainly hope you find him someday."

But this depends on Inigo advertising the promise. If he makes the vow to his father, and then quietly pursues his vendetta against Rugen without telling anyone about it, then he derives no benefit from the convention of promising. Nor does his failure harm the convention.

Either theory could argue that Inigo's promise wasn't really a promise. Expectationalists could argue that a promise to the dead isn't really a promise, but that's a dangerous claim. Wills and last requests are promises to the dead. Also, it's not death that invalidates the promise, but the dead person's inability to discover whether a promise was fulfilled. By that reasoning, promises are only obligatory if there's a chance that the promisee will find out that the promisor broke her word.

Similar logic holds for the case of a secret promise. Conventionalists might argue that promises must be public, but that would be dangerous. Suppose Inigo managed to make his promise to Domingo before he died. Now it's a public promise, but the one person who knows about it is dead. Is Inigo still bound by it? I think so, but he isn't bound to his father or to the general convention of promising: he is bound to himself.

You Are the Brute Squad

The trouble with Inigo's promise is that there isn't a promisee. Since his father is dead, no one is placing their trust in the Spaniard's word. But every promise needs a promisee to be binding. And every promise has at least one promisee, even promises to the dead: the promisor herself. Inigo's promise is as much a promise to himself as it is to his father.

This claim is controversial. The philosophical consensus since Thomas Hobbes (1588–1679) has held that there are no self-promises. The problem is that any promisor can be released from her promise by the promisee. So, if the promisor and the promisee are the same person, then the promisor can release herself from the promise at any point.

This argument holds that self-promises can't be binding, so they're not promises. Self-promises are just expressions of strong desire or resolve. If Westley promises himself that he won't break under torture in the Pit of Despair, according to this reading, he's really just committing himself to a particular plan of action. But a plan of action can be changed without any wrong-doing, while a promise can't be broken without wrongdoing.

That's the classic claim. Support among philosophers for the idea of self-promises has begun to increase recently. I maintain that not only are self-promises possible, but every promise is a self-promise. Westley's declaration to Buttercup "I will always come for you" is as much a promise to himself as it is to her.

Perhaps I Have the Strength After All

The case that every promise is a self-promise begins by noting one important and undeniable fact about promises: you can only make promises for yourself. It's possible for someone else to make a promise for you, but "proxy promises" require some prior agreement or earlier promise from you. Humperdinck can make promises on behalf of his men because they are in his employ. This gives him a limited authority to promise for them. Generally, promises are done in the first-person. "*I* promise" creates an obligation; "he promises" merely reports a fact.

A further point in favor of this theory is the fact that there is only one person guaranteed to know whether a promise gets fulfilled—the promisor. This isn't true of all promises—in some cases the content of the promise ensures that the promisee will know whether the promise is fulfilled. There's no way for Inigo to fulfill his promise to lower a rope for Westley on the Cliffs of Insanity without Westley knowing whether he's done it. But Buttercup's promise never to doubt Westley again could be broken without Westley discovering it. Only Buttercup would know.

Once we accept that it's at least plausible that promises are self-promises, the central problem of promises remains: why are they obligating? The answer is (as Thomas Hill has pointed out) that every sincere promise puts the promisor's self-respect on the line. Self-respect is the simple acknowledgment that you're responsible for your own actions. Promises put this on the line by making us responsible for taking certain actions in the future. When Westley promises Buttercup that he will always come for her, he makes himself responsible to both her and himself for those future acts. Should he fail, he wouldn't just let her down, but himself as well.

Each promise represents a commitment to making the future a certain way. Promises to others simply represent two or more people sharing a common commitment to that future. That may sound grandiose, but it needn't be. The content of a promise may be enormous or it may be simple. When Buttercup orders Westley to polish her horse's saddle or fill some buckets with water and he responds with his customary "As you wish," they are both committed to a particular future: one where the saddle is polished and the buckets are filled with water. Both promisor and promisee have a stake in this shared future. Both risk something: the promisee risks vulnerability; the promisor risks self-respect.

On the other hand, insincere promisors like Vizzini and Prince Humperdinck risk nothing. They don't commit to a vision of the future, and therefore don't put their self-respect on the line. Insincere promises are denials of responsibility, in two ways. First, the insincere promisor fails to take responsibility for a vision of the future by failing to commit herself. Second, the insincere promisor denies the promisee's responsibility for any action by manipulating their ability to choose.

If an insincere promisor fulfilled her promise, her reputation may be enhanced, but her self-respect will be unaffected, because she will know that the link between the promise and its fulfillment was an accidental one. She can conceive of herself not as a responsible agent, taking charge of her own life, but as a puppet at the mercy of fact.

Did You Say "I Do"?

Promises are more important than we first thought. Aside from our abilities to co-ordinate our actions and live together in societies, our ability to make and keep promises is the mark of our existence as beings that are responsible for ourselves and our actions. Promises make us people. That is their magic. They turn mere farm boys into heroes, humiliated children into avenging angels, intimidating giants into gentle friends. Let's see Miracle Max beat that.

4

That Moron Aristotle on the Means of Persuasion

IVAN WOLFE

Of all the titles and skills one could attribute to Westley—Dread Pirate, skilled fencer, master planner, skilled athlete—most people would not immediately jump to "master rhetorician." In fact, I'm willing to bet most people familiar with *The Princess Bride* wouldn't even think to apply the word "rhetoric" to anything in the book or movie.

However, as someone with a PhD in rhetoric, that's exactly what I see in the book and the movie—rhetoric everywhere, and Westley is the master of it all, the one who outshines everyone else, even Prince Humperdinck.

In modern times, rhetoric is often considered synonymous with political doublespeak and obfuscation, as in "Cut through all the rhetoric" or "That's just rhetoric." This is something we've inherited from Socrates, who sometimes confused rhetoric with sophistry, though this was understandable, given that the first teachers of rhetoric were the Sophists.

The Sophists were itinerant teachers who traveled from city to city, teaching whoever would pay them how to speak and argue well. 'Sophistry' usually means to use clever but false reasoning in order to convince others. In one of Socrates's conversations with a Sophist, the Sophist claimed he could win a debate with a doctor, despite knowing nothing about medicine. Socrates clearly did not appreciate such deception.

Even Socrates allowed for good uses of rhetoric (such as in the *Phaedrus*, where he decides it might be okay if used for good purposes, such as to help others enlighten their souls). However, Aristotle, a fellow "moron" (as Vizzini would put it) and "grand-pupil" of Socrates (Socrates taught Plato, Plato taught Aristotle—three generations of morons!), saw rhetoric in a more neutral light, and he was one of the earliest philosophers to write an extensive treatise on the art of rhetoric (conveniently titled Aristotle's *Rhetoric*). For Aristotle, rhetoric was a tool by which anyone, good or evil, right or wrong, could use to create more effective arguments.

By looking at Aristotle's views of rhetoric, we will clearly see that Westley mastered the art of rhetoric, and was able to use it to conquer nearly every situation he encountered.

Looking at All the Options

Aristotle's definition of rhetoric works fairly well even today. While there are different ways of translating his definition (he was writing in Ancient Greek, after all), a standard version goes something like this: "Rhetoric is the ability to see the available means of persuasion in a given situation."

Rhetoric, to Aristotle (but what does that moron know?), is more than just mere attempts at persuasion. Rhetoric aims at looking at all available options and picking the best way to change people's minds. Rhetoric is needed when there are disagreements—two or more people (or groups of people) do not agree on what to do, yet someone must prevail. Say you and your friends don't agree on what party to go to, but you're in a big group and all want to go together. Somehow, that disagreement must be resolved—rhetoric comes into play (or say you're Prince Humperdinck and you want to go to war with a neighboring country, but you need your subjects' support). Rhetoric is weighing all the options (give a rousing speech to convince the population that war is awesome? Lie about what your spies have found in order to get the public on your side? Marry a beautiful woman, kill her, and then frame the other country?) and then deciding which is most likely to convince others your decision is correct.

Now, while a skilled rhetorician will not win in every case, the most skilled rhetoricians will recognize the widest range of options and thus be more likely to succeed. What enables a rhetorician to succeed? Aristotle taught that arguments can fail or succeed because of the character of the speaker or the emotional state of the audience, as well as the actual content of the argument itself.

Nearly every conflict in *The Princess Bride* can be read as dealing with various instances of rhetoric. You have parties at odds (Humperdinck wants Buttercup to marry him, Westley wants to rescue Buttercup from Vizzini, Inigo Montoya wants Miracle Max to heal Westley, Westley needs Humperdinck to let them leave the castle), and someone must prevail.

If we look at a few instances of rhetorical interplay in *The Princess Bride*, we can see how applying Aritstotle's (possibly moronic) ideas of rhetoric helps us understand why Westley is a brilliant rhetorician, and why Humperdinck is not. Then, we might even be better able to use rhetoric in our own lives, to win people over.

I Must Court Her Now

Prince Humperdinck most likely has some training in rhetoric, as it was considered essential for a member of the court (and especially royalty) to know how to speak well and persuade others. Princes would most likely have had some formal training in rhetoric, since in ages past rhetoric was considered an essential skill for the upper tiers of society—in fact, most higher education until the nineteenth century focused on rhetorical training.

However, despite their training in rhetoric, too often royalty realized they could coast by on the mere power of their title, and Humperdinck is no exception. Many of his problems stem from his inability to be very persuasive in situations in which the force of his office is not important.

Aristotle says that an argument persuades due to the character and position of the speaker, the emotional state of the audience, and the actual content of the argument. Usually, all three occur in combination, but Humperdinck relies too much on his position as "the Prince", as evidenced by his marriage proposal to Buttercup (in the book—the movie omits this scene). After blandly declaring "I must court her now", Humperdinck rides over to her and states, "I am your Prince and you will marry me."

For most women in his country, this would likely work. However, Humperdinck does not take into account the emotional state of the audience (in this case, Buttercup). Buttercup, emotionally dead over Westley's apparent death at the hand of pirates, replies "I am your servant and I refuse."

Humperdinck, rather than looking for other options, shows his weakness as a rhetorician and continues to rely on his position of power. This does not go over well, and Buttercup continues to refuse: "Refusal means death." "Kill me then." ". . . how could you rather be dead than married to me?"

Buttercup mentions that she does not want to marry him due to marriage involving love, and Humperdinck realizes his position of power may not be enough. He capitalizes on this admission, gives a short speech on how marriage for him is about producing an heir and not at all about love. Of course, he still has to rely on his position of power, and basically tells her that if she refuses she will die, but Buttercup agrees. Humperdinck "wins" the argument, but it takes him a while, and he almost fails due to his overreliance on being the Prince. He eventually manages to win by manipulating Buttercup's emotional state. However, it's clear he doesn't really win because of the actual content of his argument.

Out-thinking the Opposition

I cannot compete with you physically, and you are no match for my brains.

Westley's attempt to rescue Buttercup from Vizzini may not seem rhetorical to most people (at least the fencing and fighting—the battle of wits is more obviously rhetorical), but it contains all the elements arguments and disagreements have. Westley wants something; to get it, he has to convince three other people (Inigo, Fezzik, and Vizzini). In each case, he has several options he could explore (such as try and talk Inigo or Fezzik out of fighting, or make a heroic attempt to kill Vizzini before his knife slits Buttercup's throat), but as a good rhetorician, he chooses the best option for winning.

For Inigo, Westley does more than just out-fence the Spaniard, he out-thinks him as well, and this starts on the climb up. The climb is tiring to Westley, but Inigo reveals that he wants to "speed things up." This would be beneficial to both of them—Westley would be less tired, and Inigo could catch up with Vizzini sooner. Realizing Inigo could just drop him, since Inigo mentions he's just waiting in order to kill Westley, Westley declines Inigo's invitations for help, but in ways that play on Inigo's mind.

'   In the book, at one point, Westley just stops climbing, with "the entire weight of his body supported by the strength of his hand jammed into the crevice." He tells Inigo he will just rest for "a quarter hour or so" in this position, which drives Inigo further into wanting the man to reach the top sooner. Of course, this position is not actually a very restful position, so the likely reason for stopping is to drive Inigo even crazier (as Inigo states, in the book, "I'm going crazy up here").

Inigo keeps trying to find ways to convince Westley he is trustworthy—and he finally succeeds by swearing on the soul of his father. This may seem like a "win" for Inigo, but really it's a win for Westley. Westley is less worn out, reaches the top without dying, and Inigo has been driven somewhat to distraction, trying to hurry things up and find ways to get Westley's trust. Then there's the duel that follows.

Inigo starts the duel left-handed merely to get some practice and allow the duel to possibly last longer. Why does Westley start the duel left-handed? Clearly not for the same reasons— Westley wants to rescue Buttercup as quickly as possible. Likely, the reason is to mess with Inigo's mind, the same way he was on the climb. For Inigo, switching to his right hand was a move of desperation, in order to win. For Westley, who likely knew he would win the duel, the switch to right hand is a way to demoralize Inigo and thus make victory more likely. Westley's character—his skill at fencing—won the day, but he also managed to skillfully manipulate the emotional state of his audience (Inigo) as well.

For his duel with Fezzik, Westley again shows his skill at choosing the best option. Knowing he cannot physically best the giant, and thus Fezzik's physical character would win the battle (or argument), he must somehow change the terms of the debate. By grabbing Fezzik's throat, and then keeping him talking (as in the movie) or just holding on for dear life (as in the book), Westley manages to render Fezzik's strength moot.

As for Vizzini, Westley came prepared with iocane powder— a good rhetorician will increase his chances of victory by preparing beforehand, and thus increasing his options. Picking up on Vizzini's overconfidence in his own intellect, Westley quickly realizes that Vizzini thinks in dualistic terms—right or wrong, black and white, conceivable or inconceivable. While there are a few other possible options for a battle of wits, one that has a third option not immediately apparent seems best, and one that leaves Vizzini dead or incapacitated is even better. (How can you get better than best? This all happened after grammar was discovered but before superlatives were standardized).

Here, Westley manages to play on Vizzini's belief in his own character, yet Vizzini's overconfident emotional state does him in (as Westley clearly anticipated). Having many possible options at hand, like a good rhetorician, Westley chose the option that would most likely lead to success.

This also helps explain why Westley hid his identity from Buttercup for so long. He had to take time to read Buttercup, to see if her character had changed (why did she marry the prince?), but he also likely realized an immediate reveal would not have the same rhetorical impact. Buttercup was most likely to respond positively to his identity at a time of more heightened emotional intensity, where it seemed like she might lose him again, rather than at a time where she had Westley and no immediate potential loss seemed apparent.

To the Pain

Westley's "to the pain" speech is justifiably a classic and oft-quoted part of the tale (but then, all of the movie is quotable), but it's also a little odd. Why did Westley choose to give a speech threatening something he clearly could not carry through on? Humperdinck has all the real power, both physically and legally (though not morally), in this instance. Westley seems doomed, and there's not much he can do about it.

However, Westley, as a master rhetorician, has looked at the situation and realized he has few options. He must persuade Humperdinck to let them go, but there seems little chance of that. The content of the argument (Westley and Buttercup have true love and belong together) has long ago ceased to be a factor in this particular dispute. Character-wise, Humperdinck has the legal authority and physical power to do what he wants, and is emotionally charged enough to do some damage to Westley's plans (and Westley has no ability to fight or otherwise overpower the Prince).

Westley needs to change Humperdinck's emotional state, and so he relies on what he knows about the Prince. The "to the pain" speech is an attempt to play on Humperdinck's cowardly nature and thus change his emotional state from anger to confusion and ultimately to fear—and, of course, it works. Westley has had very little direct interaction with the Prince, but what he has seen shows that Humperdinck prefers to have his underlings do the dirty work of harming others—the only person Humperdinck was willing to kill directly was Buttercup (not exactly the intentions of a brave warrior). As a good rhetorician would, Westley recognizes that of all his options (which are admittedly few at that point), verbal intimidation is the best, and especially verbal intimidation that strikes at the core of what drives Prince Humperdinck. Humperdinck loves the adulation and power that comes with royalty, and turning him into a deformed freak would ruin all of that. A man as vain as Humperdinck would prefer death to such a life.

Hey, Everybody—Move!

You may not have noticed one slightly depressing element of these discussions of rhetoric: how often the actual content of the argument matters. In nearly every case, the content itself is cursory. This does not fit well with our modern idea that arguments should be won on the merits, and not on whether the audience is in a receptive mood or the arguer has a position of power.

Actually, this idea is not so modern, as even in Aristotle's time the ideal was that arguments should stand on their merits. However, Aristotle recognized that other elements were often just as important as, or even more important than, the actual argument. Aristotle stated that the rhetorician must not only have a solidly presented argument, but that the arguer must also present an acceptable character and do their best to put the audience in a receptive mood.

Humperdinck relied too much on his own prestige as the Prince to truly be effective in all situations, whereas Westley, as a survivor and outlaw, had to learn to consider all options and choose the best technique for winning (and Fezzik just gets everyone to move by being so physically intimidating).

Westley, in every case, had the best argument—true love. However, he had many obstacles to overcome, and sometimes his persuasive skills involved physical force. In your own life, whoever you are reading this essay (and since you're reading a book about *The Princess Bride*, I already know you are smart, witty, and sing well), when finding yourself in disagreements, you should remember that even if you have the best arguments, the most moral cause, or the least bad option, your argument may not carry the day. The mood of your audience or the position or character of those opposed to you may have more rhetorical force.

However, if you follow the example of Westley and begin to look at all possible options in every case, you may find that your arguments carry the day more often. Then you can ride off into the sunset (and hope that no enemies pursue you).

5
Does It Mean What Vizzini Thinks It Means?

JUSTIN FETTERMAN

> What does it mean when we say, "I can't imagine the opposite of this?"
>
> —LUDWIG WITTGENSTEIN, *Philosophical Investigations*

Vizzini's intellect is truly staggering. He puts it most obviously on display in the Battle of Wits to the death with Westley. His entire scheme relies on clever planning that surely no one can decipher and follow: sailing through shrieking-eel-infested waters and going over the seemingly unscalable cliffs among the more cunning. Further, he hires underlings perfectly suited to balance out his needs and abilities: the quick swordfighter Inigo and the incomparably strong Fezzik. However, a mysterious stranger *does* work out the plan and keeps up with every move Vizzini makes.

For a man enamored of his own chess-like strategy, Vizzini is left to proclaim this turn of events "inconceivable!" As he continues to repeat the word, refusing to believe what is happening in the face of clear evidence, it is the supposedly unintellectual Inigo who puts Vizzini in his place, declaring:

> You keep using that word. I do not think it means what you think it means.

The audience laughs, believing the Spaniard has found a flaw in Vizzini's (supposed) brilliance. Perhaps, though, Vizzini is not so mistaken. Inigo speculates that Vizzini does not know the meaning of the word 'inconceivable' or is at least consistently applying it incorrectly. It remains possible that the Spaniard is mistaken and that Vizzini's overwhelming intelligence is using the word 'inconceivable' as only he (and maybe other great sages) understands.

You'd Like to Think That, Wouldn't You?

The simplest defense lies not in Vizzini's word choice but in Inigo's: "**I** do not *think* that word means what **you** *think* it means." At its most basic, Inigo's statement is merely an observation that the two men have different definitions for the word 'inconceivable.' In this case, the actual definition of the word has no bearing. They could be any two people disagreeing about any word and Inigo's statement would be justified.

An example: if, while drifting through eel infested waters, Fezzik tells Inigo "the sky is blue." Inigo responds with, "You keep using that word. I do not think it means what you think it means." Specifically, Inigo thinks 'sky' is a kind of fruit and knows there are no naturally blue fruit (blueberries, of course, are indigo). Fezzik, like most people, thinks 'sky' means the visible region of the atmosphere. Inigo's definition of 'sky' is false, but his statement about their beliefs (what they *think*) remains true. To say they think it means different things (that is, that they define the word differently), is pretty obvious. Indeed, they could both be wrong about the definition (one thinks it is a fruit and one thinks it is an animal), but the statement "I do not think it means what you think it means" remains true.

We may reach a similar conclusion by examining the word 'means,' which can be a verb for "to be defined as" or "to cause a certain feeling or reaction." Perhaps Inigo's statement is best paraphrased as "I do not react to that word in the same way you do." It is clear from Vizzini's agitated exclamation that he thinks the "inconceivable" events are cause for concern and alarm. Inigo, on the other hand, may see them as impressive and think the best reaction is one of wonder and respect. Seen in this light, Inigo's statement is not necessarily a criticism of Vizzini at all. Rather, Inigo is puzzled by Vizzini's usage and his response would imply the conclusion "I do not think that word means what you think it means, but I would like to understand how you are using it." Such an interpretation reveals more about why the line is funny: the characters take the statement seriously and at face value, but the audience reads a second (sarcastic, satirical, or even mocking) meaning into the words.

But You Must Have Known I Was Not a Great Fool

What the audience hears and what Inigo is commonly understood to say is "The word 'inconceivable' has a different definition from the one Vizzini believes it to have." This interpretation offers a much harsher critique of Vizzini's word choice and intelligence level. Certainly, Vizzini offers plenty of evidence that his intellect may be less impressive than he believes, as in his nautical instructions to "move that thing . . . and that other thing!"

The temptation is to simply crack open a dictionary and compare the definition to the situation, asking if Vizzini has applied the word correctly. We may be able to come to a quick conclusion through this method, but we would be overlooking a hidden but difficult conundrum. Which dictionary should we use? Writers like George Orwell and David Foster Wallace have argued that all language is political and that dictionaries are the prime ideological battleground. The Austrian philosopher of language Ludwig Wittgenstein explains that

> It is not only agreement in definitions, but also (odd as it may sound) agreement in judgments that is required for communication by means of language.

The foundation of communication by means of language is all the people involved agreeing that such-and-such a word means something specific. If no two individuals agree on the definition of 'sky,' then they can have no meaningful conversation about the topic, for one is constantly discussing meteorology while the other ponders fruit. We may broaden the scale and imagine two dictionaries which differ in their meaning of 'sky'; meaningful conversation could occur among all those who use one dictionary or the other, but not between individuals who refer to different dictionaries.

The world with two dictionaries gives us examples of what Wittgenstein calls "language games." The users of Dictionary A are playing language game A, while the users of Dictionary B are playing language game B. Each game functions well on its own, but they cannot be brought together, as groups playing poker and basketball enjoy their separate activities but cannot combine them into a single game. Like cards and sports, language games rely on all players agreeing on the rules. In language, we call those rules spelling, grammar, punctuation, and so on.

Inigo feels that Vizzini's usage of 'inconceivable' violates the rule of agreement in linguistic communication. The implication is that Inigo and Vizzini are playing different language games, so meaningful communication between them is impossible. Like calling the sky blue, declaring the actions of the masked man 'inconceivable' leads nowhere because Vizzini and Inigo do not think it means the same thing.

Taking this attitude, it would be unfair to criticize Vizzini's usage of 'inconceivable.' Inigo's reply that he does "not think it means what Vizzini thinks it means" would be the same as an American telling a Brit that he (the American) does not think 'knickers' means what the Brit thinks it means (namely, that 'knickers' are feminine underwear in Britain but trousers in America). Vizzini is simply playing a different language game than Inigo. We cannot determine whether Vizzini's usage is correct until we understand the rules of his language game; then we could see if he is following the rules he has agreed to.

You're No Match for My Brains

Languages often develop distinct subdivisions with different spellings or pronunciations, creating marginally different language games. Even regional variations in definition and usage are generally acceptable, as in the previous 'knickers' example among hundreds of others. While we may not always think words mean exactly the same thing, our disagreements are rarely complete barriers to communication and stem from having some form of in-group whose members do think it means what we think it means (that is, people who are participating in the same language game).

But what if the in-group has only a single member? Stripping away all the context, could Vizzini's usage of 'inconceivable' be defensible if he is the only person who uses it that way? Inigo's statement would remain correct, because the two men do think the word means different things, but Vizzini's meaning and application could *also* be correct. We can't be in any position to determine the correctness of usage until we are familiar with the rules of the particular language game the speaker is playing—just as we could not determine whether a forward pass was legal until we knew if we were playing American Football, Rugby, or Australian Rules.

Perhaps the idea seems absurd at first blush, but we accept it implicitly on a regular basis. Let's return to Fezzik and Inigo discussing the 'sky', a word they now both understand to mean the visible region of the atmosphere. Further, they both agree that it is blue. To an outside observer, this appears to be a classic example of perfectly functional communication based on agreement. If we could get into the brains of Fezzik and Inigo, however, we might discover that what they are calling the color 'blue' registers drastically differently in their visual cortex. A version of this compromised agreement happens every time someone with color blindness agrees to call a stop sign 'red' even though he sees it as green or grey. Indeed, meaning might just be whatever private associations we have with a given word.

Vizzini's usage of 'inconceivable' simply takes the concept one step further. In *The Princess Bride*, he does not find any outside agreement, even in compromise, from Inigo. Suppose, however, that he has a "private" definition and thus finds an internal agreement. Every time he uses 'inconceivable', he is remaining consistent with both his believed definition and every previous instance of his own use. That is: he is following the rules of his own language game, so Inigo and the audience should be forgiving and neither criticize nor laugh at the Sicilian—unless we could somehow come to understand the rules of Vizzini's language game, compare his usage, and still find inconsistency. In that case, Vizzini would fail to follow his own rules and be laughably inconsistent.

Wittgenstein considered the possibility of creating a private language at length in *Philosophical Investigations*, his influential and posthumously published book about the complications of mind and language. In the end, he rejected the idea by stressing the necessity of communal agreement as the basis of working language: no one can confirm what a word means by just asking themselves. This is because meanings are not attached to words outside of the way we use them. As

Wittgenstein says, "One cannot guess how a word functions. One has to look at its application and learn from that."

Even though Vizzini believes he is using the word correctly and is consistently applying it with that definition, the word effectively means nothing until someone else confirms the definition. It would always seem that Vizzini is speaking correctly because the rules for determining correctness (the rules of the language game) are known only to himself and are, thus, completely dependent on his own perception and his own judgment, which only he can confirm, which soon spirals into an infinite loop of Vizzini telling himself that he is right. There is nothing stopping Vizzini from changing the rules of his private game at will to make sure he always confirms his own rightness. The rules of any game, language games included, have effect only when they are known and enforceable. If Vizzini says to Inigo, "This is the language rule that governs the way I personally use 'inconceivable'," the language ceases to be private.

The role of communal agreement in language appears later in *The Princess Bride* when Miracle Max hears "to blave" and says "which we all know means 'to bluff'." At this point, his wife, Valerie (who is not a witch), calls Max a "liar!" However, it is not his apparent sham of a definition that she objects to. All the characters implicitly appear to agree that 'to blave' does mean 'to bluff,' even though no dictionary readily available supports that conclusion. In this case, though, everyone involved agrees to the rules of a language game that includes 'to blave' and they are free to move on to more important considerations, like true love and mutton-lettuce-and-tomato sandwiches.

You Fell Victim to One of the Classic Blunders

The upshot of all this is that we do not have sufficient evidence to determine the correct usage of 'inconceivable.' Inigo's statement is broadly defensible and Vizzini could not claim to have in mind a definition in his private language. Still, we can easily understand Vizzini using the word figuratively: The odds of these events happening are so small—nearly impossible, even—that no reasonable person would predict them. Inigo's reply becomes a joke because he is taking Vizzini *too* literally, pointing out that the events are not only conceivable but are actually happening.

Philosophy, however, contains several ideas that are inconceivable (or were considered so at one time or another). Philosophers equate "being conceivable" with "being logically possible" (that is, "could actually be imagined, without contradiction, to exist"). All kinds of ideas can be expressed in words, but are not logically possible. The classic example is "a square circle." No one has ever seen a square circle and no amount of artistry or computer wizardry can make one appear. More important, the definitions of 'square' and 'circle' are mutually exclusive. Yet we can easily find words—such as 'square circle'—to describe the impossible thing.

Naturally, the things Vizzini labels 'inconceivable' are both logically possible and easily imagined. Nothing prevents anyone imagining the Dread Pirate Roberts sailing shrieking-eel-infested waters and climbing the Cliffs of Insanity. Vizzini himself could have imagined them while making his plan, if only to picture them as scenarios he was preventing—his scheming might not have factored in the Dread Pirates Roberts, specifically, but he could easily have imagined some generic person trying to follow him.

Within philosophy, we often talk about logically impossible things like square circles, but outside technical philosophy, when we use the word 'inconceivable', we're not usually talking about what's logically impossible.

Whether we picture a world with colonies on Mars or forests with flame spurts, logic is not standing in our way. Movies, like all works of art, provides an opportunity to experience that which is beyond reality but *can* be conceived in the imagination or with special effects. Fantasy stories like *The Princess Bride* have long found power and beauty in their ability to show us that which seemed impossible. In reaction, we may declare that what we see is "inconceivable!" because we can't believe our eyes. Like Vizzini, we may prefer to disbelieve our senses than to accept that what we are seeing is true. Vizzini could, then, take comfort in knowing that when he misuses 'inconceivable', he is not any *more* wrong than anyone else.

In the end, Vizzini is perfectly justified in using 'inconceivable' as an interjection of surprise and disbelief. The audience may side with Inigo, thinking "that word" does not mean what Vizzini thinks it means, if they adhere to a strict interpretation where 'inconceivable' only means logically impossible. On the other hand, we may also side with Inigo (and be in on the joke), if we understand Vizzini's *intent* in proclaiming events "inconceivable!"

His exclamation occurs every time Inigo tells him that someone is catching up to them. Vizzini's outburst implies that Inigo must be seeing things or making it up, that Inigo is the one whose statement is wrong. Of course, the characters (and the audience) see the events happening as Inigo describes them, so we're pleased when he turns the tables and insinuates that no, it's actually Vizzini who is wrong.

We all know the Sicilian would never admit it.[1]

---

[1] Special thanks to Erin Flynn of Ohio Wesleyan University for his insights into Wittgenstein and reminders to treat the Inigo-Vizzini exchange as, first and foremost, a joke.

II

Courage and Reason

Never go in
against a Sicilian
when death is
on the line.

6
To the Pain

RACHEL ROBISON-GREENE

Sadism abounds in *The Princess Bride*. Three of the characters in the story have a particular talent for exacting pain on others. The two most obvious are Count Rugen and Prince Humperdinck. Humperdinck had a torture chamber built that would surely put any chamber in Guilder to shame. Count Rugen has, as a life goal, a desire to write the definitive book on the nature of pain. Even Westley has the capacity and the willingness to inflict pain in ghastly ways (an ability that was, perhaps, cultivated by his training to become the Dread Pirate Roberts.)

Though not a sadist myself, I would be quite interested in reading Rugen's book. He has a rather passionate view on the subject, so I can't imagine that it would be lacking in detail or ardor. He says:

> I think pain is the most underrated emotion available to us. The Serpent, to my interpretation, was pain. Pain has been with us always and it always irritates me when people say 'as important as life and death' because the proper phrase, to my mind, should be 'as important as pain and death'.

This kind of fascination with pain makes me wonder what the table of contents for Rugen's book would look like. What kinds of questions would he be interested in answering? I've brainstormed a little bit, and here is what I have come up with:

1. **Acknowledgements.** Here, I imagine, Rugen would graciously thank Prince Humperdinck for the truly astounding number and range of possibilities he has provided for the study of the phenomenon of pain.

2. **Brutes.** Are there differences between the pain humans experience and the pain that nonhuman animals experience?

3. **Intensity and Duration.** How should strength and length of pain factor into our analysis?

4. **Propinquity.** The nearness or remoteness of the inflicted pain.

I'll suggest a final chapter title, though it is not one I think Rugen is likely to include himself:

5. The Relationship between Empathy and Pain

We're still waiting with bated breath for the publication of Rugen's magnum opus on pain, but while we wait, let's try to imagine what such a work of art might look like.

The Zoo of Death

In the movie, Westley, after saving Buttercup and successfully navigating the Fire Swamp, is, sadly, captured by Humperdinck. He is brought, unconscious, to a torture chamber. When he finally regains consciousness, he opens his eyes to find himself strapped to a table, staring up at a truly horrifying-looking albino. "Where am I?" Westley asks. "The Pit of Despair," answers the albino, "Don't even think about getting out alive."

The movie is a masterpiece; it's hard to find someone who hasn't seen it (most people you find will probably be able to quote it at length). Many people who saw and loved the movie, though, may not even be aware that the movie was based on a book by William Goldman (or, for those of you gullible enough to believe it, by Florinese writer S. Morgenstern). Goldman also wrote the screenplay for the movie. One significant difference between the book and the movie is that the torture chamber in the book is not called "The Pit of Despair." It's a much more sadistic location that, in the book is called "The Zoo of Death."

The Zoo of Death was created to satiate the sadistic desires of Prince Humperdinck. In both the movie and the book, Humperdinck is described as perhaps the world's greatest hunter. Buttercup exclaims to her captor, The Man in Black, "It does not matter where you take me. There is no greater hunter than Prince Humperdinck. He can track a falcon on a cloudy day. He will find you."

Though he is, indeed, an excellent hunter, in the book it is revealed that Prince Humperdinck is perhaps a little more like a serial killer in the making. I'm sure all of us have watched enough crime TV to know that one of the three major warning signs that indicates a person might become a sociopath is a fascination with killing animals. Humperdinck's behavior should set off some major warning sirens here. Goldman describes Humperdinck's proclivities, "He made it a practice never to let a day go by without killing something. It didn't matter what. When he first grew dedicated, he killed only big things: elephants or pythons. But then, as his skills increased, he began to enjoy the suffering of little beasts too."

We see here that it isn't just the sport of tracking that Humperdinck enjoys. It is the suffering. The pain. The Zoo of Death is designed to inflict upon creatures of all types as much pain as possible (I think of it as the animal version of serial killer H.H. Holmes's "Murder Castle." It was a real thing. Google it.)

The Zoo is underground, accessible through a hole in a tree. It has five levels, each designated to animals of specific types. The first level is designated for animals that are fast. Cheetahs and wild dogs zip about this level. The next level houses the strong animals: anacondas, rhinos, and giant crocodiles. The third level is for poisonous animals: spitting cobras, jumping spiders (ick!), and death bats. The fourth level (shudder) is for "enemies of fear" and includes the shrieking tarantula, the blood eagle (which eats human flesh), and "in its own black pool, the sucking squid." The fifth level is reserved for a truly worthy opponent. Sure enough, when Westley opens his eyes after being captured, it is in this fifth level of the Zoo where he finds himself.

Humperdinck didn't keep all of these animals for the novelty of having a zoo full of the most terrifying creatures imaginable.

He kept them as subjects for the infliction of suffering and death. The Zoo was a place he could come to train to become a better killer.

Count Rugen is certainly aware of Humperdinck's Zoo and, one would think, as a connoisseur of all things related to pain, he certainly approves, though his approval is grounded in something quite different. It's academic. Goldman describes Rugen: "The Count really cared about pain. The whys behind the screams interested him as much as the anguish itself. And whereas the Prince spent his life in physically following the hunt, Count Rugen read and studied anything he could get his hands on dealing with the subject of distress."

The Zoo is like a research lab for Count Rugen. Specifically, he is in a position to observe the differences in pain behavior among different animals.

Pain is a topic that, insofar as it is a physical event, calls out for empirical investigation—scientific experimentation. Insofar as pain is also a concept that is actually fairly broad in scope, it calls out for a philosophical analysis. Certain biological events often happen when we are in pain, but those same biological events are not always taking place in every instance in which we claim that pain is occurring.

Count Rugen likely observed that most of the animals in the Zoo exhibited certain pain behaviors when they were put under stress physically. Consider the behavior that you display when you stub your toe. A non-human animal might act in the exact same way. Obviously, most of them won't use colorful language, but they might hop up and down, cry out, or pay increased attention to the area that was injured. The fact that non-human animals exhibit pain behaviors gives us good reason to believe that, like us, they are experiencing pain (in fact, this might be the best way we have of knowing that and when other humans are experiencing pain as well.) If it quacks like a duck . . .

It is this line of thinking that motivates the position of many animal rights advocates (of course, Rugen and Humperdink would have no interest in this fact). Behavioral evidence makes it pretty clear that non-human animals experience pain (except for animals like mussels and shellfish—practically ambulatory plants). They might not experience all of the same sorts of pain that we as humans experience, but they experience brute physical pains. Many thinkers (including, famously, Peter Singer) argue that to treat equal amounts of physical pain differently simply because of the kind of animal that you're dealing with amounts to something akin to racism—speciesism. Many people are vegetarian for this reason, or, at the very least, oppose animal products that were produced under conditions in which animals suffered unnecessarily.

I don't imagine that Rugen's treatise on the topic would contain much in the way of moral reflection. He would note here that many non-human animals can and do exhibit pain behavior. He would likely provide a list of the kinds of pain behavior that they exhibit. He can keep his morbid list and I'll keep my reflections on ethics.

There was one account of Humperdinck's behavior in The Zoo that I found particularly disturbing. Here's Goldman's description:

> He was ringing down the curtain on an orangutan when the business of the King's health made its ultimate intrusion. It was mid-afternoon, and the Prince had been grappling with the giant beast since morning, and finally, after all these hours, the hairy thing was weakening. Again and again, the monkey tried to bite, a sure sign of failure of strength in the arms. The Prince warded off the attempted bites with ease, and the ape was heaving at the chest now, desperate for air. The Prince made a crablike step sideways, then another, then darted forward, spun the great beast into his arms, began applying pressure to the spine. (This was all taking place in the pit, where the Prince had his pleasure with many simians.) . . . CRACK! The orangutan fell like a rag doll.

There's something about the description of this death that leaves me feeling especially squeamish and more than a little morally unsettled. Goldman has done a pretty good job of flagging Prince Humperdinck as a really bad guy. This death feels worse than some of the others. What might explain this?

John Stuart Mill's discussion of higher and lower pleasures might provide us with some guidance here. Mill is a utilitarian, which means that he thinks that the right thing to do, morally speaking, is to perform the action, which, among all the actions available to us, would produce the greatest overall amount of happiness for the greatest number of people. According to Mill, though equal amounts of happiness should always be treated equally, some *kinds* of happiness are inherently more valuable than other kinds. He argues that intellectual pleasures (what he calls "higher pleasures" are always more valuable than physical pleasures (pleasures he calls "lower pleasures"). He says, "It is better to be a human being dissatisfied than a pig satisfied. Better to be Socrates dissatisfied than a fool satisfied. And if the fool or the pig are of a different opinion, it is because they only know their side of the question."

Chimpanzees can hardly participate in the higher pleasures that Mill describes. They are unlikely to author philosophical treatises or to become chess masters. But chimpanzees do engage in more sophisticated thought than other animals that do not have a cerebral cortex developed to that degree. They are even capable of using sign language and, the evidence suggests, of teaching that sign language to their children. Some of these signs represent rather complex, even abstract concepts. The pain and fear involved in being tortured and killed over an extended period of time may be much more painful for a chimpanzee than for a wild dog because the chimpanzee may, on some level, be capable of reflecting on what is happening to her.

Based on his observations in the pit, Rugen might conclude that there is a certain kind of suffering that most creatures are capable of experiencing equally. The more developed a creature is, the greater their capacity for suffering might be.

This Being Our First Try, I'll Use the Lowest Setting

A contemporary of John Stuart Mill, Jeremy Bentham was also a utilitarian. Bentham provided us with some additional tools that might be useful in a book on the topic of pain. Two of those distinctions are intensity and duration. These are both fairly common-sense concepts. Intensity has to do with how strong the pain is. For those of you that are unlucky enough to have experienced both, consider the difference between an ordinary, low-grade headache and the pain involved when you have a migraine. If migraines aren't familiar to you, think about the difference between pricking your finger or feeling your hair being pulled on one hand, and having a toothache or an ear infection on the other. These differences would be differences in intensity.

Duration has to do with how long a pain lasts. About a decade ago, I developed an allergy that caused me to break out into hives. They were awful, but not toothache or ear infection awful. I expected that, like most allergic reactions I had experienced, they would go away quickly. Days became weeks and weeks became months, and still the hives persisted. I remember thinking, "If I knew this was going to keep going forever, I would just want to die now." Of course, I'm sure the persistent itchiness was making me a bit dramatic, but I definitely experienced in that moment the degree to which duration makes a difference (by the way, I ended up being allergic to my plug-in air freshener. Watch out for those). The length the pain is experienced should be factored into the overall severity of the pain.

Rugen seems well aware of some of these distinctions. Before Humperdinck gets his vengeful hands on The Machine, it is Rugen's plan to dole out Westley's torture bit by bit. One of the reasons he wants to take his time is to see how pains of varying intensities and durations impact Westley. The Machine is presented as one of the cleverest and most effective torture devices ever created. It isn't the first torture implement used on Westley, at least not in the book. He's tortured in a variety of ways, including the use of spinning ticks, which Buttercup had let slip were particularly loathsome to Westley. Rugen carefully observed intensity and duration, allowing the ticks to feast on Westley right up to the point where he might have died from their poison. He exhibits particular finesse with his precious Machine saying, ""I want you to be totally honest with me about how The Machine makes you feel. This being our first try, I'll use the lowest setting." How professional. The Machine is a tough customer, and even at its lowest setting, it does a number on Westley.

RUGEN: As you know, the concept of the suction cup is centuries old. Really that's all this is, except that rather than sucking water, I'm sucking life. I've just sucked one year of your life away. I might one day go as high as five, but I really don't know what that would do to you. Let's just start with what we have. What did this do to you? Tell me, and remember this is for posterity, so, be honest how do you feel?

WESTLEY: [*whimpers*]

RUGEN: Interesting.

Of course, Humperdinck puts an end to Rugen's little experiment. In a jealous rage, emasculated by Buttercup, he bursts into the Pit of Despair (Zoo of Death) and cranks the lever on The Machine from one all the way up to fifty: "You truly love each other, so you might have been truly happy. Not one couple in a century has that chance, no matter what the storybooks say, and so I think no man in a century will suffer the way that you do."

I've Just Sucked One Year from Your Life

Another of Bentham's tools for evaluating pain and pleasure is Propinquity. Propinquity has to do with the nearness or remoteness of a pain or pleasure. There is much to be said about how remoteness should be calculated, but for our purposes, let's just keep it simple. Depending on the circumstances, we might care less about a pain if it is far away. This diagnosis might have something to do with why smokers have a difficult time quitting (keeping in mind that the most important explanation, obviously, is physical addiction). A young smoker might be told about the risk for lung cancer. That consideration has weight. On the other hand, that consideration is part of some distant, unsettled future. The cigarette is available now for immediate satisfaction.

In other contexts, the remoteness of an event could make it even more anxiety provoking and, as a result, more painful. In the book, Rugen drags the strange looking machine to the fifth level of the Zoo of Death and just leaves it near to where Westley is tied up. He says:

> One of my theories . . . is that pain involves anticipation. Nothing original, I admit, but I'm going to demonstrate to you what I mean. I will not, underline *not*, use the machine on you this evening. I could. It's ready and tested. But instead I will simply erect it and leave it beside you, for you to stare at the next twenty-four hours, wondering just what it is and how it works and can it really be as dreadful as all that.

When it comes to The Machine, remoteness issues are metaphysically pretty odd. The Machine sucks years from a person's life, but it does so *from the back end of that life*. And this, apparently, hurts. A lot. The more years that are sucked away, the more it hurts. The interesting thing is that, so long as the person operating The Machine doesn't suck *all* of your remaining time away, the pain you are experiencing is the pain of being robbed of something that hasn't happened yet—of losing something that was promised to you in some distant future.

Life Is Pain, Highness

A more thorough analysis of much of what we have discussed so far would effectively fill the pages of a book on pain. Pain can be judged in terms of the capacities of the kind of thing experiencing it, the intensity, the duration, and the propinquity of the pain. This is all just a first pass. But there may be methods of pain infliction about which Rugen is ill equipped to comment or to analyze.

When the story begins, Westley and Buttercup are innocent young lovers. I am hesitant to even call them adults at this point. But when Westley learns that Buttercup loves him in return, he sets out on a quest to make his fortune. From this moment on, our lovers know real pain. Westley is separated from Buttercup by the Dread Pirate Roberts. To stay alive, he is made to perform acts of piracy. We tend to glorify pirates like we do vampires or werewolves, but pirates existed and continue to exist. Their occupation is such that they both dole out and experience their fair share of pain. What's more, Westley must have been good enough at it for the former Dread Pirate Roberts to pass on the mantle.

We learn that Westley is well learned in swordsmanship, feats of strength, general strategy, and the facts of basic human nature. What's more, he's not a sociopath like Rugen and Humperdinck. He is able to relate to other people. He befriends Inigo and Fezzik, despite the fact that both of them had, at one time, tried to kill him. He is even capable of true love, a depth of emotion that most of the characters in the book seem to believe almost never occurs. Because of his capacity for compassion and empathy, he is, perhaps, able to conceive of kinds of pain that the sociopaths could never fathom.

You might use the following exchange from the book to defend Rugen's capacity to inflict optimal levels of pain:

> "I am fascinated to see what happens," the Count went on. "Which pain will be least endurable? The physical, or the mental anguish of

having freedom offered if the truth is told, then telling it and being called a liar."

"I think the physical." Said the Prince.

"I think you're wrong." Said the Count.

This exchange makes it seem like Rugen knows that emotional pain can sometimes be just as intense as physical pain. But, though Rugen might be able to understand certain generalities about human behavior, he lacks the kind of empathy that would allow him to take fully into account the particular values and commitments of individual people.

Westley, by contrast, because he is capable of empathy, is able to really hit the egomaniacal Prince Humperdinck where he lives:

HUMPERDINCK: First things first. To the death.

WESTLEY: No. To the pain.

HUMPERDINCK: I don't think I'm quite familiar with that phrase.

WESTLEY: I'll explain and I'll use small words so that you'll be sure to understand, you warthog-faced buffoon.

HUMPERDINCK: That may be the first time in my life a man has dared insult me.

WESTLEY: It won't be the last. 'To the pain' means that the first thing you lose will be your feet below the ankles, then your hands at the wrists, Next your nose.

HUMPERDINCK: Then my tongue, I suppose? I killed you too quickly the last time, a mistake I don't mean to duplicate tonight.

WESTLEY: I wasn't finished! The next thing you lose will be your left eye followed by your right.

HUMPERDINCK: And then my ears . . . I understand! Let's get on with it!

WESTLEY: Wrong! Your ears you keep and I'll tell you why; so that every shriek of every child at seeing your hideousness is yours to cherish. Every babe that weeps at your approach, every woman who cries out, 'Dear God, what is that thing!' will echo in your perfect ears. That is what 'to the pain' means. It means I leave you in anguish, wallowing in freakish misery forever.

Because of Westley's excellent understanding of human character, he has Humperdinck quivering with fear for the time that it takes to escape. This is something that you sociopaths simply aren't able to do. Thus, our storybook hero par excellence is able to out-sadist even the most committed sadists. Perhaps Rugen should ask him to co-author his book.

7
Who Should Have Won the Battle of Wits?

RICHARD GREENE

One of the most beloved scenes in both the book and movie versions of *The Princess Bride* is the Battle of Wits between the Man in Black (later revealed to be our hero, Westley the farmboy and also the most-recent version of the Dread Pirate Roberts) and Vizzini the Sicilian.

There are many noteworthy things about the Battle of Wits. For instance, the Sicilian does most of the reasoning, or at least he does most of the talking (he's pretty much speaking for both parties). Also of note is the fact that Vizzini had no real incentive to enter the Battle of Wits with the Man in Black; he just couldn't resist. At the time, Vizzini was kidnapping Princess Buttercup and had a knife to her throat as the Man in Black approached. The Man in Black was there to rescue the princess, but so as long as Vizzini had her at knifepoint, there wasn't much the Man in Black could do. Moreover, Vizzini's future well-being actually depended on Buttercup's being killed soon.

Despite all this, he still enters the Battle of Wits, as his huge ego (remember this is the guy who called Plato, Aristotle, and Socrates "morons"), wouldn't let him decline the Man in Black's challenge. Most noteworthy, however, about the Battle of Wits, is that the battle never occurred. The Man in Black "won" the battle of wits by cheating. Recall that he put iocane powder—an odorless, flavorless poison—in both cups, but had spent several years building up a resistance to iocane powder. Although the Man in Black never actually said that he was putting iocane in one cup only (his exact words were "Your guess. Where is the Poison?"), certainly that was the implication. The whole point of the Battle of Wits was to determine which cup it was in. So we didn't truly get a battle of wits; rather, we got a battle of physical abilities. The person who had developed his body in the right way "won."

But who would have won a true battle of wits between the Sicilian and the Man in Black? There are three possibilities: the Sicilian wins, the Man in Black wins, or no one wins. For the Sicilian to win he would have to deduce where the poison is (as opposed to merely guessing right). For the Man in Black to win he would have to trick the Sicilian into guessing wrong, and the Sicilian's wrong guess would have to be as a result of the trickery—he must in some way cause the Sicilian to guess wrong. If they wind up at an impasse, such that the Sicilian has no idea and merely ventures a guess as to where the poison is, then, regardless of whether he guesses correctly or not, no one wins. This is because no one actually outwitted the other; the result was just a matter of luck or chance. So our question becomes: could either the Sicilian or the Man in Black outwit the other?

At a Picnic Table Somewhere Near Florin

In the story, the battle of wits takes place high atop a mountain outside of Florin, not far from the Cliffs of Insanity, overlooking the Florin Channel. We'll travel just a little further to a spot that looks identical to the one where the rigged battle of wits took place, but one where an actual battle of wits can occur. This would be in a parallel universe to the one described by S. Morgenstern so many centuries ago. As philosophers like to say, we need to go to a "near possible world."

The idea is that we want to consider what a battle of wits would have been like and how it would have played out, *if* it had been a true battle of wits. To do this we need to change some of the details. So what needs to change and what needs to stay the same? Clearly, we want it to involve the Sicilian and Westley. If we had a battle of wits between two persons with identical intellects and having all the same personality traits, then we would expect that the third result would obtain: no one would win (presumably, they would both be thinking the same things). And if we had a battle of wits between persons who were not intellectual equals, then the outcome would depend on the particulars of those persons.

So the question of who wins a battle of wits, depends on who is *in* the battle of wits. In other words, there is no point to discussing who will win a battle of wits, in the abstract and without reference to specific people. It's like asking who would win a game of tic-tac-toe! Thus, for our purposes, we can't change who participates. It's got to be the Sicilian and the Man in Black.

We don't need to change the setting, either. There's nothing about the fact that the battle occurs over a picnic table, atop a mountain, and so forth, that bears on who will win. Time of day and other such factors are also irrelevant in this case. I suppose that if you swapped out the iocane powder for something that is not odorless, that would give the advantage to whomever has the stronger sense of smell, but then it would no longer be a battle of wits (it would be a matter of "best sense of smell," or some such). So we should hold that constant as well—it's got to be iocane powder (or some other equally deadly odorless poison).

There are, however, two things that need to change. First, we need the Man in Black to be identical in every respect, but he must not have built up an immunity to iocane powder. Second, the way the battle of wits is played must be different. Specifically, it cannot be the case that poison is put into both goblets. There can only be one winner and one loser (or it can be a tie). So let's head to the nearest possible world in which everything is exactly as it is on that fateful day near Florin, but an actual battle of wits occurs between two people, each of which can die, but only one will.

By now you must be wondering a few things. In that world does the Man in Black die? Does Buttercup get killed and left on the shore near Guilder? Does a war break out between the people of Florin and the people of Guilder? Does Domingo Montoya's death go unavenged? Does Miracle Max get his mojo back? And, finally, do Vizzini, Fezzik, and Inigo become celebrated assassins in either land? We can now see that this is not just a thought experiment. There is an entire world (in another, but wholly real, universe, if the philosopher David Lewis is to be believed) whose future depends greatly on the outcome of our battle of wits.

The Rules of Engagement

The rules for our true Battle of Wits are simple. The Man in Black takes the two goblets of wine and, out of sight of Vizzini, places the iocane powder in one of them. He then places one goblet in front of Vizzini and one in front of himself. Vizzini must decide from which goblet each will drink. They must drink (and swallow) at the same time. The winner of the Battle of Wits is the person who does not drink the poison.

You can die in the Battle of Wits and still win, provided that drinking the poison isn't what killed you. For example, if you choke to death on your wine, but didn't consume the poisoned wine, you've won the battle. It's also the case that you can fail to be killed by the poison and still lose. For example, if you had a heart attack and died prior to the poison you consumed kicking in, you would not have been killed by the poison, but you would still be the loser of the battle. So the salient feature of winning the Battle of Wits is being the one who did not consume the poison—it's not necessarily avoiding death. Still the threat of death plays an important role. The stakes have to be high enough to give each participant an incentive to do his best.

Finally, as we see in *The Princess Bride*, there's no prohibition against trying to get your opponent to reveal something about himself. Vizzini "reasons" his way to a decision ("reasons" is in scare quotes because Vizzini's reasoning processes seem somewhat suspect and arbitrary—as we will see), by talking through the process. He is looking at the Man in Black for clues. He's also free to question his opponent, but the Man in Black is under no obligation to answer, and if he does answer, he's not under any obligation to answer truthfully. Think of it as being somewhat similar to the bluffing that goes on in a game of poker or during Alan Turing's Imitation Game, in which a computer attempts to trick a human questioner into thinking that the computer is a human being.

So Much Jiggery Pokery

To see what would likely happen in our true Battle of Wits, let's begin with what happened in the Battle of Wits in the story. Even though the Man in Black cheated, Vizzini didn't know that he would. He thought it was a battle in earnest. Let's re-examine his reasoning process.

Assuming that the Man in Black put poison in exactly one goblet, Vizzini says, "It's all so simple. . . . All I have to do is deduce, from what I know of you, the way your mind works. Are you the kind of man who would put the poison into his own glass, or the glass of his enemy?" Thus far, Vizzini has correctly diagnosed the situation. From there his reasoning is not so compelling.

He "deduces" that a great fool would put the poison in his own goblet, because only another great fool would choose his own. Since Vizzini is not a great fool, Vizzini would not choose the wine in front of the Man in Black. Then he reasons that since the Man in Black knows that Vizzini is not a great fool, and would reason this way, Vizzini cannot choose his own goblet, either. This, according to Vizzini's reasoning, puts the poisoned goblet back in front of the Man in Black. But it doesn't end here.

Vizzini also notes that iocane comes from Australia, where there are many criminals (criminals don't trust one another). Since Vizzini now cannot trust the Man in Black, he has further reason for thinking that the poison is in front of the Man in Black. Further, the Man in Black certainly would have known that Vizzini would be aware of the origins of iocane, as well as having detailed knowledge about the behavior of criminals, so he now has reason to think that the poisoned wine is in his own goblet. This goes on for another round or two, but you get the idea. At this point we've not been given anything by Vizzini to make us think that he's actually deduced which goblet contains the poison, but he asserts, nonetheless, that he has.

We all know the rest of the story: Vizzini distracts the Man in Black, switches the goblets, and drinks the iocane. Of course, both goblets contained the poison, and Vizzini drops dead.

One thing the details of the story tell about how to win a Battle of Wits, such as the kind we are currently considering, is that there are very good reasons for thinking that the poison could be in either goblet (along with some pretty bad reasons, such as that iocane comes from Australia, and what's supposed to follow from that). Thus, all things being equal, we should have about the same chance of winning such a battle of wits that we have of winning a game of tic-tac-toe. The likely outcome of such battles will almost always be the third outcome: no one wins, because no one is able to trick the other.

Another thing the details of the story tell us is that in this instance, it's not the case that all things are equal. To see this, let's look at what we know of the characters of Vizzini and the Man in Black.

Maybe Plato, Aristotle, and Socrates Were Morons, but This Vizzini Fellow . . .

The Man in Black succeeds throughout the story in no small part by being excellent at reading others. A prime example of this is when he's climbing the Cliffs of Insanity using only his fingertips. He is able to determine that Inigo Montoya, who has offered to drop him a rope, will not kill him, even though both know that they will be dueling to the death as soon as the Man in Black reaches the top.

He hears the sincerity in Inigo's voice, as he swears on his father's name. He also correctly judges that Fezzick's life should be spared (Fezzick later becomes a great ally), that Vizzini's life should not be spared, and that Humperdinck will not keep his promise to Buttercup to spare Westley's life (at this point he is no longer masquerading as the Man in Black).

There are many more examples throughout the story. In fact, the only times that Westley doesn't seem to be good at reading people, is when it comes to Buttercup. His passion and jealousy seem to get the best of him, leading him to jump to conclusions about her loving Humperdinck and not being true to him, and so forth.

Vizzini, on the other hand, seems horrible at reading people. His "reasoning" in the battle of wits is evidence of this. Also consider the numerous times he uttered the word "inconceivable." Nearly every instance comes on the heels of his underestimating what the Man in Black was capable of. Vizzini couldn't conceive that the Man in Black could climb the Cliffs of Insanity or best his swordsman and giant at their own games.

The best example of Vizzini misreading somebody is when he sums up himself. Any paraphrasing of Vizzini's assessment of his own intellect would severely fail to do justice to it. Here's how he puts it himself in the book:

> There are no words to contain all my wisdom. I am so cunning, crafty and clever, so filled with deceit, guile and chicanery, such a knave, so shrewd, cagey as well as calculating, as diabolical as I am vulpine, as tricky as I am untrustworthy . . . well, I told you there were not words invented yet to explain how great my brain is, but let me put it this way: the world is several million years old and several billion people have trod upon it, but I, Vizzini the Sicilian, am, speaking with pure

candor and modesty, the slickest, sleekest, slyest, and wiliest fellow who has yet come down the pike.

This is one reason why in a Battle of Wits between Vizzini and the Man in Black all things are not equal. On the one hand the Man in Black is a very good judge of character and human nature. On the other, Vizzini is horrible at reading people, and is full of hubris. His false beliefs in the abilities of his own intellect serve to blind him to the fact that he is a horrible reasoner.

Another reason for thinking that all is not equal lies in the fact that Vizzini is a horrible person, and a predictably horrible one, to boot. Recall that in the beginning of this chapter we saw that there were some noteworthy things about the actual-world battle of wits. In addition to the fact that it wasn't a real battle of wits (because the Man in Black cheated), we noted first that Vizzini did virtually all the talking (the Man in Black left Vizzini to decide from which goblet each would drink), and second that despite the fact that Vizzini (with his knife to Buttercup's neck) held all the cards, and had very good reason not to enter the battle of wits with the Man in Black, he simply could not resist the challenge.

In addition to being pretty evil, Vizzini, does not appear to be able to resist his own compulsions. Vizzini, after reasoning himself into an impasse in the battle, for no apparent reason tells the Man in Black to look the other way, and switches the goblets. It's as if he were compelled to engage in trickery, even though nothing in his evidence suggested that this was the right move. Furthermore, he was completely confident that he was right ("You fell victim to one of the classic blunders. . . . Never go in against a Sicilian when death is on the line"). He didn't have to do this. He simply could have said to the Man in Black, "I choose the goblet in front of you." That's what they had been discussing all along. But, of course, he couldn't resist.

Do We Have a Reason to Rejoice?

We now have all that we need for a happy ending. The Man in Black should win a true battle of wits over Vizzini, as Vizzini's predictable evil nature, along with his hubris, and self-blindness make it likely and foreseeable that he would do exactly as he did in the actual battle of wits (create a diversion and switch the goblets). The Man in Black's keen ability to recognize such behavior in advance gives him a huge advantage (Hell, if he can predict in advance that Inigo would begin their swordfight left-handed, then guessing what Vizzini would do should be a walk in the park)—an advantage that is much like the advantage adults have over young children in a game of tic-tac-toe. (It's not difficult too imagine Vizzini thinking to himself "I'm soooo good at tic-tac-toe, the I can win by starting with one of the side-middle squares.")

Notice that the title of this chapter is "Who Should Have Won the Battle of Wits?" and not "Who Would Have Won the Battle of Wits?" I'm not claiming that the Man in Black would necessarily win a battle of wits with Vizzini. I'm claiming that he would most likely win the battle of wits. To put this back into our language of possible worlds, my claim is that in a majority of possible worlds, the Man in Black would be triumphant. I'm also comfortable making the further claim that in no possible world would he lose the battle of wits to Vizzini, although in some worlds it would be a tie, and in some of those he would die.

All of this prompts the question, why did the Man in Black cheat? If after all, as I'm contending, the Man in Black would likely win a battle of wits, why didn't he just enter into a legitimate battle of wits with Vizzini? My response is that the Man in Black was never interested in engaging in a battle of wits with Vizzini. There would be no real challenge to it. The appearance of a battle of wits was all he needed to get Vizzini's knife away from Buttercup's throat.

Moreover, the Man in Black wanted Vizzini dead. So killing him with the appearance of a battle of wits, satisfies both goals at the same time: Buttercup lives and Vizzini dies. Truly entering into a battle of wits with someone such as Vizzini would somehow be beneath someone as dignified as the Man in Black.

So do we still get the happy ending? Do the Man in Black and Buttercup live happily ever after? Do the peoples of Florin and Guilder find peace? Does Inigo Montoya avenge his Father's Death? Does Miracle Max get his mojo back? Does Vizzini die?

Sure, in the possible world I'm describing these things all happen, and in many other possible worlds, too. Perhaps, it best not to focus on the other possible worlds, though—they can be kind of depressing.

8
I Will Never Doubt Again

JAMIE CARLIN WATSON AND
LAURA K. GUIDRY-GRIMES

> **WESTLEY:** Death cannot stop true love. It can only postpone it for a little while.
>
> **BUTTERCUP:** I will never doubt again.

Buttercup promised to trust that Westley would return, but then he was gone for five years. She had no word from him for five years! Plus, his ship was attacked by the Dread Pirate Roberts (who takes no prisoners). Who could blame her for losing hope?

Apparently, Westley could. In the guise of his assailant, Westley excoriates Buttercup for her upcoming marriage to Prince Humperdinck, mocking her promise to be faithful. Is Westley's outrage rational or is it simply jealously? Should Buttercup have held fast to hope despite the overwhelming evidence that Westley was dead, or is her choice to move on perfectly reasonable?

These are questions about responsible belief. Starting with the ancient Greeks, many philosophers have claimed that, in order to be rational, we must follow the evidence; we must be careful to believe for the right reasons, and the right reasons require that a belief is likely to be *true*. If our evidence is strong, we should believe strongly; if it is weak, we should believe weakly. And if it is very weak or unclear, we should suspend belief altogether. These philosophers would say that Westley is irrational to blame Buttercup for losing hope. Westley's own confidence that he would return is probably a form of wishful thinking, a type of self-imposed delusion that can mislead and ensnare someone as thoroughly as lightning sand.

Presumably, we all want to avoid this sort of wishful thinking. The world does not bend itself to our desires, whether we wish for a million florins, a miracle pill, or true love's return. But should we be strictly beholden to evidence? In *The Princess Bride*, Westley seems almost careless with his evidence (and he is our hero!). Vizzini's confidence in his evidence is not entirely unwarranted, yet he is a villain. We cannot help but admire Inigo's perseverance and twenty-year conviction that he will avenge his father, even though he has hardly any information about the identity or location of the killer and no reason to think he will find out. So, is there room for rationality in the space between strictly following the evidence and wishful thinking? Are we still rational if we allow *hope* to shape our beliefs, even if the evidence says things aren't promising?

Through studying the characters in *The Princess Bride,* we discover a reason to expand our notion of rationality. In some cases, as we will see with Westley and Inigo, it can be rational and admirable to choose to believe for reasons that go beyond the evidence. Hope, in particular, is an endorsed desire that can motivate beliefs, and those beliefs can serve us well by supporting well-being and character. These reasons are not only about obtaining knowledge; they are also about living a good life and becoming the sorts of people we want to be.

When hope pushes us into wishful thinking, we have gone too far in allowing our preferences to guide our beliefs. To avoid this trap, we need to balance hope against the evidence. Although it's important to doubt our beliefs when the evidence mounts against us, it is also important to save room for hopefulness.

Evidence and the Farm Boy's Return

The characters in *The Princess Bride* act in odd ways. Westley is motivated by his hope for the future he wants to have with Buttercup. But he has no reason to believe things will work out. Buttercup, on the other hand, is quick to accept the (quite strong) evidence that her true love is dead, and she doesn't have faith that Westley can keep his promise to return. Yet Westley's seemingly irrational optimism serves him well: he survives death; he successfully scales the harrowing Cliffs of

Insanity; he bests a great swordsman, a giant, and a criminal mastermind. Does he have evidence that we don't? On the other hand, Buttercup's well-founded resignation causes her a lot of suffering, leading her into depression and the arms of Prince Humperdinck. Isn't evidence supposed to help us have *better* beliefs so that we live *better*? Are these examples just the stuff of fairytales?

Evidence is supposed to help us form beliefs that are likely to be true, and truth is alleged to be the ultimate goal. The French philosopher René Descartes (1596–1650) tells us that his first rule of reasoning "was never to accept anything as true if I did not have evident knowledge of its truth." Scottish philosopher David Hume (1711–1776) says that "A wise man . . . proportions his belief to the evidence." If being a responsible knower requires that we have as many true beliefs as possible, then we should strictly follow where the evidence leads. Brand Blanshard (1892–1987) says the "only possible rule" for knowers is that they should pursue truth, and he suggests that the "ideal is to believe no more, but also no less, than what the evidence warrants." And some even say we have a strict moral duty to follow evidence. W.K. Clifford (1845–1879) famously says that "it is wrong always, everywhere, and for anyone, to believe anything upon insufficient evidence." If our aim is truth, then in order to be rational, the available evidence should dictate what we believe—or so goes the traditional philosophical view.

This emphasis on following the evidence is not lost on wider culture, either, as certain pop icons inspire similar sentiments. *Star Trek*'s Mr. Spock constantly advises Captain Kirk and the crew to act only on evidence, and not for other reasons like pesky human emotions. Sir Arthur Conan Doyle's Sherlock Holmes is a model of cool-headed reason guided only by the most complete and detailed evidence.

These examples suggest a very particular (and highly popular) view of rationality: a person is rational only if her beliefs match her *evidence*. Evidence is one type of *reason to believe a claim is true*. There are lots of reasons to believe something that have nothing to do with whether it's true, such as wanting to fit in with the brute squad or being threatened with iocane powder. And there are lots of bad reasons to believe something, like wishful thinking and self-delusion. In contrast with these, evidence is a *good* or *legitimate* reason to believe a claim is true. For example, when Westley and Buttercup are in the Fire Swamp, they hear a popping sound just before flames erupt from the ground. Westley rightly takes this popping sound as evidence that fire is about to spurt, and following this evidence allows him to move Buttercup out of harm's way.

The reasons for preferring this view of rationality are clear: the world is a certain way whether we like it or not, and *guessing* does a much worse job of helping us figure out what the world is like than relying on evidence. People visit Miracle Max precisely because they have evidence that his cures work (whether miraculous or not). And if we aren't relying on evidence, we might have fallen into *wishful thinking*.

By "wishful thinking," we don't mean merely wishing something were true. It's often rational to wish you were stronger or smarter or that you wrote the definitive work on pain (like Count Rugan plans to do). These wishes inspire us to achieve our desires or allow us to express regret. But when someone falls prey to wishful thinking in the sense we are talking about, she is using her *wish that something is true* as a reason to believe it *is* true, such as Vizzini's belief that Plato, Aristotle, and Socrates are morons in comparison with his intelligence. Wishful thinking involves ignoring evidence and stubbornly turning away from challenges to our beliefs, even when those challenges should be taken seriously. According to one group of psychologists (Bastardi, Uhlmann, and Ross), wishful thinking occurs "when someone engages in biased reasoning in order to support a belief in a desired conclusion."

If Buttercup had persisted in her belief that Westley would return after hearing his ship had been attacked by the Dread Pirate Roberts and after five years had passed, we would rightly regard her as irrational. To believe these things she would have to ignore good evidence in order to cling to a theory without much evidence—what we would normally regard (at least in non-fairytale worlds) as a fantasy. In order to avoid wishful thinking, then, Buttercup rationally (though sadly) believes that her beloved has perished.

Westley, on the other hand, has a tendency to believe astonishingly implausible things. When he and Buttercup are running into the Fire Swamp to escape Humperdinck and his men, Buttercup insists they will never survive. Westley objects to her conclusion on what seem to be pretty shoddy grounds: "Nonsense. You're only saying that because no one ever has." But the fact that no one has ever survived the Fire Swamp (presuming there was a non-trivial sample of people who entered it), *is* good evidence that Westley and Buttercup won't survive it. If Westley is flouting the available evidence, he's in danger of wishful thinking, of irrationality.

But are there only two ways to think about belief here? Is it only that someone follows the evidence and is rational or that he or she succumbs to wishful thinking and is irrational? Consider, again, our evidence-driven heroes, Spock and Holmes. Spock has trouble in a number of social situations, not least of which involve love. (Contrast Spock's reactions to chemically induced passion in the original series episodes "Mudd's Passion" and "This Side of Paradise.") And over time, Sherlock Holmes becomes an arrogant, reclusive cocaine addict. Can we still call these characters rational if their evidence-driven beliefs threaten their ability to live a valuable life? Perhaps there's more to rationality than just following the evidence.

Inigo's Quest and the Strange Case of Hope

Let's look at Westley and Buttercup's alternatives: likely death in the Fire Swamp or imprisonment and probably death at the hands of Humperdinck. Clearly, they have good evidence they will not survive the Fire Swamp. But they also have good evidence that at least Westley will not survive Humperdinck's wrath. Surely Westley wants to believe they can escape this trap, but is that wishful thinking? Or is Westley's unfailing *hope* that they can escape actually rational?

Hope and despair shape beliefs differently than evidence. Whereas evidence provides us with reasons to believe something is likely true, hope and despair are ways of believing that combine our evidence with what we value. Philosopher Adrienne Martin says that the standard philosophical conception of hope is "endorsed desire plus uncertainty." When our evidence is unpersuasive but we still have to make a decision about what to believe, our decision need not be arbitrary; we can turn to what makes our beliefs valuable. *Hope* is possible when our evidence for a belief is weak and yet our values tell us that belief is worthwhile. Count Rugan's Pit of Despair is designed precisely to make the evidence of Westley's impending death so overwhelming that he no longer values living.

In the Fire Swamp, the evidence for a happily-ever-after-ending is not good. Nevertheless, if they despair because of this evidence, it is likely that their prospects will diminish even further. Consider an example from the medical field, where hope—but not wishful thinking—is often encouraged. Patients, doctors, and nurses commonly believe that hopefulness can make a difference for a patient's quality of life—and even length of life—in the face of certain medical conditions. And some studies support this notion. For example, in 2002 researchers Kubzansky at al. found that aging patients who had hopeful attitudes ended up having better lung function across a ten-year period than patients who had pessimistic attitudes. Other studies (like the one by Maruta et al.) show that fatalism, catastrophic thinking, and learned helplessness are typical of people who lack general optimism or hopefulness, and such people suffer poorer health and higher risk of mortality overall. So, even when the evidence of a happy outcome is low, if the alternatives are suffering and death, being hopeful can improve your chances.

This suggests that strictly following the evidence is not the only or best way to be rational. In fact, having *true beliefs* may not be the only valuable goal. Typically, we don't just want correct beliefs; we also want to live good lives. We want to be happy and healthy and fulfilled. This combination is called *well-being*. Hopeful attitudes improve our quality of life and help us become the sort of people we want to be; we rightly admire people who are hopeful as opposed to despairing and pessimistic all the time.

But this doesn't mean that we should let wishes guide our beliefs and forget about evidence. A person can be hopeful without falling into wishful thinking. In our story, Inigo understands that the likelihood of finding the six-fingered man is very low. The six-fingered man might have died of old age or in battle. Further, he could be anywhere in the world. Nevertheless, Inigo trains to become one of the best swordsmen in the world.

Is Inigo's search supported by the evidence? No. He has ample reason to believe he will not find his father's killer. He even tells the Man in Black that, after twenty years, he is starting to lose confidence. Nevertheless, he presses on because he also values the pursuit. To him, the honorable and decent thing to do is to commit himself fully to the plan of avenging his father. He still has *hope* that he will find the killer. And if he stopped his search, his well-being would surely decrease (perhaps drastically, as we learn that Vizzini found him drunk in despair when he doubted he could complete his mission).

Inigo also demonstrates other benefits of hope. Unlike wishful thinking, hope does not lead Inigo to ignore things that make life valuable. His search does not interfere with his ability to live life normally: he works for Vizzini "to pay the bills," he forms bonds of friendship (with Fezzik), and he appreciates beauty and goodness where he finds it (Westley's swordsmanship). So even if his search for the Six-Fingered Man is irrational according to the standard account of rationality, it is not obviously irrational if we take into account all the things that make Inigo's life worth living.

In contrast with Inigo, consider Buttercup's decision to take her own life near the end of the movie, when it looks like she will have to marry Prince Humperdinck. At this point, Westley has shown repeatedly that he can keep his promise to return in spite of terrible odds. This evidence is admittedly weak now that she knows Humperdinck didn't really return Westley to his ship. Nevertheless, her despair seems irrational *not* because her evidence is weak but because it would be better for her to live and to hope for rescue. Her hope would not be baseless, since it is *possible* that Westley was able to escape his captors once again. For the sake of not succumbing to helplessness or catastrophic thinking, it would be rational for her to maintain hope. So, our question now is this: how do we balance weighing the evidence and hoping for the best?

Perhaps I Have the Strength After All

Returning to the Fire Swamp, Buttercup despairs, "We'll never make it! We may as well die here!" while Westley presses on confidently. The evidence is in Buttercup's favor; death seems imminent. So, there is a conflict between the idea that rationality requires believing solely on the basis of evidence and the idea that there are other valuable reasons to believe, such as those that contribute to our sense of self and well-being. If rationality is solely a matter of evidence, then in the Fire Swamp, Buttercup is rational and Westley is irrational. But surely Westley is the better model. He does not ignore the evidence, but he understands the alternative; he believes they will survive because it is better to do so than not. He has not only believed responsibly, we are tempted to say he believed *rationally*.

The same can be said for Inigo. He has very little evidence that he will find and defeat his father's killer, but his belief that he will is enduring. It's important to his sense of what is valuable to hope—that he will fulfill his mission. In this conviction, we see the marks of heroism.

The way to resolve this conflict between the classical view of rationality and these examples is to expand the concept of rationality to include *both* evidence-driven beliefs *and* value-driven beliefs. Evidence is surely important for responsible belief; we shouldn't ignore it for just any reason. Wishful thinking is irresponsible precisely because it leads us to follow only the evidence that supports our wishes or to ignore evidence altogether. Even if indulging in wishful thinking accidentally makes us happy in a given situation, it puts us at great risk for enormous disappointment and suffering when the world proves not to conform to our wishes. Hope, on the other hand, can take evidence very seriously. It can balance evidence against the value of a belief, particularly when that evidence is uncertain.

If all of this is right, then rationality is not simply a matter of following the evidence; it is a matter of taking responsibility for living a good life. Westley is so committed to Buttercup that he's not willing to give up hope that they will be together. Sometimes this encourages wishful thinking, as when he gets angry that Buttercup didn't believe he would return after five years. But other times, it supports a well-lived life, as when he perseveres through the Fire Swamp or when he is paralyzed on the bed, facing Humperdinck. When a person takes responsibility for her beliefs, she evaluates all the relevant reasons for belief, regardless of whether they are strictly tied to evidence. In some cases, it may be responsible to ignore everything except the evidence. But in other cases, it may be responsible to believe in spite of the evidence (as when facing a terminal disease). When the chips are down and our options are grim, hope can help us say, with Westley, "Perhaps I have the strength after all."

III

Getting Even

... now that it's over.
I don't know what
to do with
the rest of my life.

9
Why Revenge Is So Sweet

DANIEL HAAS

Inigo Montoya's quest to avenge the murder of his father is one of my favorite revenge stories. Who doesn't love Mandy Patinkin finally confronting the Six-Fingered Man and chanting "My name is Inigo Montoya. You killed my father. Prepare to die"?

Revenge is hardly the kind of motivation that moral philosophers commend. The vast majority of mainstream theories of justice and morality condemn vengeance and hold those who indulge in vengeful behavior in ill-regard. It's seen as an emotionally-driven, destructive, and primitive urge to see those who have wronged you suffer. And this is not justice. Nor is it morally praiseworthy. In fact, the very real consequence of people seeking vengeance is often an exponential increase of death and suffering.

And yet, there's something about a good revenge story that many of us can relate to. *The Iliad, The Count of Monte Cristo, Hamlet*, even the *Harry Potter* novels—all have sympathetic characters questing after revenge at their narrative cores. In fact, one of the easiest and cheapest ways to get an audience to relate to and empathize with a protagonist is to give that hero a wrong to avenge. Montoya's quest for the Six-Fingered Man who killed his father is the perfect example. There's something about a good revenge story that is relatable, and perhaps even something about the character who seeks to avenge an injustice that is praiseworthy.

Here's where it gets tricky. If we condemn the real-life quest for vengeance, why is it that we so readily relate to and sym-

pathize with revenge stories and vengeful characters? What is
it we're picking up on, perhaps indulging in, when we cheer for
the vengeful heroines and heroes of movies and literature?
Why do we want Inigo to find and kill the Six-Fingered Man if
revenge is such a bad thing? What, if anything, is morally
worthwhile about revenge?

You Don't, by Chance, Happen to Have Six Fingers on Your Right Hand?

We first meet Inigo Montoya as a hired thug, helping Vizzini,
the criminal genius, on his 'inconceivable' mission to start a
war between the kingdoms of Florin and Guilder by capturing
the soon-to-be princess, Buttercup. Vizzini and his men have
been hired by Prince Humperdinck to kidnap the princess-to-
be. Humperdinck wants a pretext for war between his kingdom, Florin, and the neighboring kingdom of Guilder.
Humperdinck's plan is to have Buttercup murdered on Guilder
lands and to make her murder look like it was done by Guilder
nobles. As Princess Buttercup is beloved by the people of
Florin, her death will give Humperdinck the justification he
needs for initiating a war. Vizzini and his men have been hired
by the prince to carry out this plot.

Despite Inigo's obvious sense of humor (Inigo and his fellow
thug, Fezzik, the giant, spend most of this first scene mocking
their boss), Inigo is initially presented to the audience as a villain. He's a mere thug, helping to kidnap and murder a
princess and to start a war. He is not a character we are supposed to root for.

It's really a few scenes later, when Inigo is tasked with
killing Westley, a.k.a. the Man in Black a.k.a. the Dread
Pirate Roberts, that the audience's perception of Inigo
changes. Westley has been pursuing Vizzini's band of kidnappers across the ocean and is gaining on them. The kidnappers
try to escape their pursuer by scaling the Cliffs of Insanity
but Westley follows. As Westley climbs the cliffs, Vizzini
orders Inigo to stay behind and kill Westley, if Westley manages to scale the cliffs without dying. Vizzini and Fezzik then
flee with Buttercup in tow.

Inigo is both an honorable and an impatient man, and
decides he'd rather best Westley in a fair fight than to stand

around waiting for the pirate to fall. He pledges to help Westley safely scale the cliffs.

Upon arriving safely atop the Cliffs of Insanity, Westley is given a few moments to catch his breath and prepare for a fair fight while Inigo relays his life-story. His father, Domingo Montoya was a great swordsmith. The Six-Fingered Man sought out Domingo to make a sword for him. After the sword was completed, the Six-Fingered Man refused to pay the full price, offering only a tenth of what he'd originally promised. Domingo found this offer insulting and refused. The Six-Fingered Man retaliated by piercing Inigo's father through the heart. Inigo tells Westley that he loved his father, and challenged his father's murderer to a duel. Inigo failed. He was merely an eleven-year-old boy and outmatched. The Six-Fingered Man spared his life but slashed him across both cheeks, scarring him. Inigo then devoted his life to studying fencing, and to becoming strong enough and skilled enough to avenge his father's murder. He pledged that the next time he met the Six-Fingered Man, he would not fail.

Backstory and motivation hashed out, Inigo and Westley duel. Westley wins the duel (he is the hero of this fairytale, after all). Being a hero, he chooses not to kill Inigo. Westley explains that it would be a grave injustice to rob the world of a great swordsman like Inigo Montoya, akin to destroying a work of art. He merely renders Inigo unconscious and continues his quest to rescue Buttercup.

It is interesting how Inigo's backstory made him instantly relatable. By the time he is defeated in battle, we don't see him as a bumbling cartoonish thug whom the hero should dispose of. He is someone who we root for because we see the virtue of his mission to avenge his father's wrongful death. And we are happy that his life is spared, and his quest for vengeance can continue.

There's Not a Lot of Money in Revenge

Revenge may make for good motivation for fictional heroines and anti-heroes, but this doesn't translate so well to real life. The real-world quest for vengeance is much more likely to be realized as the escalation of violence such as we see in gang wars or inter-tribal conflicts than as a quest to overthrow a cartoonish villain by a noble heroine. There are fairly obvious and compelling pragmatic reasons why we don't tolerate vigilante justice and personal revenge.

Philosophers have also condemned vengeance as a barbaric perversion of justice. Revenge is typically viewed as retaliation that is tied to base emotional reactions such as spite, anger, and resentment. We seek revenge to make us feel better and to hurt someone who has hurt us or ours. Just punishment, by contrast is not an outburst of negative emotion. Rather, justice is a kind of communication between the society and the wrongdoer that their action is not appropriate and possibly, in virtue of the wrong act, the wrongdoer deserves punishment.

Even if the target of revenge is someone like Rugen who is worthy of punishment, being motivated by vengeance is not to seek justice. It's more often driven by these negative emotions, by a desire to hurt someone merely because they hurt you. It's not a case of impartial, proportional justice.

There's a compelling case against revenge here. If revenge is such a dangerous and vile approach to justice, why does so much of our art praise revenge? *The Princess Bride* actually makes revenge a positive and integral plot-device. Were it not for a quest for revenge, things would go very badly for Westley and Buttercup, and the story is told in such a way that we cheer when Inigo finally takes his revenge against the Six-Fingered Man. Let's take a look at the second act of the movie to see whether we can shed some light on what's going on here.

After Twenty Years at Last My Father's Soul Will Be at Peace

The mercy Westley showed Inigo would prove to be a wise move. Disheartened by his defeat, Inigo spends weeks inebriated and licking his wounds. By chance, he meets up with his old partner, Fezzik, whose life Westley also spared. Fezzik rescues Inigo from a run-in with a soldier, and nurses Inigo back to health. While Inigo is recuperating, he learns of Prince Humperdinck's plot to start a war, and more importantly, that the Six-Fingered Man is named Rugen, and that Rugen and the prince are working together. Inigo and Fezzik are too outnumbered to take on Humperdinck and Rugen by themselves, but if they could team up with the Dread-Pirate Roberts! They'd be unstoppable. Fezzik and Inigo pledge to find Westley, and together, take down Humperdinck and Rugen.

By this point in the story, Westley, of course, has been captured by Humperdinck and is literally having the life sucked out of him in the castle's torture chambers. His screams are so loud that Inigo and Fezzik can hear them despite being nowhere near the castle. Apparently, having years of your life sucked out via a renaissance torture machine will do that to you. The two friends rescue Westley (whom they find nearly dead), restore him to health (with the help of a miracle-worker and his wife, of course), and set out to rescue the princess and defeat Humperdinck and Rugen.

This rescue mission eventually gives Inigo his long-awaited opportunity for revenge. Shortly into their raid on the castle, Inigo and his allies confront Rugen and several guards. With the guards quickly dispatched, Inigo challenges Rugen to a duel. But of course, the Six-Fingered Man, being a villain, is not about to engage in a fair fight. He turns and runs. Inigo pursues his foe, but Rugen manages to throw a dagger into Inigo's gut, while Inigo is running down a flight of stairs. It's only after Inigo is severely wounded that our villain chooses to confront him. Not to be deterred from his life-long quest by something as insignificant as a near-fatal wound, Inigo pulls the dagger from his gut, rises, and takes his well-earned vengeance against the Six-Fingered Man. Chanting, "My name is Inigo Montoya. You killed my father. Prepare to die," he engages his foe. With each chant of his mantra, Inigo seems to gain more strength, more resolve, and Rugen soon meets his fate. Domingo Montoya has been avenged, and Inigo can finally end his quest for vengeance and move on with his life (while the movie ends on a happy note, with the suggestion that Inigo will become the next Dread Pirate Roberts, in William Goldman's novel, Inigo's wound reopens as he flees the castle, suggesting that he might not survive much longer).

It's Inigo's quest for vengeance that really saves the day here. Had Inigo decided that vengeance was an immoral motivation, Humperdinck and Rugen would have succeeded in starting their war, they would have both escaped punishment for their crimes, and Westley and Buttercup would have both suffered tragic deaths. In *The Princess Bride*, as in so many other myths and fairytales, it's the motivation for personal revenge that leads to heroic victory. *The Princess Bride*, rather than condemning, praises revenge.

Given the problems with revenge we reviewed earlier, is there something dishonest, perhaps even dangerous, about this fairytale? Should we really be condemning Inigo's quest for vengeance and the positive way in which *The Princess Bride* portrays revenge? Would it have been better if Inigo had appealed to the judicial system to seek justice for his father's death?

Blood Will Be Spilled Tonight!

We don't know much about the judicial system at work in *The Princess Bride*. We know that Florin is a vaguely Renaissance-era kingdom that looks to be ruled, at least in practice, by Prince Humperdinck. While the kindly king of Florin is still alive and on the throne, he seems to exercise little, if any executive or administrative power. It's also suggested that his mental capacities are beginning to deteriorate, that he has little knowledge or input into what is actually happening in his kingdom, and that he might even be going senile.

We're definitely given the sense that what the Prince says goes, at least in Florin. We know that Rugen is a count in Humperdinck's court, and that both Humperdinck and Rugen are villains, who have little respect for judicial process. It's highly unlikely that Inigo has anything like a legitimate judicial channel through which to have his complaints about the murder of his father heard. So, appealing to the magistrate for justice is not a viable option for Inigo. In fact, given that the ruling elite of Florin are corrupt, asking for state justice would likely have gotten Inigo killed.

This really leaves Inigo with few options for seeking justice for his father's murder. Revenge looks very different in this kind of environment than it would in, say, contemporary America. It's understandable, then, in the absence of an effective criminal justice system, that he made the choice to personally avenge his father's death.

Recently, several philosophers and social scientists (including Richard Nisbett and Dov Cohen) have drawn attention to a distinction between honor cultures and institutionalized cultures. Honor cultures are cultures in which:

- Most co-operation occurs between families or close-knit groups such as clans, gangs, or small tribes (there is little co-operation among strangers).

- The protection of scarce resources is vital to survival.

- Attempted theft and raids are common.

- There is little to no state-provided justice, the land is relatively lawless.

Institutionalized cultures, by contrast, as Tamler Sommers and others have discussed, have extensive economic co-operation amongst strangers, significantly less theft and the perks of raids are significantly reduced, and there is a robust, institutionalized judicial system. These are the kinds of cultures we see throughout most of the contemporary world. In honor cultures personal retribution plays a significant role. As there is no or little access to a formalized legal system and the costs of personal attacks are high, it is a beneficial deterrent to be the kind of person that would take a personal attack such as theft or the murder of a family member as an attack on one's honor, that can only be addressed by personal vengeance. The risks and costs of personal vengeance are high, but the costs of not being the kind of person who would retaliate against an attack on your honor is worse. Given that there is little formal justice in an honor culture, not being the kind of person who will seek vengeance for an attack on one's honor would paint you as an easy-target and possibly increase the chance that you and yours will be targeted again. Institutionalized cultures, of course, remove this motivation, and give the duty to address concerns of justice to the state.

Inigo inhabits and is committed to the moral norms of an honor culture. As I said before, it's likely that there is some sort of judicial system operating in his society. But, given that the leaders of his kingdom are villains, it's also highly unlikely that this judicial system is one that takes the needs for justice of people like Inigo with any sort of seriousness. In this sense Inigo is a member of a disenfranchised group. For Inigo, there is little or no protection provided by the state and the land he inhabits is largely lawless. To the extent that the state would become involved in the life of someone like Inigo, it would be as a threat. For all intents and purposes, there is not a functional justice system in Florin. If Inigo wants justice he must take matters into his own hands.

Okay, so maybe, given that Florin is led by a villain and lacks an effective judicial system, Inigo has reasonable grounds for believing that the duty to seek justice for his father's murder falls on his shoulders. As the son of a man murdered in cold blood, he has a duty of honor to avenge this wrong. In this sense, it's commendable for Inigo to seek revenge.

But surely revenge is something that has no place in the modern world, with its relatively healthy judicial systems. We relate to Inigo's success, not because we find something admirable about revenge, but because there's a very strong psychological impulse to see people who deserve punishment get what they deserve. In a good revenge story, the hero takes it upon herself to avenge a wrong because there's no other avenue available to the character to right that wrong. We relate to and cheer on the hero out of respect for justice, not because we genuinely think revenge is of moral worth. Or, is there something, even today, that is admirable about revenge itself, and perhaps worth taking a closer look at?

He Is a Sailor on the Pirate Ship *Revenge*

What can be said in defense of revenge? The reason we're attracted to revenge in so much of our art is that a good revenge story captures the widely, albeit not universally, shared intuition that people who freely do wrong deserve certain treatment and that revenge is personal.

We've been speaking a lot about the deserved retribution portion of revenge already. The motivation and justification for revenge at least partially involves the retributive idea that people who freely, intentionally, and knowingly do wrong often deserve to be punished for their moral transgressions. While a desire to see people who do wrong get what they deserve might be what makes revenge stories somewhat sympathetic, it is not the unique feature of revenge that is absent from contemporary approaches to justice. After all, this is an idea that can be accommodated by moral and legal theories that condemn revenge.

The personal and relational nature of revenge, however, is different. Revenge is personal. It can only be sought by someone who has a personal tie to the wrong-doer or the wrong-doer's victim, and it can only be carried out by someone with a similar tie to the offense. It would not be as pleasing if Rugen had been killed by someone other than Inigo. Suppose, upon breaking into the castle to rescue the princess, Inigo had found Rugen dead, say he'd slipped and impaled himself on his own sword. Or suppose Fezzik had entered the castle before Inigo, dropped a boulder on Rugen's head, and then called Inigo. Both scenarios would be unsatisfying for Inigo and the audience. Why?

It's because Inigo would be denied personal justice that we would find these outcomes narratively unsatisfying. It's not that we merely want Rugen to suffer or die. What we want is for Rugen to suffer at the hands of Inigo. Those who are wronged have a special kind of moral standing, a relationship to those who have wronged them such that it is more appropriate for them to be dishing out the punishment (or forgiveness) than someone else. Only Inigo can give Rugen what he deserves. And revenge stories like *The Princess Bride* capture this.

You've Got an Overdeveloped Sense of Vengeance

Maybe it's not revenge that is sometimes praiseworthy. Maybe it's something else, something that often goes hand-in-hand with revenge, at least when it's written about in stories like *The Princess Bride*.

Suppose that we changed the story slightly. Suppose that instead of a convenient villain like Rugen, the real killer of Inigo's father had been Westley. It wouldn't be a huge stretch to imagine that during his days as the Dread Pirate Roberts, Westley, while out pirating, encountered and had to kill Domingo Montoya. Would we, the audience, still cheer, at the chanting of "My name is Inigo Montoya. You killed my father. Prepare to die," if Inigo was chanting this as he cut down Westley? I doubt it.

There is a sense in which we would understand and perhaps even empathize with Inigo's motivations. There would be something appropriate about Inigo avenging his father's death. We might even say it is unfortunate, but fitting, that, if Westley had killed Domingo Montoya, then it is understandable that Inigo would make Westley pay with his life for the death of Inigo's father. But we wouldn't want this. The story would be a tragedy, a meditation on the ugly costs of personal vengeance, rather than a heroic tale moved forward by a just quest for vengeance.

What we'd hope, as an audience, in this scenario, is that Inigo would be willing to give Westley a chance at atonement, an opportunity to make amends, to show appropriate remorse, and to be forgiven.

What this suggests is that vengeance stories are compelling because of the way they're told, not because of the intrinsic value of revenge. If we changed the narrative, we're reading a tragedy, or the revenge-seeker is a villain (just think of how many horror movies involve a vengeful evil). What's compelling, to us, about revenge, is that revenge stories point to something that is not often discussed outside of honor cultures. Victims have a special kind of relationship to those who have wronged them, and perhaps this is something worth taking seriously, when we think about justice.[1]

---

[1] It would be inconceivable to write a paper about revenge and not dedicate it to Mareen Redies. I've said it for years, Mareen, but it is still true to this day: "As you wish."

10
Making the Punishment Fit the Crime

JOSHUA HETER

Suppose a certain Six-Fingered Man commissions a sword maker to make him an elegant, ornate sword. However, once the sword is finished, the Six-Fingered Man demands the sword maker sell him the sword at one-tenth the original, agreed price. When the sword maker naturally refuses, the Six-Fingered Man stabs him right through the heart. Also, suppose that the sword-maker has an eleven-year-old son who, in a fit of justified and unbridled anger, attempts to avenge his father's death by challenging the Six-Fingered Man to a duel. After the Six-Fingered Man easily bests the young boy, he leaves him with a pair of facial scars.

Many of us feel that under the right circumstances the son would be justified in tracking down the Six-Fingered Man and avenging his father's death, even if that meant taking the life of the Six-Fingered Man. And of course, this thought experiment is familiar to us as it is played out by Inigo Montoya (the son) and Tyrone Rugen (the Six-Fingered Man) in *The Princess Bride*.

What is philosophically interesting about Montoya's quest is that although we feel that Montoya is justified in killing Rugen, this is not because killing Rugen will bring about some good result. Rugen is by no means a praiseworthy or virtuous character, but it's not as if he is still shaking down and subsequently murdering sword makers. So, Montoya is not justified in killing him because he must put an end to Rugen's ongoing murderous rampage.

The people of Florin are presumably largely ignorant of Rugen's crime as well as Montoya's quest for retribution. So, it's not as though Montoya wishes to deter *others* from murdering (thereby saving innocent lives) by showing them that murderers often enough lose their own life. On the contrary, Montoya's killing of Rugen seems to be purely a matter of justice. Rugen simply *deserves* to die. By murdering Montoya's father, Rugen has knocked the scales of justice out of balance and the only way for them to be brought back into balance is for Rugen, a man who has taken a life, to lose his life as well.

It *does* seem as if Montoya is justified in killing Rugen. Some would even argue that Montoya's actions are not only justified but *obligatory*. As natural as it is to defend Montoya's hunt for and ultimate killing of Rugen, it raises troubling questions about the nature of crime and punishment.

First, even if Rugen deserves to be punished, and even if he deserves a particularly harsh punishment, it's still an open question who has the right or the authority to punish. Even if Rugen deserves to pay for his crimes, it doesn't follow that Montoya ought to be the one to collect. Montoya is acting as a vigilante, and while it is perhaps important that all criminals be punished, it is perhaps equally important that punishment be carried out only by the proper authorities.

Second, even if Montoya is justified in punishing Rugen, it may be argued that the punishment that Montoya chooses—that Rugen die after Montoya explicitly introduces himself and informs Rugen of why he is about to die—is not (or is never) an appropriate form of punishment. Does Rugen deserve to die for his crime? Does any man ever deserve to die for his crime? These are important questions. And again, while many of us naturally view Montoya's actions as justified, if we are to come up with a good, solid defense of them, these worries must be laid to rest.

The Kingdom of Florin and the State of Nature

Outside the time and place of Florin, we make a hardline distinction between punishment delivered by sanctioned, governmental authorities and punishment delivered by vigilantes. When delivered properly, the former seems just and fair; the latter most often, or at best leaves us feeling morally uncomfortable. Even if a criminal deserves to be punished, we presume, ordinary citizens without special authorization are simply never the ones who ought to carry out the punishment. Even if a criminal genuinely deserves a punishment, if the proper authorities fail to deliver it, many feel that it is nevertheless inappropriate for individual citizens to deliver punishment independently of the government.

If this is correct, then perhaps Montoya should seek justice for his father (as well as himself) by some other means. Perhaps Montoya should alert Prince Humperdinck of Rugen's crime and implore him to hold a trial; and only if he is found guilty, for Rugen to suffer an official, Florin-sanctioned execution. Even if this course of action is highly unlikely to achieve the justice which Montoya seeks, some would argue, it is nevertheless the course he ought to take, as he has no right or authority to pursue justice independently of the authority of the Kingdom of Florin.

We're assuming here that only monarchs, or governing bodies more generally, have the authority, or the right, to punish. However, it's by no means obvious that this assumption is correct. The simple question here is, who has the right to punish? If governments have the authority to punish, on what basis do they have this authority? To be sure, if *only* governments have the right to punish, then Montoya is not justified in punishing Rugen. However, simply because governments are *typically recognized* as the sole arbiters of justice when it comes to punishment, it doesn't follow that Montoya may not in fact be justified in punishing Rugen

In defense of Montoya's right to punish, we will look to the political philosophy of John Locke. According to Locke (as well as many other political philosophers), the manner in which people typically live their lives, within the bounds of society and under the rule of law, is not natural. Governments, societal structures, and the rules that come with them are in one way or another artificial. While people in the land and time of Florin (as well as today) do in fact live under a state of governmental authority and control, we can imagine living in the "state of nature."

Imagine any ordinary citizen of Florin. When we ask questions about what he does, why he does it, or what he should in fact do, the place and time in which he lives offers us seemingly effortless, useful explanations for all of these questions. When Prince Humperdinck and his fiancée Buttercup ceremoniously present themselves to the citizens of Florin, our Florinese citizen bows. Why does he do this? Perhaps he does this because he respects the monarchs of his land, or because he fears their wrath. What should he do? Perhaps he's doing what he should. He ought to bow, either to conform to the not unreasonable law of the land, or because it's simply prudent. He doesn't want to risk being seen as a troublemaker (and subsequently receiving a harsh punishment).

However, thinking about the "state of nature"—what we should and should not do if there is no government—allows us to ask questions about what we do, why we do it, and what we ought to do, independent of presumably artificial governmental influences. Strip away the laws, customs, and police force of Florin, and we're forced to come up with very different answers to the questions concerning how our hypothetical Florinese ought to live. Without undue governmental influence, is there ever a time in which he should bow to any other man? If he need not worry about being hooked up to Prince Humperdinck's life-sucking Machine, how should he conduct himself on a day-to-day basis? More broadly, without undue governmental influence, how ought anyone to live life in general? What should the Florinese do were he to live solely within the bounds of nature?

If we can get straight on what the state of nature actually is, that should inform the way in which we structure our governments. Looking closely at a state of nature, where there is no government, can help us decide what governments are for and just what they ought to be able to do.

According to Locke, the state of nature is one of freedom and equality. Man is free in the sense that in his natural state, he has the right to any and all he thinks is best to secure his own self-preservation. He is equal to other men insofar as no man has the right to control or maintain power over any other man. However, when one man violates the freedom of another, it's within the victim's right to seek retribution, or payment from the perpetrator (and thus, exact control over him in some limited sense).

With this in mind, it is man's state of nature that grounds the government's authority to punish. It is true that governing bodies, such as the Kingdom of Florin, write their own laws, and deliver their own punishment when those laws are broken.

However, their authority to do so is founded upon and should aim to map onto the natural law of man's state of nature. Who ultimately has the right to punish? Victims have the right to punish. In "civil society," perhaps for prudential reasons, victims simply transfer their right to punish to the state. Whatever authority a government has to punish is given by victims who have the right (if not the obligation in certain cases) to seek retribution.

If this is correct, then we here have a ready-made defense that if Rugen deserves punishment for his crimes, then Montoya has the right to carry out the punishment. The Kingdom of Florin is by no means a civil society. It is a tyrannical government run by a self-important leader, Prince Humperdinck. Under more desirable circumstances, in which Inigo Montoya is searching for justice for his father, it would be prudent if not appropriate for him to seek retribution through different means. That is, if the murder of Montoya's father had occurred in a place where there was a reasonable expectation of justice, we could perhaps hold Montoya accountable for attempting to transfer his right, or his father's right as a victim to the state so that it could deliver punishment and justice. However, without any such a reasonable expectation, Montoya is well within his rights to seek retribution on his own. He is justified in punishing Rugen for the acts committed against himself and his father.

Prepare to Suffer a Punishment Morally Equivalent to the Crime you Committed!

So it does look as if Montoya has the authority to punish Rugen for the crimes committed against his father and himself. However, it doesn't immediately follow that Montoya is justified in killing Rugen. Is the appropriate punishment for Rugen death? Does Rugen *deserve* to die for his crimes? According to Immanuel Kant's theory of retributive justice, the answer is yes.

Imagine an island (perhaps just off the Cliffs of Insanity) whose inhabitants agree to disband and go their separate ways. According to Kant (in his *Metaphysics of Morals*), if the inhabitants do not first put to death all of the prisoners of the island who are guilty of murder (and similar enough crimes), the island's inhabitants should be regarded as "accomplices in the public violation of justice." The inhabitants of the island have contributed to the injustice in the world by failing to put to death those who deserve to be put to death.

The broad idea behind claims of Kant's retributive justice is that certain morally egregious crimes call for punishment, and that it's simply immoral or unjust to allow the crimes to go unpunished, or to allow the punishment to be disproportional to the crime. More specifically, Kant suggests that it would be unjust to allow a murderer to go on living thereby going without his just desert. If any crime calls for punishment it is the act of murder. And, insofar as it seems fairly intuitive, if not undeniable, at least at first blush, that the punishment should fit the crime, we're left with a fairly compelling reason to think that murderers should lose their own lives for the punishment of their crimes.

From the assumptions that murderers should be punished and that their punishment should be proportional to their crime, it does not necessarily follow that they themselves ought to be killed. The relevant principle of retributive justice is that a punishment should be *proportional* to the crime, not that a punishment must be of the same *type* or *kind* as its crime. Suppose that while storming the castle and pulling a fast one on Prince Humperdinck's men through his medieval special effects, Montoya's especially large comrade, Fezzik, through gross carelessness, burns down a villager's house. What is the proper moral response? If we assume a crime has been committed, and we are dedicated to making sure that (as a matter of justice) crimes don't go unpunished, nor do they received a disproportional punishment, are we committed to burning down Fezzik's house as well? Setting aside the anxiety that burning down the house of a man the size and strength of Fezzik may be asking for trouble, it does not seem as if we are.

A punishment may be proportional to its crime even if it is a significantly different type of thing from its crime. So long as Prince Humperdinck's men could actually subdue Fezzick and put him in the dungeon, there may be some amount of time Fezzik could be imprisoned that would appropriately mirror his crime. An hour spent in prison would perhaps not suffice. A life sentence would perhaps be too harsh. However, an appropriate amount of jail time (or, dungeon time) could in principle cover Fezzik's crime even though spending time in a dungeon's cell is a significantly different thing than the crime of carelessly burning down the house of an innocent villager. So (as M.A. Moore argues) proposing that the punishment should fit the crime is merely saying that the punishment should be proportional to its crime even if it looks nothing like it. If this is so, then perhaps the proper response to murderers such as the Six-Fingered Man is not necessarily to take their lives, if retribution can be achieved by some less gruesome or undesirable means.

However, with this in mind, I think it is clear what Inigo Montoya (and his defenders) ought to say in defense of Inigo's quest to avenge his father's death by hunting down Rugen and killing him: murder is a special case. While in general it's true that a punishment can be proportional to its crime without being the same type of thing as its crime, it is nevertheless also true that the only proportionate punishment the crime of murder can receive is death. Murderers deserve to die if only because there is no other punishment that carries an equal amount of weight as the crime of murder.

Recall that just before Montoya does exact revenge and kill Rugen, the Six-Fingered Man, at the behest of Montoya, Rugen begins to bargain for his life.

MONTOYA: Offer me money.

RUGEN: Yes.

MONTOYA: Power too, promise me that.

RUGEN: All that I have a have and more; please.

MONTOYA: Offer me everything I ask for.

RUGEN: Anything you want.

MONTOYA: I want my father back you son of a bitch!

Rugen is not trying to set things straight; he's not trying to pay the debt he owes for his crime so many years ago. He is simply doing anything he can to appeal to whatever avarice Montoya might have to induce him to spare his life. Still, the exchange here does seem to motivate the idea that there is no fee, or amount of service, or any other punishment that could equal the weight of Rugen's murderous crime. The only way for Montoya to get retribution is to take the life of the man who took the life of his father. If this is correct, we have a somewhat compelling justification for our intuitions that Montoya really is justified in taking Rugen's life even though not *all* crimes deserve a punishment that is the same type or kind.

But is there not still another way for Montoya to achieve justice without putting Rugen to death? If there is, then perhaps Montoya needs a special reason for choosing death over any other equivalent punishment. There are punishments much worse than death. Instead of a relatively quick death, Montoya could kidnap and torture Rugen for days on end. Also, unsurprisingly, as we have already considered, there is a punishment nowhere near as bad as death. Montoya could force Rugen to eat Miracle Max's favorite meal—a mutton, lettuce, and tomato sandwich. Both of these run the gamut of the proportionality of punishments, yet neither look hardly anything like retributive execution. So, as the objection goes, there must be some punishment which falls within these two extremes which is equivalent to the crime of murder, but nevertheless, a very much different type of thing than murder itself. There must be a punishment morally equivalent to the crime of taking a life, even though it does not involve the taking of the criminal's life as retribution. If this is so, the choice to put a murderer to death is merely arbitrary amongst the various options for equal punishment and perhaps inappropriate given its gruesome and conclusive nature.

There are two things to point out here. First, simply because there are punishments worse than and not as bad as death which are very much unlike murder and execution, it does not follow that there is a punishment literally equivalent to death. As unlikely as it is, it could be that on the scale of proportionality, the death of the murderer is the only punishment that lands directly on the right place on the scale. Second, and perhaps more convincingly, suppose for the sake of argument that we have successfully established that—even though it may not be the only punishment equivalent to the crime of murder—the punishment of killing a murderer is in fact proportional to the crime of murder. If this is so, then there is an epistemic, or practical reason to put murderers to death as opposed to punishing them in some other way. We have no way of knowing what other punishments would be equivalent to the murderer's crime. Even if Montoya has the motivation, he does not have the time nor the opportunity to sit around and figure out what some other but equally weighty punishment he could give to Rugen. Though this does not justify the claim that every murderer ought to be put to death, Montoya seems to be in a case in which the issue is relevant.

Given Montoya's, and Rugen's places in society, along with Montoya's limited resources and time, Montoya is justified in killing Rugen even if, as it turned out, there is some other, mysterious punishment that Rugen could suffer without losing his life. So, there is a fair amount of support for the idea that Montoya is justified in seeking, and achieving retribution as he does.

11

Have Fun Overthrowing This Evil Government!

TOBIAS T. GIBSON

As with many of my age, *The Princess Bride* is one of my favorite movies. It was on seemingly constant repeat while I was in high school and my early college years. It's a love story, naturally. It offers some of the finest one-liners in Hollywood history. And it has what is still my favorite sword fight ever to appear on the silver screen.

I wanted to share this movie with my children as they grew up. Admittedly, it had been several years since I had seen it, and I forgot one scene in particular: the anguish Westley feels when Prince Humperdinck uses "The Machine" to suck fifty years of his life away—famously making him "only mostly dead." That scene ruined one of my cherished movies for my sons, which changed the way I see the movie.

War-mongering for Fun and Profit

Prince Humperdinck, in both the movie and the book, spends a great deal of effort, and no doubt a great deal of money, to lead his country of Florin into a war against the neighboring country of Guilder. Humperdinck schemes to have Guilder blamed for an outrage which will cause the subjects of Florin to become angry and ready for war. Thus, preparing for war is also providing a public justification for war—the war must be made to appear as a good war in a worthy cause.

The history of Florin and Guilder has been one of frequent warfare. The book tell us that "the two countries had stayed alive over the centuries mainly by warring on each other" (p.

82). We're never told the justifications offered for those numerous past wars, but they may have all been faked or fabricated.

We do learn that Vizzini, Inigo, and Fezzik have been hired to create the illusion that Guilder kidnapped Buttercup prior to her wedding to Humperdinck. At the scene of the kidnapping, they tear a piece from a Guilderian soldier's uniform, and openly plot to murder her and leave her body on the plain of Guilder. As Vizzini says in the movie, "I've hired you to help me start a war. It's a prestigious line of work, with a long and glorious tradition."

Even after the plot goes awry, Humperdinck makes the most of framing Guilder to create the illusion that a war with Guilder would have a just cause. This is made clear with his plot to strangle the newlywed Princess Buttercup on their wedding night and blame Guilder's assassins.

If we look at the history of real-life warfare we see that this trick of going to war after fabricating some blameworthy action by the other nation is by no means a rarity. The novel, *The Princess Bride*, was written at a time of rising opposition to "a land war in Asia," with opponents of the war claiming that the justification for war—the Gulf of Tonkin incident—was faked.

Alexander Moseley has pointed out that nations can all too easily create "a pretext for war . . . by a contrived theatrical or actual stunt—of dressing one's own soldiers up in the enemy's uniforms, for instance, and having them attack a military or even civilian target as to gain political backing for a war." This description seems to fit Prince Humperdinck's fallback plan after Westley vanquishes Humperdinck's hirelings. Indeed, when remarking to Count Rugen about the new plan to kill Buttercup on their wedding night, Humperdinck remarks that

> the people are quite taken with her. It's odd, but when I hired Vizzini to have her murdered on our engagement day, I thought that was clever. But it's going to be so much more moving when I strangle her on our wedding night. Once Guilder is blamed, the nation will truly be outraged—they'll demand we go to war.

There is a philosophical theory of when and why it can sometimes be right to go to war—it's called Just War Theory. Just War Theory has a long history, and has become one of the most influential philosophical ideas in the world. It is largely based on the works of St. Augustine and St. Thomas Aquinas. Just War Theory comprises two key principles: *jus ad bellum*, or "just cause," which looks at the circumstances in which going to war is justified, and *jus in bello*, which considers what kinds of force are morally justified in fighting a war.

The Just War theorist Gregory M. Reichberg asserts that "war should never be undertaken in a spirit of cruelty or a desire to dominate, but only to in order to gain peace." Reichberg notes that historically, especially in Aquinas's formulation of just war, that "just war was . . . defined as a *response* to grave wrongdoing." Yet, some contemporary philosophers question whether Florin's war with Guilder would be just even if, in fact, Guilder had kidnapped or killed Princess Buttercup. Larry May, in "The Principle of Just Cause" argues that "in the just war tradition, punishment was normally discussed in terms of deterrence, at least long-run deterrence, rather than as *pure* retribution" (p. 59; my emphasis). Humperdinck's assertion that the citizens of Florin will "demand war" indicates that it would be a war of retribution, which is not considered a good justification for war.

Those Private Contractors

I've hired you to help me start a war. It's a prestigious line of work, with a long and glorious tradition.

—Vizzini

Vizzini, Fezzik, and Inigo Montoya illustrates an area of Just War Theory that is increasingly important: the role of "private contractors" in war. With the rise of Blackwater, Executive Outcomes, and other private military (or sometimes "security") contractors in the Iraq and Afghanistan wars, philosophers have again turned to the study of the ethical implications of the use of non-military companies and fighters involved in wars between nation-states.

While the trio don't technically engage in battle with an enemy—no matter how amazingly great the duel between the Man in Black and Inigo is—most of the current thinking on Just War Theory and private military contractors is related to just cause. James Pattison, for example, notes in "Just War Theory and the Privatization of Military Force" that use of private military contractors may violate the rule of waging war for the right reasons, as for these particular fighters the wage or profit margin is the motivation for the fight, not the righting of a wrong. Vizzini plays this motive out, especially in the book: "There will be war. We have been paid to start it. . . . If we do this perfectly, there will be a continual demand for our services."

More fundamentally, St. Augustine's explanation of just cause requires that states are the final authority in declaring war. However, Pattison points out that use of private military contractors—and in the context of *The Princess Bride* the employ of Vizzini and his hirelings—allows "a way for governments to deploy military force without the blatancy of state action." The secret purpose of framing Guilder in the kidnapping and murder of Princess Buttercup is designed to induce the people of Florin to accept an ill-begotten and unjustified war. Thus, while starting a war using such subterfuge may have a "long and glorious tradition," it also violates the just cause requirement of Just War Theory.

The activities of private contractors may also raise wider issues. James Pattison, in "Deeper Objections to the Privatisation of Military Force" notes that the use of private contractors such as Vizzini may indicate that "the sovereign is no longer the provider of national defense" and thus "individuals have less of a reason to agree to its authority and are arguably no longer bound to obey its rule." Moreover, when states employ contractors "the market, rather than the state, becomes the provider of military protection" and this puts the state's legitimacy in doubt. While Pattison is unconvinced by these arguments, he does believe that state employment of private military contractors may undermine the state's legitimacy.

Life Is Pain

"Life is pain." In the book, this line is delivered by Fezzik's mother, to him, when as a child he is beginning his career of fighting men. (This career is alluded to in the movie when he explains to the "Man in Black" how there are "different moves" when fighting a single man rather than a gaggle of men.) In the movie, the Man in Black, having revealed himself as the Dread Pirate Roberts, delivers the line, showing his lack of sympathy upon hearing that Buttercup's true love had been killed.

Although different persons in the movie and the book say that "life is pain," in both cases it foreshadows Westley's ordeal at the hands of Prince Humperdinck and Count Rugen.

One of the central components of the *Princess Bride* story is the torture of Westley. Understanding the underlying parts of the story discussed in the book sheds additional light on Prince Humperdinck's thinking about torture as seen in the movie. First, the movie version does not describe the full depth of Humperdinck's depravity and bloodlust. As loathsome as he is in the movie (I love Chris Sarandon's treatment of the character, and still openly cheer when Buttercup catches Humperdinck in his lie about sending his four fastest ships after the Dread Pirate Robert's ship to find Westley), the book's description is much more vivid. In the book, when the reader first learns of Prince Humperdinck, there is much description of the type of man he is. S. Morgenstern, through Goldman, tells us that Humperdinck "made it a practice never to let a day go by without killing something" . . . and that he enjoyed the suffering of beasts (p. 74).

There is also a major difference between the book and movie. As horrifying as "The Pit of Despair" is in the movie, it pales compared with the name and structure detailed in the book. Here, Humperdinck builds a "Zoo of Death" with five levels, and leaves the last level empty... until Westley is captured. This fifth level was "constructed . . . in the hopes of someday finding something worthy, something as dangerous and powerful as he was" (p. 75). In other words, rather than hold beasts, the fifth level of the Zoo of Death was designed to hold a man.

The type and reasoning of torture that Westley is subjected to is more heinous in the book, as well. In the movie, he is only tortured via "The Machine." In the book there are techniques administered before Rugen gets to the machine. Westley is asked who hired him to kidnap the princess, an answer he can't rightly give, of course. When he fails to answer, Rugen dips his hands in oil and sets them afire. In counsel with Humperdinck after that session, Rugen says the he feels "invigorated" and commends the Prince for asking "a perfect question" of Westley, as "He was telling the truth. We both know that." As Prince Humperdinck helps Buttercup write the letter sending for Westley (as she thinks the four fastest ships in the fleet will carry), Humperdinck tricks her into revealing Westley's worse fear, spinning ticks. And later, he exploits that fear in a torture session.

Much of the torture is meant merely to satisfy Humperdinck's and Rugen's personal penchants for dispensing pain. In the movie this is revealed only partially. The viewers are privy to Rugen's "interest in pain" and his study of torture. One of the most sadistic scenes in the movie is when Rugen is explaining how The Machine works, and his study of pain: "Really that's all this is except that instead of sucking water, I'm sucking life. I've just sucked one year of your life away. I might one day go as high as five, but I really don't know what that would do to you. So, let's just start with what we have. What did this do to you? Tell me. And remember, this is for posterity so be honest." After this query in the movie, Westley cries out, this leads all of us to understand just how painful and searing the machine really is. The book's description of the effect of The Machine on Westley is more telling: "In humiliation, and suffering, and frustration, and anger, and anguish so great it was dizzying, Westley cried like a baby" (p. 263).

Humperdinck uses torture to exact revenge for Buttercup's slight, after she questions his bravery when she realizes he didn't send any ships, let alone his fastest four, to find "her Westley." His genuine desire to humiliate and degrade Westley, and through Westley, Buttercup is on display as he throws the lever to fifty (in the movie; twenty in the book), leading to the maximum amount of pain The Machine can administer. He declares his underlying motive as he sneers "You truly love each other and so you might have been truly happy. Not one couple in a century has that chance, no matter what the story books say. And so I think no man in a century will suffer as greatly as you will." In case we miss the significance of this moment, as Westley's wail is heard throughout the kingdom, Inigo asks, "Do you hear that, Fezzik? That is the sound of ultimate suffering. My heart made that sound when Rugen slaughtered my father. The Man in Black makes it now."

Justifying Torture

There is near-consensus in civilized society that torture is wrong. The one debatable exception to this is the so-called "ticking time bomb" scenario, in which the torture of a terrorist or two not only can, but *will*, save the lives of tens, hundreds, or thousands of innocent lives. The scene plays itself out in several movies and television shows, perhaps most notably in the Kiefer Sutherland TV show *24*.

There are several reasons why we might reject the use of torture even in this scenario. First, as many have noted, torture can lead to negative unintended consequences. Bruce Hoffman, in "A Nasty Business," points out that the use of torture, even when the torture was designed to elicit illicit information for reasons similar to the ticking time bomb, leads to, at best, moral ambiguity. Noting the consistent use of interrogation techniques involving harsh methods across the globe, even in the modern age, Hoffman relates a question asked by a British intelligence officer involved in counter-terrorism in Northern Ireland: "If there is to be discomfort and horror inflicted on the few, is it not preferred to the danger and horror being inflicted on perhaps a million people?"

This is absolutely not the situation portrayed in *The Princess Bride*. Torturing Westley is only to satisfy, if only for the moment, a bloodlust, and at its worst, is combined with a desire to punish Buttercup for her insolence.

But, philosopher Michael Davis, in "Justifying Torture as an Act of War," offers what he hopes is a definitive answer to the ticking time bomb scenario. Davis takes real issue with the notion that there is any justification for the use of torture, under even the most dire of circumstances—even the ticking time bomb defense. As Davis points out:

> the ticking-bomb case seems to presuppose that we have available someone who knows how to torture effectively. This knowledgeable torturer must be from somewhere. Where? Insofar as we suppose that the torturer in question is likely to succeed, we must presuppose a skilled torturer and therefore an institution of torture to vouch for the torturer before he begins to work over the fanatic bomber. The moral cost of trying to save Paris by torturing one fanatic bomber is therefore much higher than it may seem. We must have an institution of torture—with some people tortured without any advantage but sharpening a torturer's skills.
>
> Second, the ticking-bomb case presupposes the absence of any effective alternative to torture. Why presuppose that? Less objectionable methods of interrogation seem to succeed at least as often as

torture does. "More inhumane" does not mean "more effective." There are, then, no circumstances in which we could reasonably conclude that torture is our only, or even our best, option (p. 202).

Davis's critique offers an interesting look into the justification for Westley's torture. As Rugen begins his use of The Machine on Westley, the Count informs his prisoner of his "interest in pain" and that he is doing research for his forthcoming book, "the definitive work on pain." It appears, then, that Rugen could be one of the creators of the "institution of torture" that Davis speculates about. Rugen's torture of Westley is exactly the kind of practice that Davis fears would become the "moral cost" to civil society of allowing the use of torture in the first place.

A Revolutionary Uprising

Form a brute squad to empty the forest.

—PRINCE HUMPERDINCK

All this leads to an often-overlooked, but important part of understanding *The Princess Bride*: the fact that Westley, Inigo, and Fezzik, storming the castle, killing Count Rugen, and making off with the princess have carried out what amounts to insurrection against the state of Florin.

This insurgency is a good and worthy endeavor. Prince Humperdinck has violated Just War Theory, regarding both just cause and the justified use of force, and he unjustly tortures for sport and revenge, which leads in turn to evil institutions in society. He has coerced a peasant girl to wed him, a fact that comes out more clearly in the book. In the chapter "The Courtship," the Prince's wooing of Buttercup goes like this: "you can either marry me and be the richest and most powerful woman in a thousand miles . . . and provide me a son, or you can die in terrible pain in the very near future" (p. 90). This, in combination with the misleading of Buttercup regarding sending his fastest ships after Westley and the speed of the "marriage" displayed in the movie, illustrates the type of coercion Humperdinck uses on his citizenry.

There's more evidence, best described in the book, however, of the corruption and illegitimacy of Florin's rule. When Prince

Humperdinck "fears" a plot on his fiancée, he orders that the Thieves' Quarter (Forest, in the movie) be emptied. Yellin, the Chief of All Enforcement, raises a brute squad. The description in the book of the feeling of the residents of the Thieves' Quarter is somewhat telling about the governance of Florin. "Most of the criminals had been through unjust and illegal roundups before" (p. 264).

This passage takes on all the more importance, however, when it is coupled with later dialogue between Inigo and Rugen. In what might be the best scene in the movie, Inigo finally catches up with the man who killed his father, and the sword fight ensues. Almost immediately, Rugen appears to have won, but Inigo finds his inner strength and fighting spirit, and eventually Inigo kills the Count. In both the movie and book versions, Inigo repeats incessantly one of the most famous lines in the movie while chasing Rugen around the room: "Hello. My name is Inigo Montoya. You killed my father. Prepare to die." When it becomes clear that Rugen is defeated, in the movie Inigo impales his heart, once, after Rugen is unable to give him what he wants in exchange for sparing Rugen's life. But, in the book, the exchange is more telling, as Inigo's sword enters Rugen's chest repeatedly:

INIGO MONTOYA: Can you guess what I am doing?

COUNT RUGEN: Cutting my heart out.

INIGO MONTOYA: You took mine when I was ten; I want yours now. We are lovers of justice, you and I—what could be more just than that? (p. 349)

Inigo sees killing Rugen as an act of justice. In other words, Inigo sees killing Rugen, Humperdinck's six-fingered right-hand man as a necessary means to correct a past injustice. While Rugen's death at the hand of Inigo is significantly based on avenging his father's death, Inigo—who was the last of the inhabitants of the Thieves' Quarter (Forest)—may be quite aware that the majority of his former neighbors felt that justice on the part of Florin's governance escaped them. Vindication is sweet for all involved.

The Right to Revolt

When is it right and proper to overthrow the government in a revolution? Most political philosophers accept that under certain circumstances this can be the right thing to do. Even Thomas Hobbes, the great proponent of absolute monarchy, apparently believed (according to Jean Hampton) that the monarch had a responsibility to carry out certain duties, and could be removed if he failed to do so. In his great work *Leviathan*, Hobbes asserts that the sovereign is in power to protect people's safety, and that

> The safety of the People requireth further, from him, or them that have the Soveraign Power, that Justice be equally administered to all degrees of People; that is, that as well as the rich, and mighty, as poor and obscure persons, may be righted of the injuries done them; so as the great, may have no greater hope of impunity, when they doe violence, dishonour, or any Injury to the meaner sort.

Within the Hobbesian conception of the sovereign, the people should expect that their government will provide them with protection and equality before the law, so the consistent violations of citizens' rights by Humperdinck proves him to be an illegitimate sovereign.

I make him better, Humperdinck suffers?

—MIRACLE MAX

The continuous, repeated, unjust use of state-sponsored violence in *The Princess Bride* indicates that Prince Humperdinck's rule is illegitimate. He violates Just War teaching, he fails to provide his subjects with basic citizenship rights, and he outright violates those rights consistently throughout the story. Even Hobbes, history's most apologetic philosopher for the absolute power of the sovereign, imposes certain obligations on the sovereign, and Prince Humperdinck fails to meet even Hobbes's minimal requirements.

12
Should I Really Stop That Rhyming?

WAYNE YUEN

Poor Vizzini, annoyed no end by Fezzik and Inigo! Okay, maybe we don't have a lot of sympathy for Vizzini, but we all know what it's like to be annoyed.

It's *so* annoying to be . . . well . . . annoyed! But what exactly is this feeling of annoyance and should we really worry about other people's annoyance when what we're doing is annoying other people? I want to try to answer both of these questions, without being too annoying.

Nothing Rhymes with Orange, You Doorhinge!

There are a few examples of annoyance, that are in or related to *The Princess Bride*, and each example might give us a slightly different perspective on *what* annoyance is. The first example is the one I just mentioned, the much beloved "rhyming scene" where Vizzini, Fezzik, and Inigo are leaving for the open seas. Vizzini is clearly annoyed by what Fezzik and Inigo are doing to pass the time. On the surface, it doesn't seem like there should be any good reason to be annoyed by their game of rhyme. It is a mentally fun exercise to find rhyming word pairs, it might keep them awake or amused, but it only draws annoyed glares from Vizzini.

So why does this annoy Vizzini so much? When people start rhyming on purpose, your mind can't help but try to anticipate the next rhyme. You're primed for rhyme. It's partly why memorizing poems is easier than memorizing non-rhyming text, each rhyme pair clues you into the next line. But this clueing signal forces your mind to think in a way that you might not want to think. Vizzini has other things on his mind, namely executing the plan that Prince Humperdinck hired him for. When you want to think about serious matters such as kidnapping princesses, but are being kept from thinking about that because of a rhyming gabfest that is happening around you, you'll find that annoying. So one way something can be annoying, is by hijacking your mental processes. In this case, Fezzik and Inigo are controlling Vizzini's mind in a crude way, forcing his attention on the next rhyme when he wants to give his attention to the plan.

The second form of annoyance occurs in *The Princess Bride* novel. In the novel, William Goldman[1] informs you that the story you're reading is sourced from a book called *The Princess Bride* by S. Morgenstern.[2] I read Goldman's book when I was in my late pre-teens, fell in love with it, and believed that there was in fact another book that the story that I was reading was an abridgement of.

The movie is interrupted by the grandfather[3] telling the story to his sick grandson.[4] The book interrupts[5] the story with Goldman telling us fictions about the arduous nature of the original book. Only later did I discover that this is not true, that the book is entirely fiction,[6] and is not an abridged version

---

[1] He is in fact the sole author of *The Princess Bride*.

[2] There is, in fact, another book authored by William Goldman under the pseudonym S. Morgenstern.

[3] Played by Peter Falk.

[4] Played by Fred Savage.

[5] These interruptions are also annoying since they interrupt the flow of the story to tell a meta-story that is unrelated to the actual story that is being told. The story telling device is used to create an artificial suspense. I want to know what happens in the story that is being told, not about what Fred Savage thinks about the story that is being told! The annoyance from interruption is different from the mental hijacking of rhyme, since if one is not preoccupied with other thoughts, rhyme can be entertaining. Interruption, especially repetitive interruption, is almost always annoying as it interrupts one's thought process. By definition, you have to be thinking about something else to be interrupted. The few exceptions are when one is interrupted by something more interesting or pleasantly unexpected, but even these interruptions have limits before they become annoying.

[6] Rodents of unusual size are not fiction, by definition, unless all rodents

of anything. The children and wife that Goldman makes reference to in the book are non-existent. I found this to be very annoying[7] and to this day I still get a little annoyed when people playfully (or sometimes ignorantly) talk about non-existent chapters of the book by S. Morgenstern that William Goldman edited out.

This annoyance stems from a kind of investment and expectation. The more we invest in something, be it money, time, emotional energy, generally the more important it becomes to us. Since I loved the book and read it several times, I was heavily invested in it. The romantic tale of a story being saved from obscurity was part of what I was invested in. I understood that Buttercup and Miracle Max weren't real, but surely the story surviving through time was. Nope. So in this case, a train[8] of thought was created and promised a destination, but was fictitious. Now the energy and investment I had in it, was lost, like a scam artist swindling their target of their money. In part the annoyance comes from my own naiveté and gullibility, as much as being deceived by the commentary that is supplied in the book. When a story is told to us, in the guise of fact, part of the pleasure of the story is the fact that it actually happened. A fantastic example of this is the movie *Fargo* which begins with "This is a true story. The events depicted in this film took place in Minnesota in 1987. At the request of the survivors, the names have been changed. Out of respect for the dead, the rest has been told exactly as it occurred." The promise of a true story impresses the viewer with the amazement that it isn't a fictional story that is being related, but rather that the *crazy* events of the movie *actually* happened.[9] Now this isn't plausible in *The Princess Bride* because of the clearly fictional elements,

---

were the same size. Since they are not there would have to be some rodents that are larger than the usual size of rodents.

  [7] I failed to mention this earlier, but a broad definition of 'annoying' might be simply "mental irritation."

  [8] Trains are really great!

  [9] In case you didn't know, *Fargo* is in fact entirely fictional. This hasn't stopped people from mistakenly believing that the movie is based on true events, and looking for buried treasure in the snow (although the most famous case of a Japanese woman traveling to Fargo, was in fact not seeking the buried treasure, but suicidal, and traveling to her former boyfriend's home of Fargo). I'm sure these people have been annoyed by the movie.

like Miracle Max, but the meta-story of having a boring book edited down to an amazing book is plausible.

A *Princess Bride* Convention? Inconceivable!

Finally, I think there is one more great example of annoyance that is closely related to *The Princess Bride* and this one is probably the most common example. I'm sure that because you are reading this, you love *The Princess Bride* as much as I do. So when this fact becomes known amongst people, inevitably conversations deteriorate into loud exclamations from the movie. "Inconceivable!" "I'm not left-handed either!" "My name is Inigo Montoya," "As you wish!" I, like most fans, find the movie highly quotable and I've engaged in quoting the movie to others. But usually these conversations don't do much beyond reinforcing the quotes from the movie that *every fan* knows. I could quote most of these lines to people who have *never* seen the film or read the novel, and they would still know what I'm referring to despite the lack of context of the lines. It is the *repetitive* nature of these conversations that make these conversations annoying. It's the same conversation that has been had between thousands of people. No doubt, there is enjoyment that can be had from finding common loves between people. I'm sure if I went to a convention built around *The Princess Bride* I would enjoy it. But it wouldn't be because we collectively got together to watch the movie and recite the lines as the movie was playing,[10] but hopefully because I was learning more about the interest that we all collectively share. Maybe someone could convince me that Humperdinck was the hero of the story or that it was possible for someone to actually build a contraption that could suck the life out of a person.[11] These would be reasons that I would enjoy the convention; not because I would hear "Inconceivable!" everywhere I went in the convention.

So what's wrong with being a little annoying? As I've shown, there are many different ways that something or someone can

---

[10] Okay, maybe I would find this fun, but that's only because I'm deeply geeky.

[11] I believe this has already been invented. Its collective name is reality TV.

be annoying and yet there are people who would still enjoy most of these and not find them annoying.[12] The problem is that what is annoying to one, may not be annoying to another and what is annoying in one context, may not be annoying in another, or to say it in a more succinct manner: Annoyance is both relative and contextual. Typical moral theories that would tell us how to behave, often require us to take objective viewpoints or perspectives to try to suss out what the moral thing to do is. But in the case of being annoying, it would be difficult to determine, objectively, whether or not something is annoying. It would take too long and require too much information gathering to make a truly informed decision as to whether or not one should behave in any particular way, in hopes of avoiding being annoying.[13]

There might be a way of thinking of annoyance that could accommodate this relative and contextual feature of annoyance, and at the same time explain why one of the all-time great philosophers thought of it as a moral problem at all. I'm talking about Aristotelian virtue theory. Aristotle believed that there were moral virtues that we should all strive to attain. Virtues themselves are character traits that we embody, through practice and habit, that would help us attain a good life.

The virtues themselves were always located at the "golden mean" between an excess and deficiency of the virtue. So let's take a virtue like bravery. Westley exhibits bravery, because he is neither foolish nor a coward. We see that he's no coward when he bravely follows and fights the Spaniard and the giant in hopes of recovering his beloved. But we also see that he's not foolish when he assesses the situation and determines that it would be unwise for the three to storm the castle with only his brain, Montoya's steel, and Fezzik's strength. Head jiggling aside, there is little hope for the three to storm the castle gates. But given additional resources, Westley conceives of a plan that requires bravery to execute, a midpoint between foolishness and cowardice. Would this plan work if I had been there instead of Fezzik? To give you a comparison between myself and Andre the Giant: I'm 5' 6" and 130 lbs, soaking wet; Andre was 7' 4"

---

[12] Believe it or not, some people even find footnotes annoying.

[13] I don't pretend to have given an analysis covering every type of thing that is annoying. Annoyingly, that would require me to write an entire book.

and 520 lbs. Change the parameters of the scenario and suddenly it would be foolish to storm the castle. Aristotle understands that for different people a virtue gets expressed in different ways. What would be brave for Andre might be terribly foolish for me to try, even with a holocaust cloak and a wheelbarrow.

Plato, Aristotle, Socrates? Morons!

There are two virtues, however, that Aristotle discusses that have always annoyed me. The first is "friendliness." According to Aristotle, someone who is overly complimentary and never in opposition to anything is excessively friendly. This is often translated as obsequiousness. A person who would oppose everything and never be concerned about the pains that his words might inflict on to others would have too little friendliness. The virtuous person is someone who understands when to be polite to others out of concern for their psychological pains, and who is also able to differentiate how we ought to treat close friends as opposed to strangers.

The other virtue is "wittiness." Aristotle says that the excess of wittiness is buffoonery, where a person thinks it's more important to get people to laugh, than to empathize with others' pains. On the deficiency side, are the boorish, people who can't take a joke nor put up with those who make jokes. The witty man then would be someone who could make jokes when it was appropriate, and is able to be sensitive to the pains of others when making jokes so that their jokes don't feel insulting, and wouldn't stand for jokes that he himself wouldn't be comfortable making.

Now, neither of these virtues that Aristotle describes appears to be terribly relevant to *moral* character. I'm fairly sure that even if I was a boorish person, or an unfriendly surly individual, that I could still be a morally virtuous person. So maybe Aristotle got it wrong when it comes to what a morally virtuous person is. I'm pretty sure that having dinner with "The Impressive Clergyman" played by Peter Cook would be boring, but I wouldn't say that this person lacks moral character because I wasn't entertained by his humor.[14] So why does

---

[14] Although I might be a buffoon if I simply enjoyed listening to him talk.

Aristotle make these qualities of a person into moral virtues? Ultimately, Aristotle is looking for the good life. What are the things that contribute to a perfectly good life, and what are the things that detract? If everyone wasn't friendly, then people would be constantly rankled by others, either because they were too surly or too obsequious. The same with wittiness. If people have no sense of humor, or make light of everything, with no regard to how their attempts at humor would make others feel, we would be less than happy. Moreover, Aristotle thinks that human life is fundamentally a social one. A good life isn't about individuals trying to attain moral perfection in a vacuum, but rather a good life is a community coming together helping one another in attainment of happiness. Ultimate happiness, human flourishing,[15] can only occur from people cooperating with one another.

So for Aristotle, being annoying to others, should be a serious concern. It reflects poorly on our characters and it would prevent others from attaining a flourishing state of being. And in a way, each of the vices that are associated with wittiness and friendliness are forms of annoyance. Vizzini is both surly and a boorish kind of person. Aristotle would probably argue that it is Vizzini, so deeply skewed in the deficiencies of friendliness and wittiness, who needs to alter his character in order to be a more virtuous individual.

But where does that leave us with being annoying? If Inigo and Fezzik are annoying Vizzini, is it really all on Vizzini to adjust his humor and be more easy-going when it comes to being annoyed? Aristotle's virtue ethics, by itself, doesn't do a very good job of recommending specific courses of actions, beyond, "Try to be virtuous." The subjectivity of annoyance and the built-in relativity of virtue theory complement one another, but also make it really difficult to explain what we should do in order to resolve the situation.

We might need the help of another ethical concept to shed some light on to the problem: supererogation. When Inigo tries to find the man that killed his father, I doubt that anyone

---

[15] *Eudaimonia* is the term that Aristotle uses, which is often translated as happiness, but probably means something closer to human flourishing, which is like, to borrow a psychological term, "self-actualization," but not exactly as Maslow, the psychologist who coined that term, defined it.

would say that he's *morally* obligated to do so. He could simply
live out his life being a fantastic swordsman, or maybe he and
Fezzik can become poets. Yet despite the fact that nothing is
morally *obligating* his attempt to redress a wrong that was
done to his father, he does so. Inigo is living up to his
supererogatory duties. A supererogatory duty is a duty that is
not morally required of a person, but would be really great if
they did do it.[16] A person going above and beyond the call of
duty is a person performing supererogatory acts. This concept
might help us understand why I feel that Aristotle's virtues of
friendliness and wittiness are strange moral virtues. We don't
think that people are morally obligated to be friendly or witty,
but it would be really nice if they were. Perhaps Aristotle is
looking at the moral ideal and consequently gives us these two
virtues as ideals, not as basic moral obligations to be satisfied.

So let's imagine that Aristotle does in fact mean that friendliness and wittiness are "supererogatory moral virtues,"[17]
which would put annoyingness into the category of a "morally
permissible" action but something that should be discouraged,
since the supererogatory virtue is something that should be
morally encouraged, but not required.

Fezzik and Inigo are annoying Vizzini with their rhyming,
and maybe I'm being annoying by shouting "Inconceivable!" all
the time at a convention. We could say that it wouldn't be
wrong to continue to engage in this behavior that others are
finding annoying, but it wouldn't be morally ideal either. We
can firmly say that if we want to be better people, the best people that we could possibly be, we need to embody the virtues
that Aristotle suggests that we embody, and consequently try
not to annoy others. But inevitably we will fail, in part because
what is annoying is so subjective. It makes little sense to hold
someone morally responsible for something that is so difficult,
if not impossible, to predict like what would be annoying to any
given individual. If we're morally responsible for annoying people, then we would need to be able avoid annoying people. I
mean, who doesn't love a little rhyming? If I can't accurately

---

[16] Editor Richard Greene is annoyed when I call anything supererogatory
a duty since it isn't required and so can't be a duty. So I'll call them acts from
now on.

[17] I wouldn't say that all of Aristotle's virtues are supererogatory virtues,
but at least these two might be.

predict what will annoy who in any particular situation, especially in unconventional situations or if someone particularly sensitive finds something normal to be annoying, then I can't be held responsible for the *unintentional* annoyance.

Why Inigo Needs to Be a Master Swordsman

Generally, when people are told that they have options available to them and one is not a requirement, they will typically choose not to do it. For example, I might argue that it is a supererogatory act to give money to charity (it also happens to be one of Aristotle's virtues). Without it being a moral requirement people are simply going to fail to achieve this virtue, since they bring no negative moral evaluation on themselves for failing to do so. It's supererogatory after all!

Since we've already borrowed other moral concepts to supplement Aristotle's virtue theory, we might as well try to borrow one more idea from someone else. Immanuel Kant thinks that we all have an obligation to develop our talents and abilities. He thinks that this duty is an imperfect duty, since I can't logically be constantly developing my talents and abilities. I have to sleep sometime! So if it is an imperfect duty, it is something that I don't *always* have to do, but I shouldn't take this duty to be any less serious. The reason that we have this serious duty is because if I fail in developing my talents and abilities, I fail to respect myself.

Inigo's behavior provides a good example of why Kant would argue that we need to develop our talents. Inigo wants to avenge his father's death and in order to do so, he must be an excellent swordsman, better than the six-fingered man at least. Had Inigo not spent the majority of his life honing and mastering his skill, he would fail to treat his own hopes and goals, in this case avenging his father's death, with any kind of respect and dignity. We could imagine the master swordsman, talking to his younger self and being deeply disappointed that the younger Inigo wasted his time rhyming, rather than practicing with his sword, not because there is something *inherently* good about being a good swordsman, but that young Inigo has failed to respect himself enough as a human being. By choosing not to develop his talents, he is in effect saying that the pursuits that Inigo Montoya would engage in with these talents are not worthwhile.

So this puts a lot more teeth behind the obligation of developing your own talents. You don't *always* have to develop your talents, since that would be impossible, but failing to do so would be to disrespect yourself, which would be morally bad. So it is like a supererogatory act in that you don't *need* to engage in it, but it isn't like a supererogatory act because if you fail in doing it at all, you've done something wrong.

So let's place ourselves in Vizzini's shoes. You're deep in thought about your plan to kidnap Buttercup, but the two dolts you hired to help you keep rhyming about stuff that is distracting you. I think you're entitled to be a little irritated and to tell them to shut up. But at the same time if Vizzini *never* attempted to be tolerant of a little rhyme here and there, being more friendly and aiming for good wit, then he's failed to treat himself as a person who could potentially be a better person. So it would be supererogatory for Vizzini to tolerate the rhyming and possibly be character building to tolerate the rhyming.

Of course Vizzini isn't the only party involved here. Both Inigo and Fezzik could also be more friendly, as they can see that they're annoying Vizzini. Since we understand that annoyance is subjective, it isn't unreasonable for Vizzini to be annoyed, it's just annoying that everything annoys him. If we accept that Aristotle's virtues are *ideals*, then they aren't things that we can ever attain perfectly. Aristotle agrees that it would be difficult if not impossible to hit virtues dead on every time. Fezzik and Inigo could better hit the virtues of friendliness with Vizzini, despite the fact that he doesn't seem terribly interested in being friends. Friendliness isn't about the end result of making new friends, but a particular way of treating people, in a polite and friendly manner.

I don't think that, generally speaking, being annoying is a serious moral issue. Sure, there are cases where being annoying could have serious consequences, like annoying a surgeon in the middle of a delicate surgery, but the instances in which being annoying is a serious moral wrong are far outnumbered by the everyday commonness of annoyance. I'm not implying that the commonness makes it less morally serious, but rather that we shouldn't find deep moral fault or heated disagreements about the morality of being annoying. That would be inconceivably annoying.

IV

Metaphysical Miracles

. . . you don't by
chance happen to
have six fingers on
your right hand?

13
The Shrieking Evils

JERRY S. PIVEN

> He made it a practice never to let a day go by without killing something. It didn't much matter what. . . . he began to enjoy the suffering of little beasts. . . . It was death chess and he was international grand master.
>
> —*The Princess Bride*, p. 74

> It was standard to leave the women for last . . . they also whimpered and looked to the heavens for escape—always good for chuckles around future campfires.
>
> —*The Princess Bride*, p. 420

Evil. Evil is what brings us together today. There's evil galore in *The Princess Bride*: scheming, kidnapping, lying, torture, and murder. Yet the villains are so obviously evil that we may overlook the serious badness of our beloved 'good' characters. Westley, Inigo, and Fezzik are actually shockingly wicked, if we pause to reflect.

But before we all start carping angrily like shrieking eels, let's begin with the nastiest villains. Prince Humperdinck machinates to murder Princess Buttercup and impugn Guilder to start a war. Humperdinck savors his schemes, and even delights when his plans to have Buttercup murdered are thwarted since misfortune now affords him the opportunity to strangle his wife in her sleep. He connives:

> when she died of murder on their wedding night, it was crucial that all Florin realize the depths of his love. . . . he already saw the scene

in his mind. . . . there wouldn't be a dry eye in the square. (pp. 244–45)

And later: "He was seventy-five minutes from his first female murder, and he wondered if he could get his fingers to her throat before even the start of a scream. He had been practicing on giant sausages all the afternoon" (p. 322). Humperdinck certainly seems the epitome of the conniving evil villain.

But there's more here than a stereotypically-sneaky overseer willing to commit princessicide, lie about the perpetrators, murder innocent civilians, or perform any other putatively patriotic acts. For as we discover, Humperdinck is later enraged by Buttercup's devotion to Westley: "If only Buttercup would admit that he, Humperdinck, was the better man. . . . But she would not! . . . All she ever talked about was Westley. . . . Maddening" (pp. 250–51). Later, Buttercup calls Humperdinck a coward and "the weakest thing to ever walk the earth" (p. 280). She then shows contempt for the Prince, defiantly proclaiming how she and Westley are joined by the bond of love. Flying into a frenzy, Humperdinck screams, rips at her autumn hair, drags her to her room, and plunges into the Zoo of Death. There he vents his wrath against Westley:

You truly love each other, and so you might have been truly happy. Not one couple in a century has that chance, no matter what the storybooks say. And so I think no man in a century will suffer as greatly as you will.

The fact that Humperdinck storms into the dungeon, rages at Westley, and hurls the life-sucking machine to fifty—in the book it's twenty, but either way, he throws the life-sucking machine to its maximum suckitude—suggests a dimension of unbearable envy. What is envy? It's not merely petty jealousy. That's just the surface. Envy can be a grotesque, malignant jealousy consuming the soul; a bitter, angry desire for what someone has, hatred that others have what you don't, and a humiliating feeling of being inferior and deprived for not having it. Humperdinck doesn't value Buttercup aside from her use as a pretty doll to murder and blame on Guilder. He envies and despises love because its absence signifies his worthlessness, and that is why he is so consumed with rage that he rushes to inflict agony and death upon Westley. His envy of true love drives him to seething hate and murder.

Hence Humperdinck transcends the clichéd, pompous, one-dimensional villain lusting for power. This tiny interlude teaches us how much the façade of bravado and power may conceal a deeper torment of being mortally wounded because unloved. It teaches us that those without love may compensate by strutting around with smug superiority, subjugating innocent human beings, and presiding over inferior subjects. Not even with vast wealth and power will they be loved, and thus true love is despised and must be extinguished. As Alford says, "evil is the destruction of the other because the other is *good*" (*What Evil Means to Us*, p. 71). Or as Berke writes, the malignantly-envious person "can't stand to see others full of life and goodness" (*The Tyranny of Malice*, p. 24).

Further, Humperdinck must envy and despise what Westley *is*, and what the pompous prince is not: Valiant, fearless, devoted, and willing to sail the oceans and risk his own death for another whom he loves. Of course Humperdinck hates Westley, for he embodies nobility, courage, and love while the prince is a posturing, conceited, cringing coward. Henceforth, we may look at regalia as a mask concealing inner misery, violence as vengeance for one's own inner destitution, and even political schemes as perverse antidotes for inner pain and humiliation.

This isn't about one fictitious prince, but about our own egotism and envy, as well as political massacre. For beneath the desire for power, beneath our vanity and acquisitiveness, beneath the moral smokescreens justifying conquest, torture, and vengeance may lurk humiliating inner anguish and the need for love. Beneath hatred itself—whether that hatred takes the form of racism, sexism, or moral judgment—is often excruciating, shameful envy.

The last thing a bigot or perpetrator can admit is that he's afraid and envious of the other, so instead he blames *them* for being evil and deserving of retribution, subjugation, or death. This applies whether we're talking about misogynistic attitudes, racist insults, or virtually any other ethnic, religious, or moral condemnation. Such judgments are usually smokescreens for far deeper issues, and envy (and *therefore* fear) may underlay much of that hatred. . . .

So *The Princess Bride* unmasks much of our pomp and hatred, and shows how much evil may germinate from our secret desire, pain, and humiliation, hide them as we may with personal and political excuses.

Tyronian Tyranny

If my experiments are valid, my name will last beyond my body. It's immortality I'm after, to be quite honest.

— COUNT RUGEN, *The Princess Bride*, p. 261

In humiliation, and suffering, and frustration, and anger, and anguish so great it was dizzying, Westley cried like a baby. "Interesting," said the count.

— *The Princess Bride*, p. 263

Evil isn't always the result of envy or frenetic hatred, however. Sometimes it's eerily cold and dispassionate. Perhaps more spine-chilling, the suffering of others can be a matter of intellectual curiosity and amusement to certain individuals. Enter Count Rugen, the pitiless six-fingered man who cheated Inigo's father, murdered him in cold blood, slashed the young boy's face, and now tortures people in the Pit of Despair with "the Machine." Rugen is merely a fictive character, but there are real people like this. What motivates people to inflict pain so ruthlessly?

Rugen is intrigued by torture and pain. It's for "posterity," but he's *fascinated* by it. In the book, Rugen really cares about pain (p. 245). He devours everything he can find to read on the subject of Distress (p. 245). He has to suppress his own shriek of triumph when killing a dog with his machine of death, and feels invigorated after setting fire to Westley's hands (pp. 246, 253). He claims to be "excited and proud" of his machine (p. 258). In the movie, he says: "Beautiful isn't it? It took me half a lifetime to invent it. I'm sure you've discovered my deep and abiding interest in pain." Anguish is treacle for him. He inflicts pain for entertainment, to inscribe humiliating scars on children, to make souls wail in agony and treat them like marionettes, to make their eardrums bleed and to suck the life out of their bodies, to make them die screaming in insufferable agony. There's some debauched delight beneath the dispassion. Rugen mirrors people in the real world who lack compassion but do savor the pain and anguish of others, and even make it their life's purpose.

The motivations of the torturer are complex, and while there are those who may be genetically incapable of empathy or those merely following orders, work on the psychology of people who torture or experiment in the pain of others suggests some virulent inner dynamics of displaced vengeance against their own inner persecutors, pain, wounds, and dread. Several scholarly writers, including Terence Des Pres, Carl Goldberg, and even Jerry Piven have shed light on these motivations. Beneath that placid surface (or even the enthusiastically-intrigued visage) is often an emotionally-injured person avenging his own wounds on innocent victims, to destroy their innocence and joy, to annihilate what is human and alive in them. As Becker says, sadism absorbs the fear of death (*Escape from Evil*, p. 113). Goldberg maintains that "Sade himself sought to quell his fear of mortality by striving to gain control of life and death" (*Speaking with the Devil*, p. 119).

Some researchers (such as Philip Zimbardo) suggest that torturers are just following orders or playing their expected roles. While some people may indeed be marching to panpipes and obeying orders, this doesn't account for the deliberate and even lascivious interest so many torturers seem to have. It is not true that all you can do is just surrender to orders. As Arendt pointed out, even many Nazi guards had more choice than we would suspect. In many cases there seems to be considerable freedom, and ample enthusiasm to torture. The plethora of pornographic photographs taken in Abu Ghraib is a testament to that salacious pleasure.

Rugen may be a vicious polydactylic vizier but he resembles actual torturers, who inflict violence with utter callousness and absence of remorse. He's the Nazi doctor, member of Japanese Unit 731, or Tuskegee scientist experimenting on hapless victims for knowledge and "posterity." History is full of people infecting and vivisecting victims for their own knowledge or amusement, often with the support of their respective kings and governments. History tends to suggest that Rugenesque sadists may surround us more than we realize, even if they hold respectable offices and titles. They may seem unlike us, but they aren't alien monsters or ultimate mutations. They've joined the human race. And their legacy remains in the countless victims we've left behind—ostensibly for knowledge, posterity, justice, and freedom, but more often as a reflection of our cultural cruelty.

Vizzinial Genius, Deviousness, and . . . Valor?

. . . were there limits to the cruelty of Vizzini, the devil Sicilian?

—*The Princess Bride*, p. 10

There are no words to contain all my wisdom. . . . there were not words invented yet to explain how great my brain is, but let me put it this way: the world is several million years old and several billion people have at one time or another trod upon it, but I, Vizzini the Sicilian, am, speaking with pure candor and modesty, the slickest, sleekest, sliest, and wiliest fellow who has yet come down the pike.

—*The Princess Bride*, p. 175

The Prince may be a fiend, and Rugen his twin in misery (p. 305), but compare them to the most celebrated rogue in *The Princess Bride*, the hunchbacked Vizzini. He too seems to delight in the misfortunes of others, but he's a different ilk of villain. Egomaniacal villains exulting their own genius are familiar figures in literature, film, and fairytale. And as we know, Vizzini bumptiously basks in his own brilliance: "have you ever heard of Plato, Aristotle, Socrates? . . . Morons." And the book shows us how much he relishes diabolical schemes and suffering: "Her body should be quite warm when the Prince reaches her mutilated form. I only wish we could stay for his grief—It should be Homeric" (p. 104). And again: "I just can't miss a death like this" (p. 117). So far, we just seem to have an egotistical villain reveling in evil. What's so intriguing here, however, is how Goldman insinuates that narcissistic grandiosity and villainy conceal inner anguish. He specifically informs us that Vizzini's mental machinations emerged from the childhood realization that his humped body would never conquer worlds (p. 113). Goldman curiously mentions how Vizzini suffered from unrelenting nightmares of falling, suggesting the fear and trembling beneath his bravado. And our author also illustrates how incensed Vizzini is with signs of his own imperfections, as when Buttercup unexpectedly dives off the boat: "My plan was *ideal* as *all* my plans are ideal. It was the moon's ill timing that robbed me of perfection" (p. 109). We might wager that beyond mere comedy we are being given a lesson on how evil, egotism, and malice are all masks for personal shame, misery, and self-loathing.

The social and political implications are even more profound. For Vizzini seems to have some weirdly grandiose set of moral principles, as stealing Buttercup to instigate a war follows "a long and glorious tradition." Further, he castigates the man in black for trying to rescue what Vizzini "has rightfully stolen." One can "rightfully" assault, abduct, and murder someone to initiate carnage and conquest, but rescuing her would be morally wrong. And if anyone witnesses this nefariously noble deed, he must therefore die.

Vizzini's attitude of moral righteousness amid his own sneaky scheming seems ludicrous, but it's precisely this mode of caricature that teaches us so much about moral hypocrisy in the *real* world. Vizzini teaches us that morality is often an egotistical, selfish, hypocritical attitude where we can behave in despicable ways but judge others as evil scum. That's just when it comes to mundane behaviors. Vizzini's sanctimony in the wake of his own depravity is a lesson about both everyday moral hypocrisy, and the strategems and atrocities of history.

For while Vizzini is a dissipated villain, it isn't inconceivable that people consider themselves moral whilst committing illicit and murderous deeds. Plato suggested that people commit evil acts out of ignorance, but Vizzini takes us further by ennobling deliberate deceit and murder. This is a scary reflection of those who scheme with delight in the real world, but bathe their dishonesty in a smug rhetoric of *moral principle*. If Vizzini is the comical caricature of the villain reveling in evil, consider the ominous historical and political implications. For when Vizzini appeals to prestigious and glorious tradition, he's suggesting that history is a sleazy network of selfish schemes to start wars and conquer others, cloaked in a ridiculous aura of moral righteousness. To echo James Joyce, history is a nightmare, and people have waged wars and committed genocide with such a tortured sense of moral logic that they were often passionately committed to the moral purity of their acts of slaughter. That's why Ernest Becker could argue that so much evil in the world has been inflicted in order to *eradicate* evil—our delirious, irrational, rationalized, selfish, hypocritical fantasy of evil, that is.

Fezzing Up: Unexpected Evil Among the Adored

Existence was really very simple when you did what you were told.

—*The Princess Bride*, p. 226

This doesn't exhaust our propensities for evil, however. Let's take this in an unexpectedly different evil direction. Lots of research has been done on those who are capable of inflicting pain and death when obeying authority. They're just ordinary human beings trying to survive, doing what people in their own communities and societies deem good, moral behavior. To do otherwise would even be selfish and sinful, a betrayal of their friends, family, and society. Hence Hannah Arendt could talk about "the banality of evil," since so many people are capable of participating in atrocities not out of a Rugenesque curiosity or sadism, but because they are trying to do a good job and be good people. Yet as Arendt observed:

The sad truth of the matter is that most evil is done by people who never made up their minds to be or to do either evil or good. (*The Origins of Totalitarianism*, p. 9)

As Bernstein states, "the worst evils we experience cannot be adequately understood if we think of them as exclusively the actions of demonized individuals" (*The Abuse of Evil*, p. 60).

Doesn't that bring us to some of our beloved protagonists? Inigo and Fezzik aren't malicious villains. They're lovable, vulnerable human beings who have been wronged, abandoned, and seek a sense of purpose or justice in their lives. Still, let's look at what these heroes have done. Under Vizzini's auspices Inigo's blade flashed and Fezzik's strength grew more prodigious. The "Sicilian Crowd" became famous and rich, and "nothing was beyond or beneath them" (p. 142). They were famously felonious. And of course they stalked Buttercup, assaulted her, trussed her up, and deprived her of her freedom. Debates about evil notwithstanding, readers here might agree that being yanked off your horse, manhandled by a hippopotamic land mass, thrown in a dinghy, and dragged across the sea against your will might be kind of evil. You might consider it evil if it happened to your sister or mother. (Or maybe not.) Fezzik and Inigo may have not known Humperdinck was planning to murder Buttercup, and may have been so drunk, helpless, and hopeless that they were desperate or easy to manipulate, but they were sober and aware of what they were doing when assaulting Buttercup. They were certainly willing to kill anyone trying to save her.

It's difficult to defend their actions. Perhaps Fezzik's moral failings result from childish innocence (or imbecility). In the book he's pretty slow on the uptake. Fezzik sees Westley running toward them and thinks "Inigo has not lost to the man in black, he has *defeated* him. And to prove it he has put on all the man in black's clothes and masks and hoods and boots and gained eighty pounds" (p. 153). He thinks Guilder captured Buttercup, and Inigo has to remind him that "*we* kidnapped the Princess. . . . *we* put the Guilder uniform pieces under the Princess's saddle" (p. 275). At one point he finds himself facing the most hateful, insidious bewilderment ever conceived by the mind of man—a fork in the road (p. 414). Fezzik is pretty much a drooling, cowering, trembling, thumb-sucking, sucking squid-fearing, vagina-fleeing, oft-sobbing oaf. He's afraid of bats, spiders, sharks, sea monsters, rhinorrhea (or water up the nose, anyway), and a host of other things, in addition to the squid and *byuk* (birth fluids). Allusions to his oafishness, fears, and slowness occur frequently throughout the book. Goldman even has Fezzik saying that he licked the chocolate pot (after Max made the miracle pill), and it was "duh-licious" (p. 424).

Inigo, however, is far more perceptive than Fezzick and shows a sophisticated appreciation for all the subtle schemes and machinations. So ignorance and naïveté can't really be a moral excuse for him. If Inigo was on his life's mission to avenge his father, does this justify any action furthering this ultimate task? Are assault, human trafficking, and murder permissible just because he's been wronged? Especially disturbing (and instructive) about Inigo's wanton disregard for human rights or compassion is what it suggests about the potential moral failings of those who believe themselves so wronged that they may feel no compassion when committing feral acts, or that their own higher moral purpose transcends the rights of others.

This isn't Arendt's banality of evil. While Inigo may be following orders, he's not trying to survive in his society by conforming to their moral standards. He's a loner recruited to do something he could easily have known was larcenous and violent. Inigo certainly understands what it means to be wronged, have someone stolen away, feel abandoned and emotionally devastated. Yet he willingly participates in abduction. This teaches us about those wounded and wronged people in the real world, whose sense of anguish and outrage are so immense that they are both ripe for recruitment by salacious sociopaths and willing to commit murder on the way to vengeance and justice. What is Inigo, but a destitute potential terrorist?

Just in case we think he's a good person whose intellectual thicket will be cleared when finally avenging his father, consider how the movie ends with him contemplating the idea of becoming the new Dread Pirate Roberts. Inigo has a profound sense of fairness and understands betrayal, pain, loss, and loyalty, but he's entirely willing to murder and then take a job pillaging for profit once his quest for justice is over. This too teaches us something about evil: People can be immensely principled, understand the ravages of injustice, and be kind, caring people—to their friends and loved ones. But they may still be willing to slaughter or plunder without being particularly bothered by the hypocrisy or thinking about it enough to recognize that they may be just as evil as those they've vanquished so righteously. Like Inigo we may in principle hate injustice, but feel almost nothing for people being massacred, raped, or ravaged across the sea somewhere. Yet we'll still deem ourselves morally-pure, good people. Maybe that's why we can watch *The Princess Bride* and love the characters so affectionately instead of being horrified at the vile acts they commit. It says a lot about us and what we may deem acceptable, what we'll ignore, and whom we'll adore even as that cozy character abducts, despoils, and kills.

To the Pain: Westleyan Wantonness

Blackest of all were his flashing eyes. Flashing and cruel and deadly . . .

—*The Princess Bride*, p. 100

"Woman," Westley roared, "you are the property of the Dread Pirate Roberts and you . . . do . . . what . . . you're . . . told!"

—*The Princess Bride*, p. 352

This brings us to the most beloved, beautiful protagonist of *The Princess Bride*: The farm boy Westley, that blond, flat-stomached, sun-tanned beau with eyes like a sea before a storm. The epitome of enduring faithfulness plunging through squalls, sands, and death for love may be the evilest character of all. (Shrieking eel sounds again from the remaing readers.)

Westley seems the swoonworthy paragon of Platonic perfection, but is he? As we know, Westley is captured but soon becomes the valet of the Dread Pirate Roberts. And as valet, he implicitly participates in piracy. (Pirates, by the way, reputedly engage in piracy, in addition to other unspeakable acts.) For Westley to become so accomplished that he'd replace Roberts, he'd have to show his pirate potential. One can hardly be a cringing, peace-loving pacifist and become the new Dread anything.

Ergo, Westley must have excelled in a plethora of pillagy piratey things. And Westley admits as much, confessing to Buttercup how much he *liked* piracy and possessed palpable pirate talent as well (p. 211). Let's be honest about just how ferociously debauched pirates were.

As we learn from Captain Johnson's historical account, the real Dread Pirate Roberts was a scallywag who had a flag woven to display him standing on two skulls. Roberts was famous for applying his talents to "wicked Purposes" and "vile and ignominious Acts." The fictive Dread Pirate Roberts was feared across the seven seas for being ruthless and never leaving survivors (p. 68).

Beyond that I merely refer the reader to Burg's *Sodomy and the Pirate Tradition* to get a vague idea of how pirates romanced and rollicked. And as we know, you can't become a soft pirate or it's just work, work, work all the time. So for true love, Westley pretty much pirated, plundered, filleted, and fellated whomever he had to. Now before you belay such pervy notions and call this author a lying picaroon or strumpety bilge rat, let's foreswear a hasty keelhaul and cite the hallowed text itself, for Westley "had been King of the Sea for several years, and, well, things happened" (*The Princess Bride*, p. 433).

When pursuing the abducted Buttercup, Westley doesn't reveal his identity even after he vanquishes Vizzini in a battle of wits. He's merely no one to be trifled with. Westley is testing Buttercup. He needs to know she's been faithful, and doesn't love Humperdinck. Yet he roughly rips the blindfold from her eyes (p. 179), slaps her across the face when she says she's more capable of love than a killer like he can possibly imagine (p. 182), and grasps her around the throat (p. 183). Westley seems remorseless, drags her relentlessly for hours, and calls her cold as hoarfrost (p. 184). Hence his aggression might be too excessive and his cruelty too severe to be a mere test. This is "true love," but so devoid of trust that he has to torture and pummel her to prove she is enduringly faithful? Westley could be jealous, bitter, and enraged, think her unfaithful, and might be prepared to kill her himself should she prove disloyal. The sinister possibility is that Westley is not as pure as the driven snow, but is a murderous pirate capable of slaughtering his love should she fail the test. We speculate of course.

Let's consider one last facet of Westley's love, before we exeunt. We bask in the sentimental dream of a morally pure farm boy who endures slavery to survive, all for true love. But we know he participated in perennial piracy and slaughter. Are we to believe that at no time during any of those chaotic melees could he have slipped away and escaped that life of brutality? Must he have pirated and pillaged all those years? Perhaps he'd do *anything* for true love, but this is still eerie. He's yet another person willing to ravage and slaughter so he may embrace his true love again. Does he imagine this is justifiable? Do we? Fiction is filled with "good" people wreaking havoc because they serve some higher purpose, whether they're on a mission from God like the Blues Brothers, or Lancelot trying to save the "princess" from the tower, and so on. The swath of death and destruction following in their wake is justified when we imagine them as good. But consider the carnage these sanctimonious quests entail.

Comedy and fairytale aside, this is again the transcendent idiom of the impassioned patriot who deems all carnage necessary and forgivable because the cause is incontrovertibly good and noble. It's also the sublime idiom of the terrorist, who believes his love for God justifies inhumanity and massacre. As some sinister scholars (like Scott Atran and Ruth Stein) have shown, those who slaughter aren't always seething with hatred, but are often moved by love. Those we call "terrorists" wear a variety of masks. Some yearn for true love, and hurl themselves toward love with a passion that leaves a trail of death behind them. Westley is hardly a radical devoted to ideology or vengeance, but he's willing to eviscerate innocents and slaughter anyone in his path so that he may embrace his true love once more. Perhaps we should suffer a certain touch of dread regarding Westley, rather than ignore these vile acts because we too are willing to swoon so naively at the notion of true love.

Happy Ending, or Not. . . .

Philosophically, we might reflect on our own our own propensities to ignore the swaths of slaughter we inflict in the wake of quests we deem so pure, passionate, patriotic, pious, or sublime. Evil isn't only manipulative deception, deliberate dehumanization, and wicked machination. True love may embrace the vilest evil.

And what does that say about us, if we're willing to adore such villains even though we know indisputably that they've deliberately engaged in acts of abduction, piracy, and even murder? Sounds to me like we'd just be bloving our way to the delirious fantasy of being good, when actually being fairly wicked. Or perhaps this was just all my bloviation on evil. Maybe that word does not mean what I think it means. It was all for a good cause and we can justly celebrate a delightful story, and go on killing one another like civilized people, as God intended. . . .

14
The End of Inigo Montoya

CHARLENE ELSBY AND ROB LUZECKY

Inigo Montoya maintains a singular purpose—kill the Six-Fingered Man who killed his father. His catch phrase, "Hello. My name is Inigo Montoya. You killed my father. Prepare to die," evidences just to what extent this purpose grounds his identity.

For Inigo, everything leads to revenge; revenge is the final good, his life's purpose. Inigo's revenge is presented as the completion of a just retribution. When he kills the Six-Fingered Man, we're left with the feeling that justice has been served. But what does it mean to have a purpose, anyway, and how is a purpose fulfilled?

Certainly, revenge isn't a life goal for everyone. There are tons of people wandering about whose fathers have been killed by six-fingered men, but not all of us dedicate our lives to honing our skills for an inevitable final battle with our arch nemesis. Other people have other purposes, while a lot of people wander about seemingly having no purpose at all, despairing over the absurdity of life. There's a broader question at work here, and that is: why do we do stuff at all? We might phrase this more pessimistically and ask, what's the point to anything?

Inigo Montoya doesn't have these problems. Life is just the means you use to hunt six-fingered men with your giant friends and that dude dressed in black. When he achieves his purpose, we (the audience) rejoice: we like it when people have goals, and when those goals are accomplished. It gives a nice conclusion to things. Everything's all wrapped up in a neat little package. Someone has won. But then Inigo Montoya has to go on living, and it seems that his purpose in life has already been accomplished, so he'll need to find something else to do (hopefully, he can *re*-purpose some of his already-honed revenge skills). His re-invention as The Dread Pirate Roberts signifies the true end of Inigo Montoya, the man living towards revenge, and gives him a new purpose—or at least something to do.

Why We Do Things

As with any problem, we should begin by adopting a concept from Aristotle's *Physics*. In that book, and in the *Metaphysics*, Aristotle goes into detail about causality. Nowadays, we're happy with the scientific notions of causality—stuff happens because some stuff bumps into other stuff, and since it's made of this kind of stuff, some stuff will happen to that other stuff.

Aristotle's concept of causality is broader; not only are we looking at *what happens*, but also *why*. And in this way, his descriptions of causality ring more true with the questions that plague us all. When we ask, for instance, for the *cause* of something like strangling your bride on your wedding night, we want to know why Humperdinck would do such a thing—not how strangling works and why it's such an effective method for sucking the life out of someone.

Aristotle's concept of causality is something more like *explanation*, and it includes the possibility of explaining *to what end* someone would do such a thing. Why something happens isn't really explained when you're just talking about stuff bumping into other stuff. When I ask, for instance, why Westley is going on a quest to save Buttercup from marrying Prince Humperdinck, we all know that it's for the sake of true love. If Westley's quest is successful, true love will happen, and everyone will be happy. That's *why* he's doing it. That's a cause of his actions.

We don't like this kind of causality anymore, because we like to think that in all cases the cause comes before the effect. Westley and Buttercup reuniting, on the other hand, will not happen until after the quest is complete. So how can true love be a cause? Aristotle calls it the *final* cause. It's the purpose of the action. (Things have purposes too—the final cause of the goblet of poison, for instance, is to kill Vizzini.) We might say it's more like a motivation. (That's how we can put this kind of cause before what it causes.) I have a purpose in mind when I act, and by doing a thing, I hope to bring that purpose into actuality. When Inigo Montoya is diligently practicing his left-handed fencing, it's be*cause* he thinks it will be useful for when he encounters the Six-Fingered Man.

Every action has a purpose; otherwise, nobody would ever do anything at all. We're not talking only about grand gestures performed for the sake of true love; every single little action is for some purpose. Reading *The Princess Bride* to your grandchildren has a purpose; storming the castle has a purpose, and correcting Vizzini's vocabulary has a purpose. Every action requires two things: something to do the thing (that's your animated flesh-body), and something that gets done (or, at least, is attempted).

So we could say that "everything has a purpose," but keep in mind that all we mean by this is that there's something that we mean to accomplish when we perform an action. We don't mean to say that there's some outside purpose to life, such that it would please some higher power were you to drag your ass out of bed and go seek your fortunes in foreign lands. The purpose of studying fencing is to get better at fencing. The purpose of getting better at fencing is to become a killing machine. And the purpose of becoming a killing machine is to be ready for your battle with the Six-Fingered Man.

Kinds of Purposes

It might seem that the chain of purposiveness could go on forever, but at the end of the chain, we always hope to find some overall purpose, something that's *just good*. So there are two kinds of good, corresponding to two kinds of purposes. Some things are good for their own sake, and some things are good for the sake of something else. When Westley drinks poison every day, it's not because drinking poison is good for its own sake. It's because he imagines the possibility that one day he might have to engage in a battle of wits. So drinking poison is good for the sake of something else. There are really only a few contenders for things that can be *just good*, but when we find one of those, we want to call it our life's purpose. Aristotle asks in the *Nicomachean Ethics* what the overall good for a human being is, and decides that it's happiness. The reason is that it would be stupid to ask, "Why would you want to be happy? What is being happy good for?" We just do.

When the battle with the Six-Fingered Man is complete, and he dies, Inigo's chain of causality ends. Revenge is achieved. In this scenario, revenge is the thing that's *just good*. Revenge is what Inigo Montoya lives for, and in a sense, it's what he is. Revenge is why he diligently studies his parrying technique, and it's why he eats breakfast in the morning. We imagine his thought process go something like: *Gotta stay alive. Gotta kill that guy. Better eat some toast.* When his purpose is achieved, the question isn't, "What should I do now that I've eaten some toast?" but *what to do with life*. Revenge makes him happy, sure, but he can't just sit around being happy for the rest of his years inhabiting his flesh body. The conversation goes:

> INIGO MONTOYA: It's very strange. I have been in the revenge business so long, now that it's over, I don't know what to do with the rest of my life.
>
> WESTLEY: Have you ever considered piracy? You'd make a wonderful Dread Pirate Roberts.

The problem for Inigo is that he sets up revenge as a life goal, but then life has the audacity to keep on going after Inigo gets his revenge. Inigo has previously believed that if he manages to get revenge on the Six-Fingered Man, he will have lived a good life; he will be happy. But then what? You can't just sit around being happy reminiscing about that time you got revenge on that guy. Inigo Montoya can't become that washed-up fencer who killed the guy who murdered his father that one time. Inigo Montoya has reached his end in two senses: he has fulfilled his goal, and he has himself come to an end—the end of Inigo Montoya.

Hello. My Name Is Inigo Montoya. You Killed My Father. Prepare to Die

We might think that orienting your whole life to one singular purpose, especially when that purpose is revenge, is a slightly on the south side of sane. But Inigo is nothing but sane (even though he first spells out his purpose on the Cliffs of Insanity). Inigo has got his script all planned out for when he finally meets the Six-Fingered Man; this much he relates to Westley relatively soon after meeting him (as the Man in Black). You can tell that his life revolves around revenge and exactly how it's going to be accomplished. Inigo has clearly considered every word, every pause, every verb tense of his speech. The regularity of the story indicates that Inigo is conditioning himself to act in advance of any circumstance, and to do so without waiting for the action to come about. While, we might be inclined to say that Ingio's ultimate actions are performed without thought, he is carefully training himself to act without thought, and these are the actions of a man who is, if nothing else, conditioning himself to embody his ultimate destiny.

By telling Westley what he plans to say to his father's killer, he's relating a huge part of himself. He sees this grouping of words as indicative of what he *is*—his being and his purpose.

"Hello," is a pretty standard greeting. It might not, however, be the greeting of choice when we finally meet our father's killer. He might have gone with something more confrontational, like "Die, asshole!" But he didn't. He kept it classy and most importantly, he keeps it neutral; he announces his presence.

"My name is Inigo Montoya." It sure is. But why even tell the Six-Fingered Man? Why not just find him and assassinate him? Because Inigo Montoya demands recognition, that's why. His revenge won't be complete unless the Six-Fingered Man knows who Inigo is and why he's killing him. The first part of that is just to announce yourself, and to give yourself a name. I'm here, and I'm Inigo Montoya.

"You killed my father." Now things are getting tense. Nobody likes a father-killer. This is Inigo providing the man with insight as to his being and his purpose. At this point in the pronouncement, the Six-Fingered Man should definitely be questioning what the intentions are of this overly polite Inigo Montoya.

"Prepare to die," answers that question. It's less an instruction than it is a warning. In fact, Inigo provides Count Rugen with no time at all to get his affairs in order, write a will, inform his relatives about his preferences on burial or cremation, or even have a last meal. The Count runs away (to perform his preparations, we assume), but Inigo chases him down and gets right to the fight that he has been planning for over twenty years.

The interesting thing about all of these phrases together is that, out of all of the possible things you could say to the Six-

Fingered Man, Inigo Montoya chooses these. There's definitely some significance to them, which we can infer from the fact that he chooses to say them at all. Inigo could have said anything, but decides that these exact words are the most relevant things to mention. This is all that the Six-Fingered Man needs to know before he dies. And Inigo makes sure he knows by repeating them again and again.

The collection of statements as a whole sums up the entirety of Inigo's being. He's a guy. With a name. And a purpose. That's it. But things don't go so smoothly in the ultimate battle with Count Rugen. First there is a dagger to the gut, then there is a rapier to the left shoulder and to the right bicep. It seems that Inigo's purpose is stymied, and all is lost. It seems that the wound to the stomach should be fatal and the wounds to the arms should prevent him from lifting of the blade, but something exists alongside these particulars, subtly altering their meaning and their significance. The blood from the wounds is not a marker of defeat, and the pain is not significant enough to cause Inigo's surrender.

Inigo's arms should not be able to rise, and yet they do. Inigo recites his mantra a second time, a third time, emphasizing every syllable with a parry or a thrust. Inigo's repetition of the mantra is not informative—Rugen already knows all that there is to know about Inigo, and Inigo certainly doesn't need a reminder of his situation when he is bleeding from multiple wounds and has a rapier pointed at him. No, the repetition of the mantra places Inigo in the grips of habit, which helps him to forget about the blood on his tunic and the fatigue of his muscles. The physical movements, which he has practiced throughout his adult life, are now ingrained in him, they are what he does as long as he can do anything. This is another way of saying that he is their embodiment. With his repetition of the mantra Inigo embodies the habits he has willingly formed, those all aiming at his vengeful purpose, and through which his final cause becomes realized.

Purposes and Ends

Another word for purpose is "end." The end towards which Inigo Montoya lives is revenge. Achieving this end means the end of Inigo Montoya. He literally (and by "literally," I mean literally) needs a new identity. That's the Dread Pirate Roberts (in the movie, at least). But what exactly is the Dread Pirate Roberts?

Most of the characters don't really know. Buttercup tells us that he sails on a ship called *Revenge* (coincidence?), and he sometimes frequents the coasts of Florin. We are told by the narrator early on (when Westley supposedly dies) that The Dread Pirate Roberts takes no prisoners, and we know he has been the scourge of the seas for at least twenty years. While we're aware of his general description, and some of his traits, we cannot attribute a definitive identity to him. The "real" Dread Pirate Roberts is long-since retired. We hear that the name is the important thing, the legend that incites fear in henchmen like Vizzini and the sixty palace guards. When Fezzik dons the Holocaust Cloak and sends people running, we know that he is not the real Dread Pirate Roberts, or any of the other Dread Pirate Robertses—after all, Fezzik is an "unemployed Brute from Greenland."

The obscurity that surrounds the character of the Dread Pirate Roberts is due to the fact that throughout the entirety of the movie the character is defined as little more than a name that can be taken on by various characters at various instances. That the Dread Pirate Roberts cannot be tied to a particular body in a specific place doing specific things indicates that he is awaiting full definition, and in this sense the character of Dread Pirate Roberts is analogous to Inigo after he has killed Count Rugen. Both of them are beings without a clearly defined path, who seem to be capable of nearly anything, seemingly adrift on the murky waters of an ill-specified past and directed to the uncharted waters of the future.

For all of us, the end is something that we do not know, and all we can do is train ourselves to act in certain ways and adopt habits that will hopefully carry us through our days in the Pit of Despair in Florin, or sick in bed. These habits inform our actions, and they are the things that give purpose to our lives. Our habits help us survive the obstacles we face when we encounter the Six-Fingered Man, after we've made it past the stone walls when we seem to have very few assets at our disposal. More than this, our habits have the unique capacity of giving meaning to our actions; they inform us, and our friends, what is important and why it is important. In the sense that our habits help us realize our goals, and give meaning to our ever so ambiguous name, these habits are how the final cause realizes itself.

The purpose to our actions, whether it be one action or many actions that eventually constitute a habitual mode of being in the world, anticipate an end, a finality. This is precisely our final cause; it takes us, scarred, out of Spain, defines our battles, and gives our lives an end.

For Inigo Montoya, revenge is the only purpose worth having (though there's not a lot of money in it). It's what he lives for, or lives towards. Everything aims at revenge. The eventual death of the Six-Fingered Man has (in its twenty-year conception) made him what he is. At the same time, when it actually happens, it spells the end of Inigo Montoya.

15
It Would Take a Miracle!

ADAM BARKMAN AND TRISTAN KÄÄRID

The Princess Bride presents us with a story of love that wins out against all odds. The reader or viewer is regaled with stories of fencing, fighting, torture, revenge, giants, monsters, chases, escapes, true love, and miracles—all quite essential to the making of such a timeless story. In one particularly interesting scene, the enigmatic miracle man, Miracle Max, even goes as far as to bring our protagonist, Westley, back from the dead.

Miracles make for excellent elements in a mythical story. The author of *The Princess Bride*, William Goldman (not, after all, the fictional S. Morgenstern) has stipulated that the universe where the story takes place, though very like ours, is a universe in which miracles occur. Of course, many people believe that miracles occur in the universe that we actually inhabit. Two prominent thinkers on this topic, who come to distinctly different conclusions, are David Hume and C.S. Lewis. Let's see what they have to say.

What Is a Miracle?

To begin we ask the question, what's a miracle? Miracles seem to have certain features: they are not natural, regular, or easily predictable. Though these are traits that miracles all seem to have, they don't seem sufficient to be the *definition* of a miracle, since events other than miracles might also have those traits.

We tend to rely on our senses to form our beliefs. This practice allows for a certain degree of predictability. Our senses have conditioned us to believe to some degree in the regularity in nature—in the consistency of cause and effect. For example, in the Fire Swamp, every time Westley heard popping sounds, fire spurted from the ground, so he was justified in believing that in the future, when he hears the popping sounds, it is likely that fire will follow. But this element of predictability seems to elude miracles as evidenced in this interaction between Miracle Max and Inigo Montoya:

> INIGO: We need a miracle. It's very important.

> MIRACLE MAX: Look, I'm retired. And besides, why would you want someone the King's stinking son fired? I *might* kill whoever you wanted me to miracle. (Emphasis added)

Did you catch that? Miracle Max said that he *might* kill him, suggesting that unpredictability is part of miracles.

Before we can answer the question: 'What's a miracle?', we need to distinguish between the various ways that we tend to use the word in our everyday lives. We may use the word miracle when describing something that we felt was unlikely to happen. For instance, we might flippantly use the word on an occasion when we were expecting to be late for an appointment, but arrived on time. We may let out a sigh of relief saying, "It's a miracle we made it!" We might use the word when the stakes are high and the probability of a positive outcome is unknown, when, for example, we exclaim, "It's a miracle nobody was hurt in that car crash!"

We also use the word miracle when certain effects are brought about as a result of impressive causes. When someone's cured of a life-threatening illness or (for those more sarcastic folk) in the case of a more mundane treatment, we may say that, when health is improved or restored, "It was a miracle of science!" Similarly, when a child is born, we often refer to the process as the "miracle of life."

Now we in no way, shape, or form intend to belittle the process of childbirth or to undermine the value of the other examples that we referred to as "miracles." For our purposes here, though, we are interested in miracles of a different type. It is here that we turn to David Hume.

Hume on Miracles

David Hume was a materialist, an empiricist, and a skeptic. As a materialist—that is, a metaphysical materialist—Hume believed that the material system was all there was or, at least all we had evidence for. As an empiricist Hume thought that all knowledge came from the senses. And as a skeptic—and a particularly radical skeptic—he viewed any knowledge that came by way of the senses with suspicion.

Hume was particularly skeptical about testimony related to the occurrence of miracles. He defined miracles as *violations of the laws of nature.* According to Hume, we are never justified in believing the testimony of someone who claims to have witnessed a miracle. When we hear such a report, we should consider whether it's more likely that the person providing the testimony is lying or mistaken or that the violation of a law of nature actually occurred. He argues that any explanation is likely to be a better explanation than a miracle, since we should have more confidence in our collective experiences of natural laws holding than reports of them being violated.

According to this approach, it's more likely that stories about Jesus walking on water were lies, exaggerations, or misunderstandings than that Jesus actually walked on water, since every time *we,* or anyone we have ever observed for that matter, try to walk on water, it can't be done. Similarly, if someone came to us and told us that he had seen a man get fifty years of life sucked out of him by a sadist with a giant water powered machine constructed just for that purpose, we would be in the same boat. In our experience, it is possible to take years off of someone's life by killing them prematurely, but it is not possible to suck some number of precisely specified years from their future life using such a contraption. If someone came to us with a story of such a machine, we would have more reason to think that they were lying or were, perhaps, confused, than we would have to believe that such a contraption really exists.

C.S. Lewis on Miracles

On the other side of the debate is C.S. Lewis, who was a "supernaturalist." He believed there was good evidence for a realm beyond and above the material realm—a super-natural realm, which includes an "above-nature" God. This God, Lewis thinks, made the physical regularities that we call "gravity" and the like, and if He wants to introduce a new element into the material or natural mix, He—either directly or indirectly through another entity—is free to do so. In this way, a miracle wouldn't be a "violation of the laws of nature" but would, rather, be an introduction of a *new* element into the regular stream of physical reality that God holds in existence. Miracles, then, are irregularities that are hard or even impossible to predict, but are not impossibilities or violations.

No one in Florin predicted that the Dread Pirate Roberts would spare Westley. The Dread Pirate, as a rule, doesn't take prisoners, so we wouldn't predict that he would do so in Westley's case. The fact that we would have a difficult time predicting it doesn't entail that his taking a prisoner alive is impossible. According to C.S. Lewis, neither are miracles.

You Rush a Miracle Man, You Get Rotten Miracles

Before we consider how what Hume and Lewis have to say applies to Miracle Max and the alleged miracle he performs for Westley in our movie, let's consider three independent but related questions that are raised by the movie.

First, there is Max's claim about the possibility of getting a "rotten" miracle. This raises an interesting question: can an event actually count as a miracle if it doesn't benefit anyone? What would count as a "rotten miracle"? One possibility is that instead of raising from the dead the clever, witty Westley that Inigo and Fezzik knew, Max could raise a decomposing corpse, or worse, a zombie. If Max did this, the "service" he provided wouldn't seem "miraculous" at all. The lesson to be learned from this is that nearly as central to the concept of a miracle as "unpredictability" is the notion of "benefit" to a certain party. Surely all miracles are not of benefit to everyone, and *The Princess Bride* is no exception since Westley's return from the dead is much to Humperdinck's chagrin.

The second point has to do with the way in which miracles in *The Princess Bride* universe work. The discussion of miracles that C.S Lewis provides is dependent on a world that has certain features (for instance, that someone like the Christian God exists). It's not clear that this is the kind of universe that Max inhabits (this universe might have a God, but if it does, it's not clear what traits that God would have). In Max's universe there are shrieking eels, rodents of unusual size, Fire Swamps, and miracle men. Max appears to be something like a sorcerer here, and his ability to perform "miracles" seems contingent on his confidence being "unshattered." Ever since Prince Humperdinck fired him, as his wife Valerie puts it, his confidence has been shattered. Does this mean that he can only perform miracles insofar as he has confidence in himself? In the existence of miracles? In an unpredictable, beneficial act happening?

Finally, there's the question of what it means to say that Westley is "dead" in the first place, so that that a "miracle" is actually needed. Some people believe that, the principle, "That which dies is dead for good" is an absolute or "always-true" principle, but others believe it might be merely a "generally-true" principle. All we can know from experience is that this principle to be likely true, but we can't be certain that it is true, since experience alone can never give us certainty. But here the question we are asking isn't so much as whether it's possible for the dead to come back to life, but whether *Westley* is actually dead in the first place; indeed, we are told, vaguely and in a way that is left open for interpretation, that Westley is "mostly dead." Should we take this to mean that his body has, in fact, died, but his "soul" hasn't moved on, so that it could still be reconnected with his body? Or should we take this to mean that his body isn't fully dead yet? If his body isn't fully dead, then what Max does seems less like a miracle and more like science.

Hume's Doubt

Hume was skeptical about reports of miracles happening because deception or perceptual error is a better explanation than a "violation" of a law of nature. He believed that it was often barbarous, uncivilized people who believed in miracles. He would claim that the uneducated are more likely to label something as a miracle that is not, than to see an actual miracle.

If we were to transport Hume to the universe of *The Princess Bride,* what would he have to say? (Let's imagine that he is unaware of the differences between the worlds. They look awfully similar, after all.) Hume certainly could make a case that Inigo and Fezzik are indeed barbarous and uncivilized (they are a sell sword and a brute squad member respectively, we would likely agree!). The skeptic in all of us should start to question if Westley returning from 'mostly dead' is indeed a miracle. Was Westley always going to pull through? Was Max just being deceitful?

It is, however, difficult to discredit completely those who lack a certain educated perspective. After all, it would be difficult for them to survive from day to day if their beliefs were not, at least sometimes, true. We don't know which cases are which. As a result, it could be very difficult to know when to trust another person's testimony. The best possible way, according to Hume, to form a belief in what's true, is to experience something firsthand (thought that isn't always necessary).

However, Hume's argument that miracles must be observed yields a slightly stronger point. For Hume, the laws of nature are easily assumed because we can observe and gain empirical knowledge of them. Unlike in the case of the regularity of the laws of nature, we don't see miracles happening around us. Therefore, we don't have good reason to believe that they happen. Indeed, Hume (oddly for such a radical skeptic) even seems to suggest that they couldn't happen, since a miracle, to him, is a violation of physical or natural laws. He rightly claims this, since miracles like Moses parting the Red Sea, or the splitting of the moon by Mohammad, or the Buddha's ability to change size from very large to miniscule, do seem to be contrary to physical and natural laws. It isn't surprising then that, if transported to Miracle Max's hovel, Hume would be skeptical of the claim that a miracle was performed on Westley.

Hume might conclude that Max is simply a deceiver. We're told that Westley is only "mostly dead," so we can conclude that he was not fully dead. Unaware that he is in a universe where miracles occur regularly enough for there to be consensus that they exist, Hume would likely say that it's far more probable that Max is being deceitful than that he brought a man back from the dead. Inigo and Fezzik, barbarous and uncivilized, would be prime candidates for deception. Max's insecure, slightly sarcastic, comment that "It would take a miracle" for their plan to work, may make us inclined to side with Hume here.

Lewis and the Whole Show

What if we brought C.S. Lewis into the world of *The Princess Bride*? Recall that Lewis is a super-naturalist. He claims that nature is what happens of itself or of its own accord. It is what we get when we don't take any measures to stop it. It's natural that Westley dies, since without taking measures to stop it, death will come eventually, even though we know at this point he is only "mostly dead." According to this way of thinking, it would possibly be a miracle that Westley continues to live despite having fifty years sucked out of his life (this seems quite miraculous in and of itself). Lewis views a miracle as an external force, something that is simply another unforeseen event. If we accept this view, we can conclude that it is at least possible for Max to perform a miracle. Max, after all, would just be the required external force.

Is Lewis's view scientifically irresponsible? Consider the following example. Suppose Fezzik put seventy-five gold pieces in a drawer. The next day he added twenty-five gold pieces. Using simple arithmetic, he can deduce that those exact pieces that add up to the sum of one hundred gold pieces are in the drawer. He can also expect that if he returns to the drawer the following day he will find those exact same pieces and they will still total one hundred gold pieces. Now suppose the Dread Pirate Roberts came and stole half of the pieces, now there are only fifty pieces left. When Fezzik returns he will find that only fifty pieces remain and not the full one hundred that he had expected. In this example, were the natural laws of mathematics broken? No.

Similarly, we might see the "miracle pill" as an unexpected and "external force" acting unpredictably, but not in violation of nature; perhaps the pill is from outside the closed physical system or the stream of regularity. Indeed, if people who have fifty years of their life sucked out of them always seem to die, then the fact that Westley doesn't die requires some explanation. Supernatural intervention is the go to answer for Lewis, though proving it scientifically may be pretty difficult. He may choose to analyze the miracle pill or the vital signs of a "mostly dead" person, but may have to offer a simple "we don't know yet."

There's also the neglected suggestion in the film that a miracle occurring is connected to "unshattered" confidence.

Neither Hume nor Lewis addresses this sort of thing, but it is interesting that when Max's confidence was intact he could perform miracles. Does this suggest that Max as a sorcerer plays a role in the miracle coming into being? Hume may think otherwise since a person can't violate physical or natural law, and Lewis would not view a person as an external force. In his past, was Max simply deceptive or actually performing miracles? The answer to that may call for a prequel! However, we can conclude that the Princess Bridian understanding of miracles is that it is entirely a person's doing and is dependent on confidence. In the case of Westley, Max simply needed a noble cause to get his mojo back and to get him back on the job!

It's Just a Story . . .

Of course, in stories—especially in fairy tales—we expect—and properly expect—miracles. But should we expect them in the real world?

The account of miracles presented in *The Princess Bride* might not necessarily fit cleanly into either what Hume or Lewis have to say, but it is a crucial element of the story nonetheless! Without the miracle pill, and Max, Inigo would not have avenged his father, Fezzik would not have done something right for once, and Westley would not have saved Buttercup. We need Max and his quirks, song and dance, and his quick-witted sarcasm to really complete such a fantastic tale.

Whether or not we are so encouraged by the tale to believe that miracles do happen in the real world is difficult to say, but, at the very least, the existence of miracles is necessary in many tales, stories, myths and religions. It is this tricky thing known as a miracle that has us, like the grandson, asking to have the tale read to us again tomorrow.

16

My Name Is—Hang On, What Was It Meant to Be Again? Are You Sure? Well, Okay Then . . .

TIM JONES

I came to *The Princess Bride* later than most people I know, and almost certainly by a different route. I'd filed it away in my head as one of those Eighties movies I should probably check out sometime but would probably never get around to watching, and I didn't even realize there was a book too. I know what you're thinking: inconceivable! But I like writing about popular culture and I especially like the heavy thud as the postman drops the complimentary copies of Popular Culture and Philosophy books down on the doormat. So once I knew this book was in the works, then onto Amazon I went, and less than a day later (thanks, Prime) I had both novel and Blu-ray in my hands.

From everything I'd heard about it, I was expecting the most wonderful thing ever. Action! Romance! Cliff-top escapes, sword fights, derring-do on an epic scale, with the good guys and the power of true love itself winning out over the forces of evil!

How shocked I was when I realized that every person raving about these qualities had been totally blind-sided by the efficiency of the fictionalized version of William Goldman's interference with S. Morgenstern's original work. *The Princess Bride*, as it comes to us now, isn't the most beautiful love-story ever told at all. It's a *warning* about how easily our identities can be seized from our own control; about how open we are to being shaped by other people for their own self-interest and amusement; and about how powerfully these manipulations can twist us into new forms that think and speak beyond—and maybe even against—what we'd ever have imagined ourselves thinking or speaking.

159

My Name Is Descartes, Prepare to Think about Identity!

If we were to go back to the time of French philosopher René Descartes (1596–1650) and get him to read or watch *The Princess Bride*, then he wouldn't see the urgency of this warning at all. You might've already heard of his most famous phrase: "I think, therefore I am." This is generally reckoned by philosophers today to place the self completely above and beyond the world around it. To view it as a completely *transcendent* point from which reflections upon the outside world can calmly and objectively emanate, but which remains undisturbed and uninfluenced by this world.

A few hundred years later, American social thought comes along and reaches a very different take on things. American pragmatist philosophers William James, Charles Cooley, and George H. Mead, amongst others, take the self down from its Cartesian pedestal and mire it thoroughly in the whirl of the world around it. As James states in his 1892 book *Psychology: The Briefer Course* (which if you check out of the library you'll see is *not* particularly brief), "a man has as many social selves as there are individuals who recognize him." Day-to-day interactions with ordinary people are suddenly recognized to influence our identities in substantial ways, so that we might even take on a completely new self in the eyes of every single person that we meet. Identities are no longer transcendent at all, but set fluidly in motion via all of their myriad social interactions in the wider world, and therefore ever shifting, ever changing . . .

You might think that this is something to be pretty pleased about. Surely we can take advantage of this plasticity at the heart of this idea of selfhood, and shape our identities for ourselves to best get through the situations we find ourselves in. We can be whomever we want, whenever we want!

Just look at how completely our hero Westley is able to reinvent his own identity in order to survive some pretty trying circumstances, shaping it from that of a lowly farm boy into the Dread Pirate Roberts, following the long screed of people who've likewise taken advantage of the mutability of their own identities and taken on this mantle before him. And as soon as it's safe for Westley to reveal his true identity to Buttercup, he's able to stop being a scary pirate and take back the identity of the man she loves, yet newly possessing the added skills and strengths necessary for carrying the two of them through the rest of their trials.

As contemporary sociologists James A. Holstein and Jaber F. Gubrium say about the advantages that seem to come from this new understanding of the self, Westley confirms how "individual agency combined with social feedback yielded a self that could move competently and confidently through the world, both reflecting and responding to changing needs and circumstances." The "changing needs and circumstances" here being those of ending up in the grip of fearsome pirates, and then facing the wrath of the girl you love, because she's a little too convinced that you're a fearsome pirate. Each of these situations is perfectly survivable for Westley, when it could have gone pretty badly, because of his skill at molding his identity.

I'm not necessarily saying that *you* could choose to become the next Dread Pirate Roberts yourself, or that it's as easy as dropping this book and embarking straightaway upon a quest of plunder and pillaging across the high-seas. Though it might be fun to try! (Disclaimer to the Feds: I am in no way encouraging my readers towards a life of piracy.) But what Westley does here is basically just an exaggerated version of what these new theories of identity suggest that we're *all* free to do, outside of the book or movie. The flexibility our identities enjoy to reinvent themselves around the needs of the situations we're in could see you deciding to make yourself more assertive in the face of a demanding boss at work, or to step up and become brilliantly witty in front of a hot guy or girl at the bar downtown.

If you take a look at the extras on *The Princess Bride* DVD, then you'll see the guy who plays Inigo Montoya, Mandy Patinkin, talking about how he took advantage, as an actor, of exactly the kind of freedom we see Westley using in the story itself. Mandy gives a pretty moving account of his father dying of cancer and explains that he channeled his anger at the disease into his portrayal of Inigo's quest to kill the more physical and tangible murderer of his own father. "When I killed that Six-Fingered Man, I killed the cancer that killed my father," Mandy tells us with a bewitching smile on his face, "and my fairytale came true."

Becoming Inigo wasn't just a matter of an actor playing a role for the money or the critical acclaim. It was also a vehicle giving Mandy the opportunities to process emotions he experiences in the real-world. It's like he wasn't just pretending to be Inigo on a purely superficial level, but genuinely became a man on a winnable mission to get revenge on his father's killer, and then felt, as Mandy, the deep catharsis that fulfilling this quest delivers.

The successes that come from both Westley and Mandy taking advantage of the mutability of their identities are obviously dependent on this mutability remaining once a new self has been taken on, so that they can step out of it when required and go back to the old ones. I doubt Westley would have ended up with Buttercup if he'd remained stuck as the Dread Pirate Roberts. At best, it would have led to an awkward first date. And it certainly wouldn't have been much fun for Mandy if he'd been doomed to keep repeating the famous "Hello. My name is Inigo Montoya. You killed my father. Prepare to die!" wherever he went. Grocery shopping would become pretty difficult amongst all of the weird looks and police interventions.

But this doesn't seem a problem for people either inside the story itself or involved with it on the outside. When Mandy is introduced on the special features, it's as Mandy, and not as Inigo. So the amorphous model of identity theorized by people like James, Cooley and Mead doesn't only carry obvious advantages through the opportunities it creates for us to navigate the situations we find ourselves in—these advantages are pretty safe, too, as you can always go back.

So *why* is the mutability of identity something we should be scared of like I suggested at the start?

Seizing Identities

What exactly *is* this story that we're perfectly happy to call *The Princess Bride*?

We hear in a featurette from 1987, included on the most recent DVD release, that it's "a tale of true love and high adventure, told to a sick child by his grandfather." And Mandy Patinkin says on a more recently recorded extra that when he asked the movie's director and co-producer Rob Reiner this very question, Rob gave pretty much the same answer: *The*

Princess Bride is "about a little boy who's sick" and whose granddad "goes over to read him a story and tell him that the most important thing in life is true love."

Fair enough. You'd have to be pretty hard-hearted to have a problem with any of that, right?

Well yes, we would. If that's what *The Princess Bride* really is. But this isn't what *The Princess Bride* really is at all. Or, at least, it isn't what *The Princess Bride* was within its own fictional universe, originally, a long time ago (in a land far away, like the fictional S. Morgenstern's homeland of Florin). We've just fallen so in love with the manipulated version of the story that we don't tend to look very closely at the poor original version that's been so thoroughly mistreated.

Holstein and Gubrium describe a bunch of grad students chewing the fat about the consequences of our identities being understood as so mutable, and realizing, in a slightly power-drunk fashion, that perhaps this is more dangerous than we initially think. What if this mutability doesn't only mean that we're able to adapt to our circumstances, like Westley and Mandy show us? What if it also means that we're open to being shaped according to interests and motivations that aren't our own at all, but belong to other people? Holstein and Gubrium think it *does* mean this, describing the mutability of identity as creating a "virtual Pandora's Box of possibilities that are not as positive as originally intended" (*The Self We Live By*, p. 5). Once the box was opened by Americans like James, Cooley and Mead, ramifications about our identity might have spilled out that we wish we could put back in, only we can't.

Thanks, guys!

Because if our identities are so elastic and so readily changeable, it raises pretty important questions about who's in control of this process. Are *you* always in perfect control of exactly who you are at any moment in time? Or have you ever felt coerced by the situations or the people around you into being in any way other than the person you consciously set out to be when you got up that morning?

This is where William Goldman comes in. Or, at least, this is where the fiction*alized* version of real-life author William Goldman, who shapes the fiction*al* author S. Morgenstern's original novel into his own unique work, comes in. And if you focus on this aspect of the story, the aspect that's about a fictionalized version of William Goldman encountering the fictional Morgenstern's original (albeit fictional) version of *The Princess Bride* and turning it into a very different text of his own, then you might reckon that the *real* Goldman has actually written a novel that doesn't praise the mutability of identity, as it seems like it's doing through Westley's arc, but that gives a rather big warning about how open this mutability leaves us to being manipulated by other people and their own selfish interests.

My argument here might kill one of your favorite childhood movies. Sorry about that. Maybe read one of the other chapters before you put this book down. They'll probably be nicer to it.

But what the fictionalized Goldman does to Morgenstern's text is just like what would happen if *you*'re ever forced to become someone you don't want to be—if the mutability of your identity is ever taken advantage of in ways you're not entirely happy about, but can't do anything to resist. Does *The Princess Bride* even *want* to be Goldman's *The Princess Bride*, or would it rather be its original self before Goldman grabbed hold of it and changed it into something different? The book's "original" self might not actually exist in the real world, but if that problematizes my argument here a bit too much for you, then bear in mind that Westley doesn't actually exist in the real world either—a fact that hopefully didn't invalidate my arguments about him earlier! It still leaves the book of Goldman's that you have on your shelves a story that's about a fictional man encountering a novel that exists within his own fictional world and going 'Hey, I'm going to twist this thing into what *I* want it to be!'

This would be a bit like Mandy Patinkin being mobbed by crazed fans and forced to repeat his famous line, to become Inigo on demand whenever other people wanted, when he actually just went out and sat at his favorite café for a cup of coffee and some cake. *This* would be an identity being forced on Mandy for the gratification of the people around him, rather than him stepping into it himself to work through his own emotional baggage about his father.

Mandy *does* mention on the DVD interview that saying the famous words nowadays is usually a joy for him, because it immediately makes him feel twenty years younger. In these cases there's no problem at all, as it's another example of the mutability of identity being advantageous for a guy due to him taking advantage of his *own* mutability for himself, just like Westley does when he becomes the Dread Pirate Roberts. But what if he were having an off day and just wanted to chill out on his own? Then it'd be a case of the mutability of his identity being taken advantage of by other people, for their benefit rather than for his.

The difference is *who* is doing the shaping of *whose* identity, and whose interests this shaping is serving.

The Princess Bride by ~~S. Morgenstern~~ William Goldman

The twenty-fifth anniversary publication of *The Princess Bride* has a lovely new introduction. Goldman starts it off by having his fictionalized persona say, in the very first lines, that the fictional Morgenstern's original work is "still" his "favorite book in all the world." "And more than ever," he goes on to say, "I wish I had written it. Sometimes I like to fantasize that I did" (p. vii).

This is pretty ironic, right? I mean Goldman's fictionalized self has changed the book he was supposedly so in love with so much that he might as well have written it!

Just look at everything that's been cut out of the version of the novel that exists within the fictionalized Goldman's universe. We're glibly told at the beginning of Part Two that "sixty-six pages of Florinese history" has fallen just like that. Um, okay. I guess getting insights into other peoples and cultures is usually pretty boring, right? No one ever wants to do that. And soon afterwards there's a big section about Florin's Queen Bella traveling to see Guilder's Princess Noreena, which is also totally cut. I guess if that chat between two named female characters had stayed in, then the book and the movie would have passed the Bechdel test, and we can't have that, so that's cool, out it goes. It goes on like this for much of the book. There's Buttercup training to be a princess; S. Morgenstern's authorial interjections to his wife; lavish-sounding descriptions of Florinese festivities . . . All gone!

Sure, the fictionalized Goldman openly admits in his new introduction that this version is his "abridgement." But by being so candid here, he actually leads us away from noticing that there's much more interference going on than he acknowledges. If the fictionalized Goldman had merely abridged

Morgenstern's work, then all he would've done would be take chunks out of it, leaving a text that was pretty much all Morgenstern's words, only far fewer of them. At least that's how *I* understand the verb 'abridge'.

It isn't really the best (or most honest!) word for the fictionalized Goldman to use here. Beyond the book being dramatically cut down to size, there's also the copious insertion of lots of his own writing. Even if we ignore his new introduction for the twenty-fifth anniversary edition, there's thirty-one pages about the fictionalized Goldman's family struggles, his writing career, and his time hanging out by a swanky pool in Beverly Hills, before Morgenstern's story even gets going. An abridgement doesn't tend to be something that adds a load of details like this, which not only aren't in the original work, but often have nothing to do with it. And so all around the events that were actually in the version by Morgenstern that existed in this fictional universe, and have survived in the 'abridgment' (particularly heavy scare quotes), we get lots of pretty self-indulgent stuff about the fictionalized Goldman that continually interrupts and influences our reading of what's left of the Morgenstern.

I don't want to be *too* hard on any of this, really. The new story that all of this manipulation gives us is really charming. Like I said, it's "a tale of true love and high adventure, told to a sick child by his grandfather." But this simply isn't what's there in the original story that the fictionalized Goldman claims to adore. The first half of that description is produced by the omission of everything in Morgenstern that's there in addition to these elements; the second by everything about the fictionalized Goldman's own life that he splices into what's left.

The version of *The Princess Bride* that we're left with *is* everything the quote from the featurette suggests. It's not wrong on that count. And we can even be pretty sympathetic about the fictionalized Goldman's reasons for re-shaping the fictional original the way he does. He's trying to reconnect with the experience of being read the same truncated version by his dad, at a time when what sounds like a really hectic work schedule was keeping him from allocating much attention to his own child. But given what had to be done to the original to make it into what the quote is describing, we might also call the new version 'a tale of a guy taking an innocent book and manipulating its identity so thoroughly that it barely resembles its original self anymore'. Only this wouldn't make such a sweet intro for a gushing retrospective.

The Princess Bride might like being the new version of *The Princess Bride* that the fictionalized Goldman has twisted it into. It's evidently given joy to millions of people, which is no mean feat. But it didn't really have much of a say in the matter. It was completely defenseless in the face of the fictionalized Goldman's tampering with it. And it might prefer to be the more politically and culturally substantial text that it sounds like it was originally, in the fictional universe inhabited by the fictionalized Goldman—one that wouldn't be quite so dizzily exciting, but which would have kept its nation of origin, and its ways of life and its history, alive in the mind of every reader who read the book and cherished what was actually there. It might be the textual equivalent of a quiet, serious, bookish kid being forced to hang out with the popular children, while wishing he or she could just be left alone doing his or her own thing.

It might then wish it had the power over its own identity that Westley and Mandy Patinkin show that they've enjoyed over theirs, so that it could escape the fictionalized Goldman's grasp and return to being the story that *it* wants to be.

Who's in Control?

So *The Princess Bride* leaves us with a bit of a dilemma about whether or not we should be happy with the line of thinking about identity started by the American pragmatists, James, Cooley, and Mead, in their move away from the transcendent self imagined centuries previously by Descartes. Inside the story through Westley, and outside the story through actor Mandy Patinkin, we can see examples that suggest that a flexible and mutable self is a really good thing. But the fictionalized Goldman's actions with the text by Morgenstern that exists in his fictional universe are there to remind us how easily this mutability leaves us open to being shaped not according to our own interests and agency, but to those of other people who can come along at any time and turn us into what *they* want us to be.

What you should probably do now is prove my cynical reading of *The Princess Bride* wrong by putting down the book, getting on out into the world and being exactly the person you want to be. Take advantage of the power you enjoy in shaping your identity and become whomever you choose!

Though I guess that thanks to me you're now someone who's just read a chapter about the mutability of identity and is worrying about whether or not that's something to be happy about, when you probably weren't either of these things before. So your ability to be in total control of who you are at any given moment might already be looking a little shaky.

17
The Miracle of True Love

CHARLENE ELSBY AND ROB LUZECKY

The miracle of the tale as old as time is that it shows us a world in which opposites are not as clear-cut as some would like to believe. It's a tale where the hero seems to die, and then turns out to be alive, and then seems to die again, and then miraculously lives.

Yet this is not a tale of rebirth, as the hero never really *fully* dies—he just comes within a hair's breadth of death after his encounter with The Machine. If this were a tale told by a pessimist, it would be the end of the movie. But *The Princess Bride* is more magical than those sorts of stories that (like their heroes) are born, rise to a modicum of fame, and then fall into an obscure death. We might say that Westley cheats death, but he's really only "mostly dead" (and mostly dead is slightly alive). In *The Princess Bride*, death and life are not necessarily opposed, and miracles can happen.

Still, Westley needs a miracle, one that will cost Fezzik sixty-five somethings, plus the intervention of Miracle Max's wife, plus an appeal to Miracle Max's bitterness towards Prince Humperdinck. We can't cite a flaw in the machine, and we can't cite the good will or incompetence of Count Rugen as reasons for Westley's continued survival. Rather, we must look to the nature of life and death, these things we call "opposites", and the possibility of exploiting a loophole in the whole life and death opposition. In the *Princess Bride*, miracles can conquer Westley's state of being mostly dead, while true love conquers death itself.

Life and Death

We tend to think that life and death are opposites. When we say this, we mean it in the most general sense of "opposite," though there are many senses of the word. When I say that two people are complete opposites, I mean something different than when I say that life and death are opposites. In Plato's *Phaedo,* Socrates makes the argument that everything comes from its opposite. (And, some philosophers would argue, he takes advantage of this ambiguity in the term "opposite.") He uses this claim to try to prove that the soul is immortal. Starting with some relatively familiar examples, he demonstrates how opposites arise from one another. After all, if something gets stronger, it must have been weaker to begin with. And if something gets faster, it must have previously been slower. In the same way, he argues, what is dead comes from what is alive (obviously), and what is alive comes from what is dead—that's the sticky point. In this argument for the reincarnation (and immortality) of souls (we call this one "The Cyclical Argument"), Socrates is assuming that the opposite of life is death. But in what sense?

There are different kinds of opposites. Consider, for instance, something that has never been alive. We might not say that it's dead, but instead, we'd say it's just *not alive.* The kind of opposites that describe the case where one of the opposites is just *not* the other we call "contradictories." Any pair of contradictories takes the form of "something" and "not something," and Aristotle tells us in *De Interpretatione* that you must be one or the other. (Modern logicians call this the "Principle of Bivalence".)

Applying the Principle of Bivalence, we know that everything is either "alive" or "not-alive." The Law of Non-Contradiction (we can thank Aristotle for that one as well) adds that, in addition, nothing can be *both* alive and not-alive. If the law of non-contradiction holds, Westley can't be *both* "alive" and "not alive." (The Law of Non-Contradiction states that nothing can be both X and not-X, in the same respect and at the same time.) It does leave a little wiggle room, though, because of the "in the same respect" clause. When Westley starts coming back to life from his state of mostly dead, we might say that his head alone is alive, while his feet remain not-alive.

We never say, though, that Westley is both alive and not-alive. He's both mostly *dead* and slightly alive. When we speak in this way, "alive" and "dead" are not contradictories, but contraries. Contraries are things that cannot both be true of the same thing (at the same time, in the same respect), though they *can* both be false. The rock Fezzik uses to warn Westley of his upcoming sportsman-like death, for instance, is neither dead nor alive. We wouldn't call it dead, because it was never alive (and it's not alive either). It's *neither* dead nor alive. When we say that contraries are opposites, it's because of the fact that they can't both be true of the same thing. Westley can't both be dead and alive at the same time—or so we think.

In fact, he can be mostly dead but slightly alive. So we can't just say that life and death are contraries and leave it at that. We need another concept to get Westley's condition right. Normally, we might think of someone slightly alive as being not dead at all. We're used to thinking that if you're alive *at all*, you're not dead yet. Otherwise, it would be time to go through Westley's pockets for spare change.

But, we're told, Westley is both mostly dead and slightly alive; Miracle Max says that these are the same thing. So life and death in this sense are like two opposite things that can both be true of the same person, at the same time, *in varying degrees*. This is why Westley's being alive and dead can't be fully explained by calling them contradictories or contraries. We know he can't be both fully dead and fully alive—but he's neither dead nor alive. He's "mostly dead". And he's not "alive", but "slightly alive." Our previous way of dealing with opposites doesn't allow for any in-betweens. We need to be able to deal with these degrees of deadness and aliveness.

Life and death, for Westley, exist on a spectrum. At any point, there's a degree to which he is alive, and a degree to which he is dead, and these are related inversely—that is, as he becomes more dead, he's less alive, and as he gets more alive, he becomes less dead. While The Machine has made him mostly dead, Miracle Max's miracle pill counteracts its effects: we can see him get more and more alive as it kicks in. So, in *The Princess Bride*, both life and death are "spectrum concepts"—there is a spectrum of aliveness and a spectrum of deadness, and where you are on the one is the opposite of where you are on the other.

This is all well and good, if we're assuming that the opposite of death is life. In *The Princess Bride*, though, we know that there is another opposite to death. The thing that conquers death, in the end, isn't life. The happy ending isn't just when Westley *survives*. What conquers death, *why* he survives, is true love.

True Love and Death

Not only is true love one of the reasons Miracle Max concedes to help Westley overcome his state of mostly deadness, it's presented in the movie as another kind of opposite to death. When the Man in Black finally reveals his identity to Buttercup, we learn something about the nature of death that should make us rethink the technical discussion of opposites above. (That kind of logic doesn't allow for miracles.)

True love and death are first set up as opposites when the Man in Black reveals himself. Westley wants to know why Buttercup has not waited for him. It turns out, she mistakenly believed that Westley's death was the end of true love.

> WESTLEY: I told you I would always come for you. Why didn't you wait for me?
>
> BUTTERCUP: Well, you were dead.
>
> WESTLEY: Death cannot stop True Love. All it can do is delay it for a while.
>
> BUTTERCUP: I will never doubt again.
>
> WESTLEY: [*quietly*] There will never be a need.

Westley sets her straight, though. But what kind of opposites are these? In order to explain how true love is the opposite of death, we need to appeal to one of the qualities of so-called opposites. That is, some kinds of opposites can be thought of as destroying one another. When someone gets stronger, their weakness is destroyed. When someone gets faster, their slowness is destroyed. In a world of grand concepts and miracles, we oppose good and evil, grand schemes and their foils, characters and their intentions.

Opposites stand in conflict and, in the end, one of them prevails. And when true love exists, death cannot stop it. Where there is true love, death cannot exist. Had Buttercup known this, she would have assumed that Westley and true love itself were alive.

The Miracle of True Love

Perhaps the most direct way to understand the nature of true love, and understand how it can overcome death, is to look at people who seem to express true love, and discern their character. We'll start with Westley: he is a farm boy, a servant, who is assigned menial tasks by Buttercup. He fetches water, he does chores without complaint. All he wants to do is win Buttercup's affections, but in seeking his fortunes in the world, his efforts are stymied, and he is led to piracy, which results in his donning the guise of the Man in Black. Yet even as the Man in Black, he seems to be good-natured. He attempts to save the damsel in distress, he employs gentlemanly tactics in his duel with Inigo Montoya, and he does not attempt to kill Fezzik, even though he is given the opportunity. When he finally faces off against Vizzini in "a battle of wits" we see that Westley merely tries to save himself, and the fact that Vizzini dies is an unfortunate outcome. Two things can be gleaned from this sketch of Westley's actions. In none of these situations is Westley motivated by simply utilitarian motives to win and maximize his happiness by any means, and, just as importantly, in none of these situations does Westley manifest any degree of malice. Indeed, Westley seems to be going through the actions necessary to enact his destiny: the fulfillment of true love.

We would like to say that Westley cheats death because of his character, but this answer seems insufficient. Of course Westley has good character; evil jerks don't even get the concept of true love. (They just want to get married to start wars.) Westley cheats death thanks to a miraculous (chocolate-covered) pill that allows his slightly aliveness to conquer his mostly deadness. But why did Miracle Max make the pill to begin with? He was a disgraced miracle man, who thought that he had no miracles left, least of all the miracle of bringing back to life someone who is mostly dead. Max didn't want to open the door to admit the strangers, and even after using the bellows pump on Westley, he (intentionally) misinterpreted Westley's purpose of true love. Max's reluctance to save Westley's life is rooted in his lack of confidence. There's something more than cynicism behind his refusal to resurrect Westley; his doubt is in his own abilities. Valerie picks up on this and reprimands Max for his weakness of character. In practical terms, Max gets dragged into making the Miracle pill, and as soon as he agrees to attempt to resurrect Westley, Valerie cheers him on.

This brief scene allows us to give some clarity to the ill-defined concept of true love. The question that arises is, are Westley and Buttercup just following some predetermined destiny? We recognize early on that Buttercup, though she's engaged to Humperdinck, *can't* marry him. She *has to* marry Westley. But that makes it look like true love is going to happen whether anyone likes it or not, and Westley and Buttercup had better get used to it. Rather, while it does seem that they are destined to end up together, true love does not simply have its origins in passive acceptance of your circumstances. While it might seem that true love is something that they succumb to, that is passively received—note that the origin of Westley's and Buttercup's true love was the passive willingness to do "as you wish"—it can also be kindled in the acrimonious exchange between a defeated husband and a wife, who knows that he can be more than he thinks he can be. Even as Westley and Buttercup succumb to their destiny, they must continuously act to preserve it (sometimes, by marching through Fire Swamps and fighting ROUS's.)

Miracle Max and Valerie seem to have been married for about a thousand years. Is their love any less true? Is that how we'll see Westley and Buttercup after they settle down and start criticizing each other for their lackadaisical attitudes towards true love? That true love has many forms, that it might be exemplified by either acceptance or acrimony, indicates that it is something that is not defined by any particular type of action. Rather than thinking of true love as something limited to the main characters and the fulfillment of their destinies, we might think of it as the sort of thing that emerges from the combination of various actions and that is amplified through various acts. In this sense, true love is a sort of harmony that links various characters. The particular things involved are different, but the relation between them remains the same. It is not *only* the kiss shared by Westley and Buttercup in the final scene of the movie, though we certainly see it here, and it is not *only* the trading of barbs between

Valerie and Miracle Max. It is that sort of thing that animates these characters, that binds them in harmony.

This brings us back around to Socrates. One of the arguments raised against him in the *Phaedo*, as he's trying to argue for the immortality of the soul, is the idea that a soul is a harmony. When the lyre exists, claims Simmias, one of the people Socrates is arguing with, the harmony can exist. But when the lyre is destroyed, the harmony must certainly disperse. Now if Simmias's argument is right, true love exists between particular people, and if one of them dies, so should true love. True love would be entirely dependent on the people between whom it exists, and when the people cease to exist, it should just disappear along with them.

Westley would have shown up after having been missing for five years, discovered Buttercup's engagement, and thought to himself, "Of course she would. I was dead, and therefore true love was dead as well." But this view is only part of the story, and only part of the miracle of true love. To understand how true love conquers death, we have to understand how it arises out of the relations between these characters, bound up with them, and their actions. When I write a beautiful song on my lyre (as we all do from time to time), the song does not cease to exist when the strings have broken. It's just the same as when a good person dies—in that case, goodness itself does not cease to exist.

True love and goodness seem to go together. Why, for instance, do we not think that Max is some sort of diabolical sorcerer and that Valerie is really a witch who is going to lock up the hero in the Pit of Despair? Why don't we think that Westley is really a villain, even when he wears the black mask? We all know that people in masks shouldn't be trusted. Yet, we know that these characters are good, because throughout the combination of all their acts we see them as embodying good intentions. It isn't just the existence of the characters that's important, it's how they exist, in the world, in relation to other people, and how they and their actions harmonize with a world of inherent goodness, miracles and magic. Their being harmonizes with the universe in which they exist, and they themselves harmonize with one another.

This gives us a crucial clue to the miracle of true love defeating death. It winnows it down in the same sort of way that the grandfather dispels the young boy's doubts about the value of the story. We turn another page, we take another breath, and orient ourselves to what might happen, trying to make our actions harmonize with that which we did before. Trying to achieve harmony is not a flawless method in the sense that it is certainly leads to immediate rewards—after all, Westley still ends up being tortured. But we remember that true love isn't just one moment, and it is certainly not just one defeat. Rather, it's the relation that binds particular moments, particular people, particular actions together.

In this sense the true lovers, wherever they are, whatever they do, all embody one quality; they participate in the creation of a harmony that subsists beyond their material being—a relation that breaks down the opposition of life and death. Instead, true love, as a harmony, persists beyond death, beyond the particular characters whose existence in relation gave rise to it, and in this way, conquers death.

V

Life Lessons of a Fairytale

No one would surrender to the Dread Pirate Westley!

18

I Know Something You Don't Know

RANDALL E. AUXIER

The Spaniard apologizes and says that Westley is too good; he is obliged to fight with his dominant hand. The scene pushes on for another minute or two and, sure enough, the Spaniard is going to win unless Westley makes a similar admission: "I'm not left handed either."

I have spoken with my friends who fence. I have spoken with a couple of thirty-something men who *learned* fencing because of this scene. They all assure me that the difference between fencing *with* the left hand, and *against* the left hand, is as great a difference as one is likely to find in any sport—whether it descends from forms of combat or not. Peyton Manning throwing passes with his left hand would be about as easy as switching hands in fencing. Clayton Kershaw launching fastballs with his right hand would be about as easy as switch-fencing.

And yet, as all fans know, Mandy Patinkin and Cary Elwes actually performed every frame of the film and it is good enough to make real fencers go "Wow!" The actors were trained by Bob Anderson, the legendary British Olympic fencer and fight choreographer, who has many grand fight scenes to his credit, but probably nothing to equal the scene in *The Princess Bride*. An analogy for those who better understand other sports: Kevin Costner in *Bull Durham* vs. Robert Redford in *The Natural*. I'm sorry folks, but Costner is an actual ballplayer and Redford, well, as a baseball player, he's a good movie director.

Yet, Patinkin and Elwes knew nothing, I repeat, *nothing*, about fencing going into the production of *The Princess Bride*. I am told that you can't really teach what they did with those swords to most people, with *one* hand, let alone *both*. I assume that Patinkin and Elwes harbored natural talent that they probably knew nothing about. It was difficult not to smile as I recently watched Elwes flash the saber at Battery Wagner as the executive officer of the 54th Massachusetts Regiment in the 1989 film *Glory*—he was rather more convincing with that piece of hardware than was Matthew Broderick (Ferris Bueller, in charge of a whole regiment?). I confess that I envy these actors their latent talent. If someone out there should contradict my fencing friends, I will have to challenge them to a duel—a test of wits, since I am clearly not anyone's physical match. But that brings me to a point.

In the classic three challenges that Westley must overcome to gain possession of his princess (anyone ever heard of Eros and Psyche? Thetus and Ariadne?), this particular tale places a strange, even uncanny, emphasis upon *fair play*. But the case is not simple. Let me remind you:

1. The Spaniard announces in advance (before Westley made it up the Cliffs of Insanity) that he would fight left-handed to make things interesting.

2. The Spaniard then helps Westley up to the level ground and allows him to rest before engaging in the fight.

3. Westley, having gained the advantage, decides he could sooner break a stained glass window than kill such an able swordsman (and this is on top of the significant exchanges of genuine admiration that punctuate the sword battle).

4. When Fezzik throws his first boulder at Westley, he misses on purpose and declares himself to have done so in order to make the encounter a sporting encounter.

5. When Fezzick and Westley are differentially armed and able, they decide upon the oldest form of struggle (hand-to-hand wrestling).

6. When Vizzini is confronted with the clear physical superiority of our hero, he assumes that the hero will accept an (honorable?) exchange of wits, albeit to the death, in exchange for a physical contest that would be unequal.

The three tasks completed, only he who has, by his inordinate pride, secured his own death is in fact dead. On the other hand (and that would be the left hand), there was nothing fair in this contest of wits between Westley and Vizzini, since both cups were poisoned and our hero had immunity. Should he have been trusted? That was the act of a fool? Well . . . let's return to this question later. Perhaps Vizzini was foully murdered, perhaps not. Let us make *that* our test case in this . . . shall we call it a test of wits?

All's Fair . . .

. . . in love and war. You've heard that saying, haven't you? Who said that? You're thinking Shakespeare. You are wrong. It was Francis Smedley. Yes, the Immortal Smedley said that. I hope I didn't ruin your day. What you need to know is whether I'm the kind of person who poisons the cup in front of himself or the one in front of you. But here are a few thoughts you might not have considered.

First, consider that both The Spaniard and Fezzick would have killed Our Hero if they had won their fights. Of course, then there would be no story, so at one level it's impossible, but at another, there is every reason to believe that both were intent upon killing Our Hero, which was, after all, their job, and no reason not to believe it. Had either succeeded, they would have been murderers, and there is at least some evidence to believe that both had killed before. They are, at best ne'er-do-wells, and at worst, simply terrible people.

Second, Our Hero has been, for some years, The Dread Pirate Roberts, who leaves no one alive. Surely he has been doing some pirating in these years, at the beginning as the First Mate of the former Dread Pirate Roberts, then as Dread Pirate Roberts with the former Dread Pirate Roberts as his First Mate, then alone. Not leaving anyone alive involves murder. Piracy is stealing, and this is not Men in Tights, so there is no suggestion of giving the booty to the poor. Our Hero is, therefore, an exceedingly dangerous and wicked individual.

Third, while it's true that the Prince, Vizzini, and the Six-fingered Man are wicked, are they really any worse than Our Hero and Montoya and Fizzick? I'm not trying to get all literal and factual about a fairytale. I understand how fairytales work (although I want to say something about that in a minute). All I want to do is "level the playing field," morally speaking to give the bad guys a sporting chance in what follows. So just remember, everyone is a wanton murderer in this comparison, and while we know very little about how many people they have killed, the evidence points to the clear likelihood that Westley is the worst of the lot.

An Odd Little Man

Here's a fairytale for you. There was an odd little boy born in California not far Sutter's Mill during the last days of the California Gold Rush. His parents had crossed the prairies and the mountains in 1849, *real* forty-niners, not the kind who play football. The boy was odd. He looked a bit like an insect (according to his own wife, in a later comment), with an enormous head and flaming red hair. He was a solitary, bookish boy, with a vivid imagination. His cat ran away when he was eight and he wrote an entire book (*Pussycat Blackie's Travels*) imagining the cat's adventures, though that book wasn't published until *much* later. The boy's name was Josie, which was short for Josiah.

Josie's family was very poor and he was often hungry as he grew up. They had to move to a big city when he was eleven where his father could look for work, but he still went to bed hungry and with nothing but straw to sleep on for years. But he was smart and good at school, and even though the other boys picked on him, because he was funny-looking and quiet, he never caved in to their jeers and name-calling. He stood up for himself and that led to frequent fights, in which he was always whipped but never humbled.

In time, Josie grew up and got married to a very smart and beautiful and wealthy woman (who didn't mind that he looked like an insect) and they had three sons. He became one of the most famous and creative philosophers in the world, teaching at Harvard University and lecturing all over the world. From rags to riches—well, not riches in gold, but in fame and achievement—he went. He was an odd little man, but he was very widely loved and universally admired. I wish I could say the story had a happy ending, but he died relatively young and suffered many tragedies in his life. One son was mentally ill and died at twenty-seven. He lost his closest friend at the same time. But he kept writing beautiful and profound books. When a Great War broke out in 1914, it broke his heart and his spirit because he had loved Germany, where he had learned so much and had so many friends. By the end he was very sad. Some people said that the War really killed him from sadness.

But Josiah Royce helped a lot of people with his creative ideas, and there were many, many such ideas, things no one had ever thought of before. One was the idea that we could understand the meaning of life, and its purpose, by cultivating our loyalties in just the right way. And that's the idea I want to bring back to our story about fighting left-handed.

Philosophers have always talked about the meaning of life, and about what is the best life for a human being. Since they are philosophers, they never agree—Bertrand Russell once said that the only thing two philosophers can ever agree upon is the incompetence of a third. But Royce's idea about loyalty was a new suggestion about the best life. Here is what he thought: Our lives get meaning from the service we give to causes that are bigger than ourselves. When we willingly pledge our devotion and make daily sacrifices and deeds of service to a cause we have freely chosen, the result is that a "self," an "individual," gradually comes into existence—the person who has done all these deeds and whose life is dedicated to the furthering of this freely chosen cause. We come to be part of a community through this service, we come to have friends, camaraderie, belonging, and most importantly a life plan that provides a purpose for our lives.

The best life for a human being, then, is a life of loyal service, with others who share the cause and whose purpose is the same. Through service we overcome our selfishness, our egocentricity, our isolation from others. A lot of people didn't like what Royce was saying because they were worried that people can serve evil causes and might still become, well, relatively fulfilled in their lives while doing very wicked things—there could be honor among thieves, for example, but that doesn't mean that the best life is one of thievery, right? It may be pretty clear by now why I want to talk about the ethical ideas of that odd little man, since he has some interesting answers to the complaints about honor among thieves.

Honor among Thieves

The argument about whether there really can be honor among people who are doing bad things together, or separately, is at least as old as the Common Era. Cicero talked about it in 45 B.C., and he had ample reason to worry about it. It wasn't clear whether the new dictator of Rome, Gaius Julius Caesar, was or wasn't a rogue. The world still hasn't decided that question, but it ultimately cost Cicero his life. It's a fair thing to wonder about. Can people just keep doing bad things (although *they* may believe them to be permissible or even good) indefinitely, without the wickedness or wrongness of the deeds eventually catching up to the evil-doers? Is there no justice in the universe?

Here we really have to make a space for fairytale logic and hold it apart from the way life really is. Not many philosophers talk about fairytales, but Susanne Langer, a very accomplished American philosopher, did. She says:

> The fairy tale is irresponsible; it is frankly imaginary, and its purpose is to gratify wishes, "as a dream doth flatter." Its heroes and heroines, though of delightfully high station, wealth, beauty, etc., are simply individuals; "a certain prince," "a lovely princess." The end of the story is always satisfying, though by no means always moral; the hero's heroism may be by slyness or luck quite as readily as integrity or valor. The theme is generally the triumph of an unfortunate one—an enchanted maiden, a youngest son, a poor Cinderella, an alleged fool—over his or her superiors, whether these be kings, bad fairies, strong animals . . . stepmothers, or elder brothers. (*Philosophy in a New Key*, p. 175)

This all sounds pretty familiar, doesn't it, right down to the Rodents of Unusual Size? We all know the logic of fairytales, but sometimes we forget that *morality* has little to do with it. How can that be? Doesn't every story have a *moral*? Not in the case of fairytales. Fables do, and that is their purpose, to convey a moral lesson. But fairytales are about wishes, not about lessons. And satisfied human wishing is, well, shall we say, somewhat different from what satisfies our moral demands.

Yet, Royce's philosophy of loyalty cuts through this veil between the real world and Neverland. I think it throws a lot of light on Our Hero and on why we find his conduct satisfying, if not precisely moral. The reason Royce can do this where other philosophers cannot is that he takes account of our process of maturing. When we're young and we have to make a life plan, we're also too naive to grasp what life is really like—the compromises we will have to make, the mistakes, the human weaknesses and frailties, the unforeseen tragedies and occasions of fortune, and so on.

A young person making a life plan is not so very different from a character in a fairytale. Young people can easily believe that war is glorious, or that they will not themselves make the mistakes their parents made. Young people believe they see clearly and that they choose their causes with open eyes. They do not yet understand all of the unconscious forces that move within their own depths and they usually don't realize how resistant the world is to being changed, or even bent a little, in the direction they desire. They don't know the hardness. Yet, they are capable of loyalty and they are able to serve. *That* is very real and it changes both the community and the individual who serves.

It isn't surprising that we choose to serve conflicting causes. Royce wrote an interesting essay on football in 1908, when football was in poor repute and there was widespread talk of banning the game. There he says:

> I know some public servants, men now devoted to the noblest and hardest social tasks, who assert that they personally first learned unselfish devotion, the spirit of "team work" (that is, of social service) on the football field; and who say that the "roughness" and perhaps their own broken bones, first gave them the needed moral lessons in what have since proved to be the most delicately tender and the most earnestly devoted forms of loyalty. ("Football and Ideals," p. 216)

So, a process of maturation that passes through such teamwork is a part of developing into a better servant. But it is only a part. Losing the game with one's teammates, is more instructive than winning it. Finding a way to "pick up" a teammate who has disappointed the team, and turning the mistake into a gain somehow—this and dozens of other lessons of loyalty are crucial to later life. I can certainly attest that I have professional colleagues who could have benefited from being repeatedly put on their asses by a physically superior opponent, and that no application of their wits would save them from having the same happen again on the next play, until the game mercifully ended. Let us invoke the cliché: it builds character (to have your ass handed to you, repeatedly). One assumes that Westley and Fizzick and the Spaniard all endured these humiliations in the process of becoming good enough at what they do to prevail over those who have not been so humiliated. Yet, this is only the beginning of what Royce calls "training for loyalty."

The first phase of life can become an obsession, a purpose that does not open the way to anything further. In considering the Spaniard and the memory of his father, we also see that he has given his life, his all, to the relentless and cruel pursuit of the father's killer. He is loyal to the cause of revenge, in a highly particular sense, and it is a great motivator in learning swordsmanship, but it doesn't do much to prepare a person for anything beyond that (unlikely) goal. That is part of the reason he is in no position to be anything except the next Dread Pirate Roberts by the end—to steal and leave none alive. But this training also prepares him to appreciate excellence in swordsmanship for its own sake.

There is something he learns, almost incidentally, which is how to recognize and appreciate anyone else who has given such devotion to the perfecting of combat with a sword. And yet, in doing so, Montoya becomes not a person but a stained glass window; he is a thing of beauty, and that is impressive because there is nothing easy about it, but he is lost without a commission, without a direction given by a guiding hand. He becomes a sword for hire, even though it is beneath his artistry, and thus is prone to serving the shifting ends of a no good weasel like Vizzini. Seeing this, Westley spares him for the sake of art, not for the sake of goodness. A similar tale may be told about Fezzick. But Westley belongs to no other man, and that is interesting.

Songs of Innocence, Songs of Experience

When young people imagine their lives, they haven't got much more to work with than Fred Savage had when Peter Falk read him *The Princess Bride*. One of the best parts of our favorite movie is enjoying that contrast between innocence and experience we get with those two, and the benevolence of grandfather as he *sees* one story while his grandson *sees* quite another. But

Rob Reiner captures a point of contact, a poignant sense that the youngster *knows* his grandfather *knows* what the youth *cannot know*, and senses the difference between them. But they tacitly agree to pretend it doesn't matter, at least for the time they have together—*story time*, and they are in it *together*. (That is the real reference of my title, btw.) By conspiring so, they give the audience permission to love fairytales, too.

Still there is a lot more. Westley is the one who sees the limitations of Fezzick and The Spaniard, and he grasps how they have come to where they are. For them, struggling against him is a *sporting* proposition, but only because they have gotten the benefit of their own process of maturation: they have outgrown the cause they serve (currently Vizzini's business deal with the Prince), and they know how causes come and causes go. They have become artists of a high grade by following the paths they were on, and what was once mere utility has become, for them, an exercise that brings its own inherent (if temporary) reward. They have come to the point that what is serious for others is merely play for them. Westley sees this and understands it. These artists do not have to be killed, they need to be directed into causes worthy of their achievements, and they have some understanding of the emptiness in their lives. They are suitable for higher service, in their innocence.

This situation does not hold for the Six-Fingered Man, who has sunk into a debauched enjoyment of physical power over others, and is now a sadist. This does not describe the Prince, who is locked in a Machiavellian Game of Thrones and cares nothing for anything in which the stakes are lower. And this does not describe Vizzini who has become an arrogant mercenary who will sell his unusual services to anyone who can pay his price. These are pathologies of sex, power, and gain. With interventions at earlier stages, these loyalists might have been saved, but by the time Our Hero encounters them, all innocence is lost. They have chosen their own ends, as the fairytale makes perfectly plain. Our test case, then, is complete. Vizzini got what he had chosen.

Lost Causes

Westley and Buttercup are a different story. Royce says that you don't advance beyond the fairytale version of your own life-plan until you've failed, and that can happen in a lot of different ways. There are two important ones. The first happens to people who rise higher and higher *within* the service of their cause, until they can no longer distinguish themselves from the causes they serve. These people always eventually betray their own causes, deliberately. The cause doesn't fail, but the individual does. Having done so, such individuals occupy a position of ignominy and humiliation. Nothing can be done for them until, gradually, the community that remains begins to pick up the pieces of their betrayal and to do the work of atonement, rebuilding the community.

Such is ever the fate of the powerful, and this is the fate of the Prince in our favorite movie. We don't see what happens, but our Grandfather points out that it is better if he has to live through the repairing of the damage he has done, although the grandson expresses his disdain for this outcome. Still, you know and I know that it *is* more satisfying that the Prince should live with his ignominy and wait to see whether anyone will reach into the abyss he inhabits and remind him "you are our prince, after all, worthless as you are." Thus does the traitor to his own cause rejoin his community, and we know the repair work is never entirely successful.

But that is not what happens with Westley and Buttercup. Neither one has really betrayed the "cause," which is their love, but each lives in the abyss of loss and failure. That love, that union, was their cause. They serve not one another, but their *union*, as an ideal. When Westley leaves to make his fortune, it is for the sake of the cause; and when news filters back to Buttercup (and it is not false news) that his voyage has fallen prey to the DPR, their union becomes, as far as she knows, a lost cause. Westley is in limbo, not knowing whether he can ever reclaim the cause, but unlike her, he actually knows there is a slim hope. That hope inhibits his moral development in a way that hers is not inhibited. She serves a lost cause. Royce says:

> The lesson of the history of lost causes . . . has deep importance for our individual training. We do not always learn the lesson aright. . . . Defeat and sorrow, when they are incurred in the service of a cause, ought to be a positive aid to loyalty. . . . they enable us to see whether we have really given ourselves to the cause, or whether what we took for our loyalty was a mere flare of sanguine emotion. When sorrow

over a defeat in the service of our cause reverberates through us, it can be made to reveal whatever loyalty we have. (*The Philosophy of Loyalty*, p. 136)

In the permanent loss of our cause, we face ourselves in the raw, so to speak, and know what we have been. The structural weakness in *The Princess Bride* is that the person who suffers this loss most fully, Buttercup, is passive. She doesn't do anything except wait and, ultimately, in despair, gives up on serving the lost cause. The person who suffers defeat, Westley, is unable (or unwilling?) to return to serving the cause until it is (truly) on the brink of being lost—the impending death of Buttercup, or her marriage to the Prince, either of which will transform Westley's cause into a lost one. Thus, he never really travels through the abyss of the lost cause, as she does.

This moral differential may explain why Westley does not emerge from his experience of confronting the Dread Pirate Roberts, and then becoming the Dread Pirate Roberts, as a morally purified symbol. Why, after all, did he wait so long to return? Was he just too busy *being* the Dread Pirate Roberts until news reached him that Buttercup was actually going to be obliged to move on with her life? Couldn't take a holiday? Really? Just couldn't send word? I will now make an inference: I do not think Westley grew up. He was off playing pirate. I think he learned some valuable things and became the cleverest but not the wisest of the boyz. That is one reason he needed to die—well, mostly. He actually hadn't come back from the lost cause until Billy Crystal raised him from the dead. Then and only then is he fit to lead his band in the triumphal reclamation of his cause.

Build Me Up, Buttercup

Seriously? That's supposed to be a woman's name? No. It is the name of a placeholder, not a woman. But geez, is Robin Wright ever a total babe—then and now? Still, I need a *real* princess for the bride in this story, a three-dimensional woman. There really is something to be said for seeing Buttercup as Jenny in *Forrest Gump* and as Claire Underwood in *House of Cards*. I *need* that complexification, supplied by the amazing actress, in order to imagine the character of Buttercup in something more than cartoon terms. Buttercup is the only character in the story who is really in a position to *grow* from the arrangement of her external circumstances. So . . . Claire Underwood is the one who would *really* understand the meaning of "As you wish." Jenny needed to find a way to escape the abuse of her childhood and never could see love for what it was, or appreciate it. Together, these three women, with Robin Wright's help, become something of a full-blooded woman. And now I have a question for you to consider: what use would Claire Underwood have for Westley? She might do better working with the talents of the Prince, or, better yet, the Six-Fingered Man, don't you think? Now *there* was a fellow with some prospects. Just needed to find his match and helpmeet.

But Buttercup, even as the helpmeet, is something less than a fully developed moral person. It's not just that Claire Underwood and Jenny are a mess, it's that all of us must learn to idealize our lost causes. Buttercup had more to gain, morally speaking, from Westley's permanent demise than from his return. When we serve a lost cause, we idealize the cause and it becomes for us something we could never have served with the same devotion when it was achievable. The memory of what might have been is more powerful, morally, than the striving for what might be, Royce says. That may not seem very cheery, but remember, the man looked like an insect.

That's an interesting way to go through life. But there is something to what he says. If you want to grow up, really grow up, you learn to respond to what is best in others, which is the earnestness with which they pursue their causes (even when their causes conflict with your own). Royce calls this being loyal to loyalty itself. I see you serve your cause, and you see me serve mine. What is best in me, my loyalty, hails what is best in you, your loyalty, and even if both of our ships are sinking, we are friends in a deeper sense; we are the legion of the loyal, of those who have fallen in love with the world, and whose service has been in earnest.

Revisiting our amazing swordfight, we can see that what's best in Westley hails what's best in Montoya, and there is genuine joy and admiration in their combat. And, if Royce is right, that would not be spoiled even if one did kill the other. There is such a thing as loyal killing. Westley spared Montoya not for moral reasons but for aesthetic reasons. And there was recognition across conflicting causes—neither cause being particularly exalted, but one commands our sentiment while the other does not, in that moment.

When we're allowed to see Montoya in service of his true cause, we're inspired to sympathy. I notice that Montoya does not fight with his left hand against the Six-Fingered Man. Sometimes we don't need to give people a sporting chance. That happens when they serve only themselves and their twisted egos. In cases like that, it is more merciful to put them out of their misery, which is, after all, what they have chosen. It isn't revenge, it's mercy, which is one form loyalty to loyalty can take. Or at least, that's how the story goes, as fairytales become life-plans and life-plans become legends.

Whether Westley and Buttercup lived happily ever after, well, maybe you know something I don't know, but if I had to choose Westley, or Forrest Gump, or Frank Underwood, I would think the one who knows the most about lost causes and loyalty is in the middle. As he once said to Buttercup, "I'm not a smart man, but I know what love is." Besides, I'm pretty sure Westley died bravely at Battery Wagner, two years later, serving a very fine cause indeed.

19

The Medical Ethics of Miracle Max

BRENDAN SHEA

Miracle Max, it seems, is the only remaining miracle worker in all of Florin. Among other things, this means that he (unlike anyone else) can resurrect the recently dead, at least in certain circumstances. Max's peculiar talents come with significant perks (as Fezzik and Inigo discover, he can basically set his own prices!), but they also raise a number of ethical dilemmas that range from the merely amusing to the truly perplexing:

- How much about Max's "methods" does he need to reveal to his patients? Is it really okay for Max to lie about Valerie's being a witch? Just how much of the truth does Max have to tell his patients?

- Let's suppose that Humperdinck had offered Max his old job back. Would it have been okay for Max to accept this offer? What about if Humperdinck wanted him to do experiments at the Zoo of Death?

- Is Max obligated to offer his services to everyone who needs them, such as the (mostly) dead Westley and friends? Or is he free to pick and choose?

These are all questions in *medical ethics*. Ethics is the study of right and wrong behavior, and medical ethics is about what's right or wrong in medical practice and in biomedical research. It may come as a surprise, but Max's dilemmas are not *too* different from the sorts of dilemmas that many medical professionals encounter in their daily lives.

We can study descriptive ethics—meaning that we try to find out what standards of right and wrong people actually abide by—or normative ethics—meaning that we try to decide what are the *correct* standards of right and wrong. In descriptive ethics, we try to describe how people think and act according to their own standards of behavior. In normative ethics, we try to discover how they *ought* to act.

So, for example, consider Prince Humperdinck. Descriptively, it seems safe to say that Humperdinckian ethics allows things such as the kidnapping and murdering of spouses, the construction of giant torture machines, and the instigation of wars with neighboring countries, so long as such actions advance your career goals. As a matter of normative ethics, however, we might decide that Humperdinck's actions are wrong—these are surely not the sort of things a decent person *ought* to do!

The distinction between normative and descriptive ethics will prove valuable to us when we start to consider Miracle Max. It is a matter of simple economics that Max *can* get away with charging a very high price for his services—after all, the services he offers (such as raising the dead) are highly valuable ones, and he is the only person who is able to offer them (talk about a monopoly!). With this in mind, we could look at the prices Max actually charges and simply *describe* Max's ethics when it comes to pricing. Does he charge rich people more than poor people? Pretty people more than ugly ones? Heroes more than villains? If we did this, we would be engaging in descriptive ethics. In general, however, we'll be more interested in answering questions about normative ethics: for example, how much *should* Max charge various people, and how *should* he determine this?

The Principle of the Thing

Among people who study medical ethics, by far the most popular theory today is called Principlism, a point of view explained by Tom Beauchamp and James Childress in their book *Principles of Biomedical Ethics*.

According to principlism, medical ethics should be governed by four fundamental principles:

- **autonomy**

- **nonmalificence**

- **beneficence**

- **justice**

A working knowledge of these principles is valuable not just for medical professionals, but for anybody who wants to think clearly about what it means "to do the right thing" as patients, caregivers, voters, and citizens more generally.

Lies, Lies, Lies

When Inigo and Fezzik first go to seek Max's aid, he isn't entirely honest. He begins by implying that he can't help (he can), states that his wife Valerie is a witch (she isn't), tells Valerie they've offered twenty gold pieces (they've offered sixty-five), claims that Westley is saying "to blave" ("to blave" in the movie, "to blove" in the book), which Max maintains means 'to bluff', when he's really saying "true love," and assures them the miracle pill will last for sixty minutes (it will only last for forty).

Max lies, in short, to both his patients and the other members of his medical team, and doesn't tell the heroes that (due to medical error) the miracle pill won't last as long as he'd originally said. While many of these lapses are understandable, given Max's low self-esteem and rusty skills, they serve as examples of an all-too-common dilemma in medical ethics: just what sorts of information *should* a medical professional reveal to patients?

These questions all pertain to the Principle of Autonomy, which states that medical professionals should respect and support the abilities of competent patients to make their own decisions about treatment. Among other things, this means that the medical professional needs to *accurately* describe the diagnosis, prognosis, and possible treatments to the patient.

While everything turns out okay for Max in the end, he makes a few mistakes along the way. First, he exaggerates Valerie's skill (by saying she's a witch) and then radically downplays his chance of success because of his fear of failure. While Max's failings here are comical, his *motivations* for lying (a "harmless" exaggeration of a colleague's skill, a sense of risk aversion overly focused on preserving professional pride) are, unfortunately, all too realistic, and they can easily be the sorts of things that cause medical professionals to mislead patients.

Ideally, a medical professional could meet the demands of autonomy by sitting down with a patient, explaining the proposed treatment in detail, and having the patient give his or her verbal or written *informed consent*.

In practice, however, this is often impossible. For one thing, patients are often unconscious, as Westley is when Fezzik and Inigo bring him in. In addition, patients who *are* conscious may be unable to understand the proposed treatment. By the time we encounter him in *The Princess Bride,* for example, it may well be that old King Lotharon (Max's old employer) is incapable of making autonomous choices about his own treatment. Even if patients are both conscious and capable of understanding, there may be some *other* factor that prevents them from making their own choices. So, for example, it seems unlikely that Max really ought to go along with his patients' requests if he suspected these requests were due to mental incapacitation (Fezzik's getting hit in the head with a rock, Inigo's still being drunk) or because of external threats (perhaps Vizzini has tricked them, or Humperdinck threatened them).

In cases where a patient's autonomy is compromised by any of these factors, the medical professional will have to rely (as Max does) on the decisions of *surrogates,* and on what was known of the patient's wishes back when they *were* capable of making decisions. In the case of Westley, this is thankfully not too difficult—the treatment Fezzik and Inigo propose (saving Westley's life) seems to be clearly in the patient's best interest, a fact that Max is able to confirm by asking the (deceased) Westley what is worth living for. In many other cases, unfortunately, matters are not always so clear-cut, and medical professionals may need to carefully consider how to weigh seemingly conflicting evidence about what the patient "really wanted."

Why Working for Humperdinck Is a Bad Idea

The idea that medical professionals should respect and promote the ability of patients to make their own, autonomous decisions is of a relatively recent vintage. By contrast, the idea that they should avoid *harming* patients is very old, going back (at least) to the ancient Hippocratic Oath, with its promise to "do no harm." In the language of Principlism, this is called the Principle of Nonmalificence. You can violate this principle either by directly harming others through your actions (Count Rugen killing Inigo's father), or by negligently allowing a person to be harmed when it was your responsibility to prevent this (Yellin not doing anything when Humperdinck reveals his plan to murder Buttercup).

In the case of Westley, Max is at little risk of *directly* causing harm (Westley is already dead, after all). However, it's worth thinking about what *exactly* Max was *morally* required to do, once he recognized that Westley has slipped from being "somewhat dead" to "mostly dead." Surprisingly, according to many traditional interpretations of "do no harm," Max was required to do almost nothing for Westley, even if he'd already signed on as his physician.

One traditional view holds that while medical professionals should never "withdraw" life-saving treatment (no taking the miracle pill out of Westley's mouth), they are perfectly free to "withhold" it (not giving the miracle pill in the first place). Another common view states that while Max's *killing* Westley would be wrong, there would be nothing wrong with Max "letting him die," even if there were measures that could save him. A third proposal requires that Max provide Westley with "ordinary treatment" (perhaps CPR?), but not that he undertake "extraordinary treatment" (a category that surely includes miracle pills).

While these sorts of guidelines may provide certain psychological benefits for physicians by making things "simple," Max's experience suggests that they may be bad ways of thinking about nonmalificence, and about what it means to avoid harming *patients*. Instead, it seems that, if we have good reasons (as Max does), to think that a treatment could work for a patient (and that the patient would consent to it), then the treatment ought to be attempted. Conversely, if a treatment will not help (or if a patient does not or would not consent to it), it should be withheld or withdrawn.

Another application of the Principle of Nonmalificence concerns its application to medical *research*. What should Max say, for instance, if Humperdinck were to offer his old job back, but on the condition that he carry out experiments at the Zoo of Death? This would surely involve harming both humans and animals, and so it would clearly violate the principle. However, this does not (by itself) entail that Max ought to refuse. After all, he would need to consider the possibility that the violation of nonmalificence was outweighed by patient autonomy (if human research subjects gave informed consent) or by the goal of beneficence (if animal experimentation promised some great benefit). In the case of the Zoo of Death, neither of these criteria are met, since Humperdinck's and Rugen's main interest seems to be in inflicting as much pain as possible. In the real world, however, these three principles would need to be carefully weighed against each other, both by individual professionals such as Max and by the Institutional Review Boards (IRBs) commonly called upon to determine the ethics of proposed research.

Max the Beneficent

When Inigo and Fezzik go to seek Max's aid, they are able to offer Max a hefty sum of gold for his services, a fact that goes a long way toward overcoming Max's initial reluctance to help. Unfortunately, it seems unlikely that the average resident of Florin could afford this price, even though they could definitely make use of Max's services. So, what should Max do when these people show up at his door, asking for help, but with no way to pay? Or what about when he is out for a walk, and he encounters a mostly dead person on the side of the road? Is he required to stop and help, or is this going above and beyond the call of duty?

In Principlism, questions such as these fall under the Principle of Beneficence, which requires medical professionals to take positive action to benefit others, or to prevent them from being harmed. In very general terms, the principle says that we are obligated to help people when 1. we notice they are at risk of major harm; 2. we think it is likely we can help them without too much cost or risk to ourselves; and 3. all things considered, it seems that our actions will do more good than harm. This principle would imply, for example, that Max *ought* to help a recently dead person he finds by the side of the road, should he have a soon-to-expire miracle pill in his pocket, and no particular plans for it. By contrast, Inigo and Fezzik are clearly going above and beyond the Principle of Beneficence when they put themselves in danger by rescuing Westley from the Zoo of Death. Similarly, Westley's "as you wish" agreement to all of Buttercup's demands at the beginning of the book goes well beyond the sort of beneficence he would owe to a random stranger (though perhaps not to the love of his life).

Beneficence becomes even trickier when it conflicts with other principles, or when actions that have good consequences for *some* people have bad effects for *others*. So, let's say that Valerie has developed a new miracle pill that she would like Max to test. When people hear about this (even more miraculous!) pill, they will surely be eager to try it. However, in order for Valerie and Max to figure out whether or not this pill *works,* they will have to test it rigorously. And in order to do this, it may be that they *can't* give it to everyone—instead, they'll have to give it to some people (the "experimental group"), while denying it to others (the "control group") in order to compare the outcomes and see what happens. In this case, it seems like beneficence toward the large number of *future* patients who would benefit from the new pill will sometimes trump beneficence toward the one or two particular patients who might benefit. On the other hand, if the new pill looked to be *truly* miraculous, and immediately and permanently cured everyone of everything, beneficence may well require hurrying it to market as soon as possible.

In other cases, beneficence may conflict with respect for autonomy, non-malificence, or both; as when a patient refuses to undergo a painful procedure that could save their life. Suppose the King refused to take a life-saving miracle pill on the grounds that it "gave him a stomach ache." In this scenario, it seems like Max should at least consider tricking the King into taking it (perhaps by sticking it in ice cream?). As with many "tough" cases in medical ethics, there may simply be no hard-and-fast "rule" about how such cases ought to be decided.

Fixing Florin's Healthcare Problem

As the only remaining miracle worker in Florin, Max is in a peculiar position: his decisions to treat (or not treat) patients are (quite literally) matters of life or death. So, for example, if he had not agreed to treat Westley, then Westley would have remained dead—the heroes simply had no other options. Given this monopoly on health care, how should Max distribute his efforts? Should he simply treat whomever pays the best? Charge a set price and do "first-come first-serve?" Or something else?

These sorts of "who gets medical care?" dilemmas fall under the Principle of Justice, which says that people should "get what they deserve." Among other things, this means that people should not be *denied* medical care because they happen to have certain disadvantageous properties (such as being born a giant, or having your father killed by an evil count) that they had no control over. Conversely, it says that people with undeserved advantageous properties (such as being born a prince) do not deserve *privileged* access to medical care. Just as with the other principles, it's highly unlikely that we could ever be "perfectly" just, since doing so would almost certainly involve substantial violations of autonomy, nonmalificence, or beneficence. Nevertheless, the principle requires that we "aspire" toward justice, even if this (sometimes) means making sacrifices in other areas.

So what does this mean for Max? This is where things get tricky. According to philosophical *libertarians*, Max should be able to offer his services to whomever he wants, for whatever price he wants (so long as his doing so doesn't violate anyone else's rights). By contrast, *utilitarians* hold that Max should distribute his services in whatever manner *maximizes* the total happiness experienced by *everyone*. However, both of these views, at least in their simplest forms, may have consequences we don't like. Specifically, libertarianism seems to entail that Max has *no* duties to help anyone in Florin (no matter how desperate their situation, or how little it would cost him to help), while utilitarianism may well require that he spend nearly *all* of his time (beyond that required to meet his own basic needs) helping those who are worse off than he is.

A third—and perhaps more palatable—proposal might involve Max balancing a commitment to doing *something* for the poorer citizens of Florin, while also reserving some of his time and resources to do as he wished (such as spend time with Valerie!). This general attitude fits well with the *liberal egalitarian* idea which holds that while everyone (including both Max and his potential patients) has certain indefeasible "rights" to live their lives without interference from other people, society *also* has a duty to distribute necessary resources in a way that maximizes the position of the worst off. Unlike libertarianism, this view clearly suggests that Max should do *something* to help those who truly need it. In contrast to utilitarianism, however, it does not say that Max must devote all of his effort to doing this (since this would violate his own rights).

In the real world, ensuring "justice" is largely a matter for large governmental or health-care institutions, and not for individual providers such as Max. However, Max's simplified case brings out a number of issues relevant to debates about justice in health care. For example, the Principle of Justice (regardless of your theoretical approach) does seem to imply that people do have a right to a basic level of health care, even if this requires others to make sacrifices. However, because resources are limited (and because citizens have priorities besides health care), it seems implausible that people have a right to *unlimited* health care. Ideally, then, Max might recommend to Humperdinck that he finance the training of some new miracle-workers, and that he put some money aside toward manufacturing miracle pills for those in need of them. Florinese politics being what they are, however, it seems likely that Max may well have to content himself with treating the occasional wounded adventurer.

Too Much or Not Enough?

So, what would Max think of our four rules? Given the (sometimes questionable) state of his memory, he might ask if we could somehow simplify things—maybe just include three rules, or two rules, or even just one? Conversely, he might ask why we needed principles at all—why not just figure things out on a case-by-case basis? While these objections both have long philosophical pedigrees, there are real advantages to adopting Principlism—which is exactly why Principlism is so popular among today's medical ethicists.

First, in allowing for a larger number of principles (as opposed to just one), we can account for the fact that questions in medical ethics problems are often *complex* (they can't be solved by "mechanically" applying a single rule), and they may be genuine *dilemmas* (with no clearly correct answer).

Second, in saying that there are *some* general principles that stay the same between cases, we can actually "learn from experience" by identifying specific commonalities between cases. So, while Max's experiences in Florin differ wildly from those of most real-world medical professionals, the principles used to assess them are the same, a fact that allows us who live a long way from Florin to *learn* from Max's failures and successes.

In the end, the value of Principlism (as with any theory of normative ethics) lies in what it allows us to *do* with it, and in what problems it enables us to solve. In this respect, it is precisely the fact that Principlism allows us to learn something relevant to solving new moral problems by considering the outcome of *previous* or *hypothetical* cases that makes it so valuable. And this is possible only because Principlism attempts neither to reduce morality to a single, mechanical rule nor to throw out rule-based reasoning altogether. So, while Florin is (unfortunately, and despite my childhood confusion about this point) a fictional place, this doesn't mean that *The Princess Bride* has nothing real to offer us.

20
The Good and the Gracious

ELIZABETH OLSON AND CHARLES TALIAFERRO

You seem a decent fellow. I hate to kill you.

The Princess Bride contains a kidnapping, killings, murder plots, torture, a near suicide, a hero who lies to the heroine . . . and yet it remains a charming tale, a tale of twoo wuv.

One of the primary elements that moves the forces of goodness forward in the story is a genteel, formal, humorous (but ostensibly earnest) sometimes elaborate display of good manners. We first notice this in the encounter between Westley and Inigo Montoya. Although Inigo means to quickly dispatch Westley in a sword fight, in their conversation and duel both men are more than gracious in their effusive, shared compliments. The next encounter, between Fezzik and Westley, is similarly graced with commiseration, polite chit-chat, and cordiality.

In contrast, the politeness and cordiality of Humperdinck and Count Rugen is skin deep, if apparent at all. Humperdinck uses the manners and mannerisms of the court to deceive Buttercup and (ultimately) to plan her murder as an excuse to launch a military attack on the neighboring kingdom of Guilder. Surely these are manners at their worst.

Philosophers are divided on the status of manners. As we might expect, Niccolò Machiavelli, in his sixteenth-century masterpiece on how to achieve and retain power (*The Prince*), would have us use any number of polite gestures to mask our true intentions. Machiavelli's approach to manners, in simple terms, is entirely instrumental. Not so, for two major thinkers, west and east: Plato and Confucius.

For Plato, the virtue of what in Greek is *sophrosyne* and is usually translated as temperance or self-control, is better translated (as A.E. Taylor has argued) as 'good form'. For Plato, there's something ugly or even incoherent about linking the vices of hubris, cowardice, and injustice with external "good form." Rather, *good form* must go hand-in-hand with justice, wisdom, and courage. Indeed, maintaining good form might naturally be seen as requiring a sense of justice, that is, a sense of what is truly wise as opposed to merely clever, and, in particular, it may require courage in the form of forbearance.

It may not be easy to retain good form when someone is trying to kill you in a sword fight. In Confucian philosophy, the Chinese term *Li* is central; it is often translated as ritual or custom, but it can also be translated as etiquette and appreciated as the way in which we are to express proper reverence to each other. In stark contrast to the use of manners in *The Prince*, in Confucian thought and practice, good manners can serve to remind us of what our roles in life should be; they are not instruments to be used for covert, wrongful action, but if they are instruments at all, they can act to instruct and steady our sometimes wayward temptations.

Manners as a Vehicle for Humor

In Goldman's *The Princess Bride*, manners act as elements of humor, and they create an affectionate satire of the fairytale form. No one expects the Man in Black (a.k.a. the Dread Pirate Roberts) to have such gracious manners—we as readers (or viewers) immediately sense something is amiss—he is not so dread at all. In fact, we rather like him. But we also like Inigo Montoya, intent on avenging his father's death, and bored of mediocre fencing partners. It becomes all the more surprising and delightful when the two men fence and each recognizes the other's genius. Our expectations are challenged, and a tense situation is defused. Although they continue fencing, we're relieved because the two men clearly do not despise each other.

The display of manners in this chapter of *The Princess Bride* is both funny and somewhat accurate in terms of reflecting situations in day-to-day life (even if the majority of us do not fence atop the Cliffs of Insanity). As in *The Princess Bride*, manners in everyday life have the potential both to defuse tension and to subvert expectations. For instance, *society* requires that we not kill another person even if we temporarily feel like doing so (for their poor grammar, say, or opting not to use a turn signal). *Manners* require you to remain (mostly) calm in such a situation and they thus defuse tension. When expecting rage, compassion can actually delight and humor a person (or at least that can be true for the bystanders—in this case, the viewer or the reader of the novel).

As the *Princess Bride* novel suggests, manners can both amuse and defuse, and in this way, they indeed reflect some of humankind's best virtues—humor and forbearance.

The Role of Sincerity in Good Manners

Inigo Montoya's compliments to Westley are genuine and effusive. It is his genuine admiration of Westley that makes us overlook Montoya's original (and very impolite) goal of killing him. Humperdinck, on the other hand, is well-mannered in the traditional sense, but the insincerity of his flattery and the hollowness of his expressions of love for Buttercup rightly lead us to cast Humperdinck as a cad and a schemer.

The critical element of genuineness, or sincerity, cannot be ignored in thinking about the role of manners. Is it possible that good manners require a degree of sincerity, that you can't exhibit good manners without some genuine care for the other person? Perhaps that's the reason why manners in *The Prince* seem like what Thomas Hobbes once called "small morals" in referring to the ordinary polite ways in which we show some cordiality. From such a point of view, our manners may tell us little about what is really at the heart of human nature. But what if our manners are not really small matters at all— perhaps they truly can tell us something about ourselves when we show good form or manners with sincerity and compassion.

A historically interesting case of someone using good manners to make a substantial point is the incident (recorded in Booker T. Washington's autobiography, *Up from Slavery*) of how General (later President) Washington encountered an African American who tipped his hat to Washington, to which Washington responded in kind. Washington was reprimanded for this by a (probably deeply racist) colleague: why would he, Washington, a white man show respect to a Negro? Washington replied (this is paraphrased): I am not going to be outdone when it comes to showing respect by anyone. Essentially, Washington turned the tables on his accuser, implying that if he, Washington, did not do "the polite thing" he would have been exposed as inferior in manners. In this incident "manners" were used as a way to hint at a desire for more respect between persons of different races even if, tragically, Washington did not think greater respect demanded he free his slaves during his life time (albeit Washington did free his slaves at the end of this life, in his 1799 will, the only slave-owning "founding father" to do so.)

Humperdinck and Rugen exhibit good manners on the outside, but the fine manners are nothing but a cover for their vile characters and evil plans. They seem fully aware of the depth of their deception and the harm they do to Westley. In the torture scene Humperdinck informs Westley that he will probably suffer more than others because he, Westley, truly loves Buttercup and so the loss of her will be especially grievous.

What is it that changes genuine care and compassion into a codified set of rules (manners) that can be manipulated and used to deceive as in Humperdinck and Rugen's cases? It comes back to connection—care and compassion spring from a sense of connection—to other people, to the earth, to a specific community. Good manners as inspired by compassion and respect cannot be codified and commodified, and compassion and respect cannot be dictated as societal manners must by their very nature, be dictated and codified. In economic terms, sincere care and compassion are not scalable—they cannot be replicated on a large scale (at a lower price). Care and compassion on an individual level are labor-intensive and often involve irrational behaviors, such as delayed gratification or sacrifice. Human beings feel care and compassion because they are connected—to a person, to a place, to an institution. That sense of connection provides room for manners that amuse, redeem, surprise, and even act heroically.

Let us quickly note, though, that although genuine manners cannot be codified or commodified, the *appearance* of genuine manners is easy to codify and commodify (see any one of several editions of Emily Post's etiquette guides). It's frequently difficult to tell the difference between the genuine article and a decent copy. This is not necessarily a bad thing—even if someone is having a bad day, we would prefer that person to greet us with a pleasant 'Good morning' rather than spit at us. In this instance, many, but not all of us would prefer good—if insincere—manners. We register one exception, however, in the case of over the top, highly exaggerated fake good manners. If you are not happy to see us, we would prefer the sound of silence rather than being treated to a huge fake smile along with effusively "cheerful" greetings in multiple languages.

The way in which manners can be instructive and lead us toward virtue comes out in the early stages of the courtship between Buttercup and Westley. In this sequence, Buttercup is at first not only failing in grace and graciousness, she is prepared to use threats to get her way:

> The horse's name was "Horse" (Buttercup was never long on imagination) and it came when she called it, went where she steered it, did what she told it. The farm boy did what she told him too. Actually, he was more a young man now, but he had been a farm boy when, orphaned, he had come to work for her father, and Buttercup referred to him that way still. "Farm Boy, fetch me this"; "Get me that, Farm Boy—quickly, lazy thing, trot now or I'll tell Father."
>
> "As you wish."

The change in Buttercup comes through Westley's return in disguise, their forging through the fire, the wrestling with beasts, Buttercup's display of loyalty when she is willing to take her own life rather than to consummate her marriage (which of course turns out to not be valid because the vows were not said properly) with Humperdinck.

Allied with Power and the Ruling Class

In contemporary Western society, manners are often equated with etiquette and used to connote social class—knowing which fork to use, showing good breeding, and signifying that you belong to the club of people who know the code. Manners in this case are used to signify "us" and "them," to reinforce "otherness." Humperdinck and Rugen do this repeatedly—and even Buttercup does this when she ridicules the boys from the village and refers to Westley (as we have seen) as Farm Boy.

As Plato and Confucius might observe, this aspect of manners really does reflect a deeply held common human trait (universal might be overstating the case, but it has to be close to universal): the need to create hierarchy. We do this in so many ways— through money, title, beauty, and sometimes, through manners.

In our day and age, for example, reality TV provides an easy way to create "us" and "them," and a good part of this has to do with class—using manners as a proxy for class. We have a large appetite for the Honey Boo Boos and Duck Dynasties of the world, and a lot of that is about creating 'us' as different from 'them'. Manners are a quick shorthand for that—"we" do not eat that kind of food, or have those kinds of fights with our family in public, or treat one another like that.

The problem with this is that "we" can also easily use manners to cover up a multitude of sins. Those nameless financiers who brought about the Great Recession caused a great deal of suffering, but they probably all used the correct fork. Good manners clearly do not equal good character, or genuine compassion and caring. Lovely manners are nice to have, but who is to say that we don't act worse than reality TV stars when we ignore or marginalize or act disrespectfully toward another being?

In *The Princess Bride*, we see deceitful manners from those who most closely represent civil society (Prince Humperdinck and his minister, Count Rugen), and we see genuine care and compassion—good manners—from those on the fringes of society (Fezzick, the Dread Pirate Roberts, Inigo Montoya). This does not surprise us—literature is rife with examples of vengeful kings and scheming queens, corrupt ministers, and unscrupulous people in power. Still, though, in a fairytale, in the "natural order of things" (which is neither natural nor ordered, but let's pretend . . .), leaders are supposed to be good and strong and beautiful and compassionate, and their manners will reflect this. It is a fly in the ointment for someone to be a leader and strong and beautiful and . . . bad.

The Princess Bride uses this counterpoint to good effect—we are full-throatedly cheering for the fringes of society (Westley, Fezzick, Montoya) as soon as we learn of Humperdinck's treachery and Rugen's vile character. And we are dismissing their good manners as yet another tool used by the powerful to deceive and exploit the powerless.

Why Bother with Manners at All?

So. Manners deceive, manners enable manipulation and exploitation, and manners divide one from another. Manners are fake (see any number of quotes from *Catcher in the Rye*). Why must we mind these manners at all?

Manners in and of themselves are neither good nor bad. They are a tool, a shorthand about cultural expectations and a way for us to live in community without constantly negotiating our behavior. It is easier for Vizzini—and more pleasant for everyone involved—to know that he is supposed to say "Excuse me" if he would like someone to get out of his way than to wonder if he should push that person or challenge them to a duel of wits.

Imperfect as they are, manners act as a floor—the price of entry for living in community. Fezzik is an excellent example of this—his primary concern left over from childhood is his abject fear of being left alone, out of community. He is willing to do what it takes, follow any rule, complete any task, so that he is not left alone. If he did not care about other people, he would do as he pleased. Hermits, on the other hand, do not worry about their manners, and by definition do not live in community. People living in community cannot make their own rules on a consistent basis, and most don't want to—it takes a great deal of time and thought to be a rugged individualist, outside of societal norms and mores. Furthermore, if you, as a rugged individualist living in an apartment building decided that vocal exercises on the balcony at 6:00 A.M. were the thing, you would not be part of the community for long.

Manners are something of a double-edged sword. Sometimes false, sometimes stifling, sometimes manipulated to create "other" or difference, they are also the mechanism by which we live with one another with a shared understanding of expectations and customs. In *The Princess Bride*, manners propel the story, add to its humor and sometimes, they act as a reflection of our better selves.

"You seem a decent fellow. I hate to kill you."

21
Buttercup and the Eternal Feminine

CHELSI BARNARD ARCHIBALD

Philosopher Simone de Beauvoir pointed out that women are often thought of as "the other"—they are not defined in their own terms, but, rather, in terms of their relationship to men. Moreover, they are not generally regarded as autonomous beings. In *The Princess Bride*, Buttercup begins her journey as a woman who shows natural leadership and management skills, but is relegated throughout the movie and by the end of the story to a helpless victim, trapped inside a male world.

De Beauvoir says that even when women are victimized they are also blamed and humanity assumes that a victim is at fault, that she is "losing her way." By examining Buttercup as a born leader in a sphere where gender is a social construct, we can pinpoint the ways in which the patriarchy around her squanders her philosophical and intellectual contributions to the events occurring in her very own life.

Femininity, the Construct

Simone de Beauvoir, in explaining how a woman is defined by society, claimed that "One is not born, but rather becomes, a woman." Buttercup is first introduced to audiences as one who manages her family's farm, rides her horse whenever she likes and to wherever she pleases, while executing orders to various farm staff, specifically to a young man named Westley. He in turn treats her with respect and reacts to her authority in appropriate ways. Because he is kind, respectful, and treats her as an equal, she falls in love with him and shares her heart.

De Beauvoir states that femininity is a construction of civilization and that all are born human, yet women are historically treated as less than human. Buttercup does not fall for Westley because he is the only man around, nor the only employee on the farm, but rather because he treats her as an equal. Buttercup's family estate grants her the right to marry a lord or landowner of her own status, but she and Westley choose one another not based on status, tradition, obligation, or arrangement. The audience gets no sense that Westley chooses her solely for her beauty or for the fact that she is the only available woman in his surroundings. Westley simply loves her for being herself, a leadership-oriented, outspoken, and intelligent human being.

In fact, there is no narrative mention of Buttercup's physical appearance, even in the original screenplay. The audience assumes from actress Robin Wright's presence on the screen that Buttercup is indeed beautiful, but it isn't until Prince Humperdinck mentions this specifically when he debuts her to the townsfolk as his intended bride that she changes her appearance to a more acceptable feminine form. The screenplay also describes Buttercup as wild, unkempt, and tomboyesque but when Humperdinck introduces her, he does so as "once a commoner" but as one who is "not so common now" as she has been ultra-feminized and remains silent in front of the crowd.

In the book *The Second Sex*, Simone de Beauvoir writes that male expectations and female expectations are not natural norms, but are instead created by society. Gender reflects only the differences of circumstance and situation rather than personality traits, qualities, or talent. Your situation determines your character; a woman is not born fully formed but is gradually shaped by her upbringing.

Westley leaves to earn money for his wedding to Buttercup, but later disappears and is presumed dead. While it seems that Buttercup is born a natural leader and has the courage to live authentically, she is consumed by society's expectations, and her marriage to the Prince is arranged.

According to de Beauvoir, a woman learns her role from men and others in society. Woman is not born passive, secondary, and nonessential, yet the forces of the external world shape her to be so, whether it is true to her essence or not. Every individual self is entitled to subjectivity or the ability to judge things based on personal experience and feelings rather than by the external worldview. In the eyes of de Beauvoir, gender destiny is not an unchangeable cosmic force, but rather a human choice that is the result of culture and circumstance.

Buttercup is a prime example of how the ability to choose is hindered in women who become a commodity rather than being considered an independent human entity. While she makes suggestions about her own fate and what she wants for her life, Prince Humperdinck constantly keeps her from the truth and controls her surroundings in order to silence her and take away her autonomy. Buttercup's relationship to Westley is constantly defined by a choice throughout the movie (to love or share her heart) whereas her relationship to Humperdinck is defined by her beauty, her femininity, and her ability to comply with his reign as King.

Buttercup pushes the Dread Pirate Roberts down a ravine, but when he calls out his famous phrase, "As you wish!", their secret code for "I love you," she immediately realizes that this is Westley, and then chooses to follow him into the dark. When they've both navigated the Fire Swamp and are headed off by Humperdinck and his men, Buttercup again chooses to give up her autonomy in order to save Westley's life, and demand that the Prince let him go free.

The Myth of the Eternal Feminine

De Beauvoir discusses the mythology of what she calls "the eternal feminine." This is the philosophical principle that idealizes an immutable concept of "woman," the belief that men and women have different core "essences" that cannot be altered by time or environment, despite their innate uniqueness and individuality. De Beauvoir pointed out that if the behavior of a real flesh-and-blood woman contradicts "the eternal feminine," then people conclude that the woman is in the wrong—the woman is "not feminine"—instead of deciding that the eternal feminine is a false entity.

The life of every woman is divided between her rights as a unique individual and the demands of "otherness." Otherness is the difference between the self and gender. Women are defined as "other" than male, not by their individual traits, talents, and contributions outside of their reproductive identity. Where man represents both the positive and negative aspects of humanity or of a complex human history, woman is defined as simply an accessory to the male story, not a key player. This is not a choice that she is able to make, but a presumed destiny that is forced upon her.

The rare woman who refuses to be a passive, elegant, and silent, is called defective, unattractive, and unfeminine. Once Buttercup gives up Westley to Humperdinck upon their emergence from the Fire Swamp, she has a nightmare of once again being presented to the public as Prince Humperdinck's chosen bride and an old woman admonishes her for being the "Queen of Slime, the Queen of Filth, the Queen of Putrescence. . . Rubbish! Filth! Slime!" and "Muck." The narrator tells the audience that "Buttercup's emptiness consumed her" and the only joy that she gets at this point is a daily ride on her horse, the very metaphorical definition of freedom.

De Beauvoir reminds readers that when women assert themselves, as Buttercup does frequently in the movie, they are considered by society as "not real women." Buttercup is punished for putting her humanity before her femininity, a recurring theme that haunts her while she sleeps. The core problem, de Beauvoir argues, is not an individual woman like Buttercup, but the complex mythology that imprisons her and corners her into an ill-fitting narrative. If the "definition" of femininity is undermined by the behavior of actual "flesh-and-blood women," de Beauvoir suggests that the problem is not with an individual like Buttercup but with the people in charge.

Independence, Intellect, or Insurrection?

After her betrothal to Humperdinck, Buttercup begins to reflect on her surroundings rather than her authentic self, but stills inserts her intellect into conversations as much as possible. Buttercup often states facts about her current situation to the men around her, but they downplay her intelligence and often ignore her advice. In many cases, Buttercup's conversational contributions would have saved the men from unneeded stress or negative consequences, yet they do not heed her word.

Because history is written and defined by those who are in charge and who are often the victors, the personal stories of women are rarely told or represented accurately. De Beauvoir explains that notions of femininity originated in man and that men have defined the "eternal feminine." Society insists that women remain mediocre, do not cause waves, or stand out separately from the system to which they are bound. When women have no voice they cannot be a problem nor can they advocate for any changes. Theirs is a silent narrative. De Beauvoir compares this to the plight of the blacks or the Jews throughout history, whose stories were downplayed and made to feel unimportant and their troubles to be imaginary in the eyes of their oppressors.

Unlike blacks in America or Jews in Europe, females constitute slightly more than half the human population at any given period in history, so they are not actually a minority. This, however, is at odds with the role that is thrust upon them: the role of being subordinate to men. Despite her lower caste, woman has always lived alongside her master as an equal partner in the creation of history and of civilization. Just as Humperdinck needs a Queen in order to be a King, man requires woman in order to exist, be born into the world, and to survive as a species. For de Beauvoir, their mutual dependence makes their inequality even more confounding.

When the three men, Vizzini, Fezzik, and Inigo, kidnap Buttercup and take her onto a sailboat bound for looming dark cliffs, she makes an effort to escape her situation. Buttercup jumps from the sailboat into shrieking-eel-infested waters. Vizzini immediately warns her that if she decides to continue in this environment on her own, she will most certainly meet her death. The shrieking eels become louder and more taunting as they close in to consume their prey.

In this moment, Buttercup's decision to jump and brave the unknown world on her own is an obvious sign of courage and independence while the shrieking eels represent society's admonition against a woman deciding her own destiny. Just as contemporary society shows women being metaphorically eaten alive when they publically venture outside of the norm, Buttercup would be literally consumed by death if she asserts her autonomy rather than continuing to be a helpless victim in a male war strategy.

In society the assertions are often the same, a woman who breaks away from wife, mother, femininity, or submission is destroying the human family, wrecking the future, and acting inappropriately and dangerously. Those around her assume that she is most likely to meet her doom. The audience later finds out that Prince Humperdinck hired Vizzini to kill Buttercup in order to enrage his people into supporting a war with Guilder and to gain more land in the process. This seems an accurate portrayal of how women are used as accessories throughout history to fulfill the unethical and brutal schemes for power by the males in their lives.

Privilege as a Cage

"Woman enjoys that incomparable privilege: irresponsibility," said de Beauvoir. In *The Second Sex*, she issues a plea for women to take charge of their own destiny, as impossible as the task may seem. While society forces women to rely on the privileged male for survival, women are historically not afforded the same amount of opportunity or ease to shape their future. Women rely on men for shelter and sustenance, as well as for their intellectual narrative, and this limits them in the community. De Beauvoir contends that when a woman is unable to contribute any economic gains to her household and is solely relegated to menial household tasks, civilization does not count her work as having any historical value.

Women can hardly be treated with justice if they are assumed to be no more than a passive, silent part of the background. Yet, because of the high demands society places on women to be all and do all, most women throughout history have been forced into the life of passivity and have embraced the comfort of compliance over the perceived conflicts of liberty. Yet Simone de Beauvoir maintains that any successful relationship between two parties grows from mutual liberty.

Buttercup waits for five years for Westley to return before she finally gives in to her betrothal to Prince Humperdinck. Although the narrative isn't specific, we can assume that it was nearly impossible during this time period for a young eligible woman to remain single and manage her family's estate when a wealthy royal gentleman demanded her hand in marriage. Historically, a woman may be put to death for resisting such arrangements on her behalf, and many women and young girls around the world are still punished or killed for running away from arranged marriages.

De Beauvoir issues a challenge to women and encourages them to be brave enough to take responsibility for their own actions and pursue an active role, regardless of the dangers it may hold. While it is less demanding and exhausting for Buttercup to abdicate all responsibility for her own future to Humperdinck, it stifles her individual self and makes her suicidal by the end of the movie. While men can oppressively discourage a woman from asserting her independence, many women refuse the opportunities available to them and in doing so discover that the "privilege" of compliance is actually a curse, in love and in life.

True Love and Mutual Liberty

Westley becomes incapacitated and crippled during the film and is ultimately saved by Buttercup's ability to protect and shield him from harm once the Prince has found them in her bedchamber. Inigo and Fezzik lose track of Westley while fighting others in their storming of the castle. It's clear from Westley and Buttercup's relationship by the end of the movie that both share equal responsibility in their destiny once she is liberated and he can travel next to her on horseback as her partner in life. Prior to her liberation Buttercup rode her horses alone, but afterward they ride together as one.

22
The *Dao* of Master Westley

Darci Doll

William Goldman consistently acknowledges that any merit in his abridgement of *The Princess Bride* is due to the brilliance, the wit, and the detailed, yet dry, account of Florinese history and foliage of S. Morgenstern.

So much is Goldman's work dependent upon Morgenstern that it resulted in trouble from Kermit Shog, legal representation of the Morgenstern estate. What's been left unsaid, however, is how the undercurrent of Daoist philosophy makes Morgenstern's and thus Goldman's book and movie about *The Princess Bride* so filled with wisdom and insight.

* * * * *

This is me using fancy italics to let you know I'm making a comment or remark to you. If you're interested in the legal troubles with which Goldman was plagued, read the introductions to the twenty-fifth and thirtieth anniversary editions of The Princess Bride. *If you're not interested in learning about that, well, you know what to do (or rather, not do). If you want to focus on just the nuts and bolts philosophical discussion of the* Princess Bride *and don't give a Florinese hoot about these comments, skip these sections. Proceed as you wish.*

Let Me Explain *Dao*. No, There's Too Much. Let Me Sum Up

Some general explanation of ancient Chinese philosophy is needed to really understand the full scope of its presence in

The Princess Bride. Out of respect for your interests, I'll try to keep my summary as quick as, and hopefully more concise than, Buttercup and Humperdinck's wedding.

* * * * *

Me again. Further possible evidence of the similarity between Chinese philosophy and Morgenstern could be the way in which both tend to give and rely on lengthy detailed accounts of history. These sometimes tedious descriptions can result in a distraction from the good stuff; hence Goldman's near total removal of Florinese history in his abridgment and his movie. However, as ancient Chinese historians and philosophers don't own exclusive rights to lengthy historical accounts, we can't be sure that Morgenstern is mimicking them in this regard.

* * * * *

Dao is essential to all Chinese philosophy. Each philosopher may have a different interpretation and application of *Dao,* but each still depends upon its incorporation. *Dao* refers to the cosmic order, truth, and reality of the universe. It is the pattern that provides cosmic coherence and organization to all things in the universe resulting in a comprehensive, interdependent, interconnected, natural system.

When the parts (including humans) act harmoniously, or according to nature, there is balance; a condition that we may refer to as being good. When there is discord, when things are acting inharmoniously or contrary to nature, the balance is disrupted and we may be tempted to refer to this as bad. Goodness and badness are intended to be relative or comparative; they identify whether a natural coherence or balance is present.

To know *Dao* is to know the right way, or the path, one ought to take. Someone who's highly tuned into this natural order, someone who can rightly predict the path to harmony, may be identified as a sage or a master depending on the circumstance and degree to which the mind is tapped into this cosmic order. Praise, elevated status, and qualification of being good are proportional to the balance with respect to *Dao.* It's recognition of the relative degree of natural coherence and harmony. Those who lack this status are deficient with respect to *Dao,* but it doesn't mean that they're necessarily morally inferior to those who are more in tune with *Dao*.

Each of the primary characters in *The Princess Bride* exemplifies a relationship with *Dao*. Some are significantly deficient and contribute to discord, mainly Buttercup, Vizzini, Count Rugen, and Prince Humperdinck. Fezzik, Inigo, and Westley provide examples of a more harmonious relationship. Categorizing them in these ways creates a job for us, and a problem to work out. Vizzinni said that when there is a problem with a job, you go back to the beginning so back to the beginning we'll go.

The Law of the Land Gives the Prince the Right to Marry Whomever He Wants

According to Confucius, performing your social role through ritual and tradition is acting consistently with the *Dao*. The importance of following tradition is something some people in *The Princess Bride* have in common with the Confucian approach. Prince Humperdinck and the citizens of Florin show this most clearly. The people of Florin follow the long and rich Florinese traditions and accept Prince Humperdinck (*and I suppose the King, too, but we don't see much about the role the he really plays as a leader. We definitely see that he's fulfilling a role by maintaining his presence and by remaining the King*) as the representative and enforcer of these traditions. When he decrees Buttercup is now royalty, they bow to her.

Buttercup herself knows that the law of the land gives him the right to marry whomever he chooses, so she agrees to become his bride despite the fact that she does not love him. When the law says that Buttercup was once a commoner but is now to be the future Queen, the people accept that she's no longer common. All that matters is the following of the law and of tradition; no more is required of people, according to Confucius.

These examples of meeting social responsibilities through following tradition are supported by a Confucian view of *Dao*. The Florinese people, including Humperdinck and Buttercup, are focused on creating a social harmony, on fulfilling their duty to their families and fellow Florinese citizens, and establishing a harmonious existence. If we were to look at this from only a Confucian point of view we could end the discussion here and say they've proven themselves in the way of *Dao*. But let's not move too quickly. There's a problem. When you rush a philosopher you get rotten philosophy.

The problem is that, if we accept this view, someone as terrible as Prince Humperdinck could be viewed as acting in accordance with *Dao* in keeping with the Confucian tradition. Humperdinck was able to work in planning a murder and starting a war in addition to planning a wedding and a five-hundredth-anniversary celebration *because* the people of Florin were motivated only by tradition (*or at least primarily. I don't want to pretend to know about all of the motivations of the Florinese people, especially since I've not had the luxury of studying their history. Suffice it to say that from what Morgenstern and Goldman tell us we can infer that the people are highly motivated by tradition*). Humperdinck, aided by Count Rugen, was able to conduct acts that are contrary to *Dao* (war, murder, torture) because of tradition. If *Dao* were only fulfilling obligations through tradition and ritual, Humperdinck's plans wouldn't be possible because of the discord and imbalance that results from them. Because tradition *would* allow such plans, *Dao* can't be just adhering to tradition. (*Before you object that the chaos comes from Humperdinck's* not *following tradition keep in mind that starting wars is part of a long and glorious tradition of the time. Second, if people weren't just following tradition, they'd see him for what he is and would thwart his diabolical plans.*) The inconceivability of *Dao* being tradition means we have to try to uncover the truth elsewhere.

We've Failed. We Need to Dedicate Our Life to *Dao* so the Next Time We Will Not Fail

While Confucianism merely incorporates *Dao*, Laozi's *Daodejing* is often viewed as the origin of *Daoism* as a cohesive theory.

* * * * *

This is despite the fact that it's not clear who actually wrote the Daodejing; it's possible it was composed by several people over an extended period of time. Knowing the author doesn't determine the value of the work, though. After all, you'd still love The Princess Bride *if it weren't really written by S. Morgenstern. Right?*

* * * * *

Whereas Confucius's discussion of *Dao* involves promotion of civility and cultural traditions, Laozi focuses instead on a return to nature, a departure from cultural traditions. Within the *Daodejing,* Laozi identifies several different definitions of *Dao* but what's most relevant for our discussion is *Dao* with respect to ideal human behavior. For Laozi, humans need to be acting in accordance with the natural way, or *Dao. De* is the term Laozi uses to refer to those who have virtue, or who are able to act in accordance with *Dao.* The potential for this ideal behavior lies in each of us; those who have achieved the ability to live consistently with *Dao* have achieved the great virtue of *De* and are living well. Part of this is to cast off the social values as they may cloud the ability to see *Dao* and to achieve *De.* Laozi also introduces the virtue of passivity, or *wu-wei.* One who has *wu-wei* has inactivity of thought, desires, and actions. More importantly, this means not interfering with the natural process. Laozi is telling us to follow *Dao,* to act when nature requires it of us, to be passive when action would interrupt the natural way.

Focusing on nature instead of culture and tradition may help us avoid the problem presented by Confucius. Humperdinck, Vizzini, Count Rugen, and Buttercup all lack understanding of *Dao;* they all lack *De* and *wu-wei.* They assume to have knowledge when they have none, take action when they should be still, and are still when they should be active. Vizzini and Humperdinck get closest to Laozi's ideal because they're in tune with nature enough to have areas of strength and to know some of the areas that are their weaknesses.

Vizzini knows better than to try to best the Man in Black at hand-to-hand combat. He knows that he'd lose to Westley in this arena (*spoiler alert: Westley and the Man in Black are the same guy!)* and knows that this is an instance requiring inaction (or *wu-wei).* His failure, however, is his fatal over-certainty in his intellect. He is *so* certain of his superior intelligence that he fails to realize that in order for the classic blunder of going up against a Sicilian when death is on the line to be pertinent the Sicilian needs to have *Dao*. By failing to realize that his being a Sicilian wasn't the advantage he presumed it to be he was bested by his own false sense of intelligence and invalidated the second most famous classic blunder.

Vizzini may believe that he's smarter than Socrates, Plato, and Aristotle, but he is mistaken; Socrates knew full well when he was drinking poison and Aristotle was smart enough to know how escape before having to drink poison. If Vizzini had true understanding of *Dao*, he'd have knowledge of the things he didn't know, or if he had paid attention to Plato and Socrates, he'd have learned that Socrates's "knowledge" was that he didn't know anything. He would have been able to anticipate the Man in Black's move, to sense the iocane powder, or at least would have known not to engage in this particular battle of wits if he wanted to live. He would have realized the possibility that the reason someone shouldn't go up against a Sicilian when death is on the line is because a Sicilian with *Dao* will only engage when the Sicilian rightly believes he can win. Vizzini may have been in tune with nature enough to know some of his weaknesses but without *Dao* couldn't have true understanding of himself, the world around him, nor was he capable of *De*.

Prince Humperdinck, on the other hand, is so attuned to his surroundings and to nature that he can track a falcon on a cloudy day. His ability to understand nature is so strong he was able to give an accurate account of the battles between Westley, Inigo, Fezzik, and Vizzini despite not being present. This ability to recount the details is owed entirely to his ability to recognize and categorize the disturbances in nature around him. Surely, though, someone like Humperdinck cannot be the person Laozi describes as having *De*. After all, someone who would murder his wife to start a war doesn't seem to be going with the flow in the sense Laozi had in mind (*and if you've read the book his "zoo" hardly seems one with nature*).

When Humperdinck said, "I always think everything could be a trap which is why I'm still alive," he gave us the real clue behind his shortcomings. While Humperdinck believes he's showing his cleverness what he is really demonstrating is inability to reliably distinguish between situations that are a trap and those that aren't; his apparent skill is actually accident, luck, or the advantage of paranoia. If he really had *Dao*, he wouldn't have to assume all things to be traps; he'd be able to sense which things are traps and which ones aren't. This is reinforced later when he says he believes Westley is bluffing.

Humperdinck suspected it was a bluff but he didn't really know; he couldn't really know because he's not aligned with *Dao* and lacks *De*. A person who has *Dao* and *De* is one who is situationally intuitive; he is aware of his intellectual and physical limits and is able to identify the right course of action by following the natural pattern presented by *Dao*. (*This doesn't mean the person sees the whole pattern presented by* Dao, *or that they are able to see the ways in which all things are connected. It means they're able to notice and listen to the natural signs that present themselves in a moment*). So it's clear how Vizzini and Humperdinck fail to live up to Daoist standards. Now I'll show how Buttercup fails as well.

Now, I know what you're thinking: You wrote that wrong! Obviously the likes of Vizzini, Humperdinck, Rugen are lacking in *Dao*, but how could one dare to lump Buttercup in with them? Here's how. Buttercup is the opposite of those three in that they all have some degree of expertise whereas she has none. (*I know we didn't address Rugen but his specialty is his scientific dedication to torture and pain. That's not a good thing, according to Daoism. It interrupts the natural cohesion instead of promoting and sustaining it.*) While we can easily identify Vizzini and Humperdinck as being a challenge to ideal behavior because they're, well, rotten and evil, it's harder to understand how Buttercup fits in. Buttercup doesn't provide a challenge to different interpretations of *Dao* the way Humperdinck does, and she's not deficient because of over-estimating her value the way Vizzini does.

The shortcoming with Buttercup is that she lacks the ability to know what is in accordance with the natural order, or *Dao*. Humperdinck and Vizzini are bad people who are lacking *Dao* and *De;* Buttercup is a decent person who happens to lack *Dao* and *De*. (*An additional difference is the law and tradition that granted more opportunities to men than to women. Buttercup lived in a time and a country where she was denied the opportunity to master skills and to attain knowledge to the same degree as her male counterparts. To say she lacks* Dao *and*

De isn't to condemn Buttercup. Rather, it's further evidence that Confucius was wrong to think that Dao *was just tradition, since tradition can deny people, like Buttercup, the opportunity to find* Dao *and cultivate* De.)

When we're introduced to Buttercup we learn that "Her favorite pastimes were riding horses and tormenting the poor farm boy who worked there." We learn nearly immediately that Buttercup has misaligned priorities with respect to *Dao*. Her entertainment (riding horses or tormenting the farm boy) is questionably passive or passive-aggressive. We may say there's some *wu-wei* in riding horses but that's not sufficient grounds to establish the presence of *Dao* and *De*. When Westley is captured, Buttercup allows herself to be consumed by emptiness and becomes even more inactive. When Humperdinck chooses her as a bride she passively goes along with it and again finds comfort only in riding her horses.

We learn that unlike his true love, Westley uses his capture to his advantage; he adapts and uses his surroundings to improve himself. Buttercup, however, continues to accept things at face value. To her credit, Buttercup does eventually attempt to assert herself and takes action that she feels is correct. Unfortunately, without *Dao* her decisions do not have the effect that she thinks they will. (*The times she tries to save herself involve jumping in with the shrieking eels which are more of an immediate threat than her kidnappers, pushing Westley down the cliff and only realizing he was her love after she'd attacked him, trying to kill herself after she gave up on true love*).

Buttercup's lack of *Dao* can be demonstrated by her inability to know the character of the people around her. She trusts Humperdinck is a man of his word and has resolute confidence in his motive for saving her. While Buttercup is correct that he'll be able to track her, she's wrong about his nature. She assumes he'll track her to save her; she's forgotten that he tracks prey and doesn't realize that she may be of no more value to him than his other trophies. She trusts that Humperdinck will be a man of his word and will release Westley unharmed. Her faith in Westley and true love is inconsistent. She doubts and fails to recognize him even while looking into those eyes that are so like the sea after a storm. She says she'll never doubt him again, yet when confronted with Humperdinck and Count Rugen she surrenders, believing

Humperdinck to be a man of his word and Westley to be unable to beat the odds. (*This is despite the fact that Westley has already demonstrated that he was capable of convincing the Dread Pirate Roberts to keep him as his lone survivor, of beating all three of her kidnappers including surviving after ingesting iocane poison, and being the first known person to survive the Fire Swamp.*)

She professes the utmost faith in Westley returning for her before she's married, yet attempts to kill herself when he doesn't show up. Buttercup's failure of the *Dao* is demonstrated through her inability to understand the character of those around her as well as the circumstances that require action or inaction. And so the peasant who mocked her and called her the queen of refuse may not have been far off. Her true love lives and she was going to marry another. The peasant realized there was another way; Buttercup could only consider the options her immediate perception presented to her.

The *Dao* Certainly Does Keep You on Your Toes

While Laozi laid the foundation of Daoism, Zhuangzi gave us a more complete, less stringent and less elitist version of the *Dao*. Zhuangzi stresses that *Dao* can be learned in the most basic of lifestyles; he says we can learn more from a butcher than from an educated master. The parable of the butcher and the oxen is one of the more well-known teachings of Zhuangzi. The long and short of it is that when the butcher began, he only saw the ox. When he mastered his skill he relied only on instinct until a new or difficult situation arose and he had to become one with the new situation.

Zhuangzi builds off of Laozi's ideas of *Dao* and identifies the ethically ideal person. This person will be unafraid of any danger, will be able to survive the harshest of conditions, will have little to no use for plans, will not presume to have knowledge when ignorant, will have such a grasp on nature that they can master anything they encounter (for after all, who needs plans when *Dao* will tell you how and when to act or to be inactive?) and will accept their fate. Like the butcher, this person will be so skilled that instinct will be all they need and they'll quickly be able to adapt to new or difficult scenarios.

Fezzik and Inigo get close and if anyone reaches this point it's Westley.

According to Zhuangzi we learn from people who have experienced *Dao*, but not through rigid instruction. These individuals help us model our behavior and hone our instincts. One who wants to find *Dao* may need to seek out a master, but not the elite type of master Laozi or Confucius had in mind. We're shown that having *Dao* involves the ability to assess the context around us and to use that to guide our action. Any person has the potential of becoming a master or student.

* * * * *

Zhuangzi does draw a distinction between the practical and the perfect. He believes that in the realm of Dao, *a person will be unobstructed and all will be acting in accordance with* Dao *naturally. In the realm of men, though, we cannot have that type of perfect harmony and have to learn to identify and address obstructions. A person who has* Dao *doesn't have to attain perfection; they just have to be able to assess and understand whether the situation at hand requires* wei *or* wu-wei.

* * * * *

Here we see more clearly the similarity between Eastern philosophers, Goldman, and Morgenstern. *The Princess Bride* uses analogy to illustrate ideal person via the examples of Inigo, Fezzik, and Westley, and to help us see the problems that await one lacking *Dao* by the examples of Vizzini, Humperdinck, Rugen, and Buttercup. In addition to demonstrating through analogy, Morgenstern and Goldman use a poor farm boy as their master of *Dao,* a choice of character that's more consistent with Zhuangzi than with Laozi or Confucius.

Since Fezzik and Inigo are both ridiculed by Vizzini for their lack of intelligence and worth, it may be unclear how they are his superiors. Both Fezzik and Inigo demonstrate more *Dao* in their skills.

Fezzik is a master at using his strength, whether fighting a group for a local charity, or fighting one person. He is able to fight without thinking—the way the butcher prepares his oxen. Perhaps more importantly, Fezzik doesn't use his strength for tasks that will go against nature. He doesn't think it's right to kill an innocent lady, insists on fighting the Man in Black in a sportsmanlike way, fights against the gangs instead of with them, helps Inigo avenge his father's death, and helps reunite Westley with his true love.

Similarly, Inigo dedicates his life to mastering swordsmanship so that he can right the wrong of his father's murder. Inigo is a swordsman unlike any other. Some may say he is a master, others may say he is a wizard (those others being people who've read the book and know about the wizard class). His mastery of the sword is *Dao* in action; he is able to go with the flow with his right and left hands. Both Fezzik and Inigo, however, are looking for a leader. They need someone to help them find *Dao* in areas other than their specific crafts. Even with a limited experience with him, they recognize the man who can be their sage.

They need the Man in Black. He bested Fezzik with strength, bested Inigo with steel, out-thought Vizzini. A man who can do that can help them find *Dao* any day.

Westley (alias the Man in Black, alias the Dread Pirate Roberts) is our *Dao* master in *The Princess Bride*. A poor farm boy is taken captive by the Dread Pirate Roberts who takes no prisoners. Yet, he is able to convince the Dread Pirate Roberts to take him on as a valet and spends the next few years learning and mastering anything anyone will teach him. He becomes Zhuangzi's ideal man: dedicated to learning every possible craft and skill, unafraid of heights, able to beat the best of the best without breaking a sweat.

Evidence of Westley's relationship with *Dao* is the calculated means by which he approaches his adversaries or challenges. What appears to many of us as reckless and rash is not so to him. He climbs the Cliffs of Insanity because it's a challenge he can conquer; he engages with Inigo in a swordplay because he has reason to believe he'll win; he knows that he is at a disadvantage with Fezzik in hand-to-hand combat so he goes for the chokehold. Even when he faces the Fire Swamp—something no one's ever survived—he is able to adapt to the conditions and escape essentially unscathed (even with a cumbersome Buttercup in tow). Physically his body is so in tune with nature that even iocane powder can't kill him.

Westley knows to trust Inigo when he makes the promise that Westley will reach the top alive because Westley knows a false promise from an empty promise. Like Inigo, his swordsmanship is fluid and flawless even when fighting left-handed (which he's not). He knows that killing Inigo would be as wrong as it would be to break a stained glass window or to destroy an artist; he knows that this would be an inappropriate kill. Because he has *Dao* he knows that Inigo is worthy of his highest respect.

The same hold true with Fezzik. When given the chance to kill Fezzik, Westley knows this would be against nature and instead exhibits *wu-wei*. This, however, isn't the case with Vizzini. Westley knows that a death in the battle of wits is an appropriate death for Vizzini, just as he knows that a lifetime of cowardice is the worst punishment for Humperdinck. Additionally, Westley is able to read Count Rugen and knows that they are both men of action and lies don't become them, and that Rugen has no intent to return him to the pirate ship *Revenge*. With instinct, with *Dao*, Westley understands all of his adversaries, knows how to best them, knows how to leave them. When Fezzik and Inigo need a leader they start with Vizzini, but realizing his shortcomings (as well as his being all the way dead) they seek out the ideal man; the Man in Black.

Master Kong, Master Lao, Master Zhuang, and Master Westley

I don't want to pull a Morgenstern and give you the entire history of the significance of Chinese names. I do, however, want you to be aware of the basic meanings behind the names should you encounter them somewhere else. Confucius is a westernized form of Kongzi, or Master Kong. Laozi or Lao Tzu is Master Lao. You're probably guessing that Zhuangzi or Zhuang Tzu is Master Zhuang. You're so clever!

These titles have been passed on to these individuals in recognition of their being sages; leaders from whom we can learn to be the best version of ourselves as well as the way to *Dao*. *The Princess Bride* may not tell us that Westley is a sage in so many words, but it's the underlying message. As the grandfather says to the boy, "Now this is a special book. It's the book my father used to read to me when I was sick and I used to read it to your father. And today, I'm going to read it to you."

The sick boy is analogous to the sick spirit—the one out of sync with *Dao*. By learning from Westley we are pointed towards understanding *Dao*. Like the boy, we may be hesitant to take the effort (or non-effort) to succumb to *Dao*. However, at the end, we welcome it and want to keep learning from it. We see the way Westley has evolved, the way he's helped Fezzik and Inigo to become better versions of themselves, the way he resolutely commits to Buttercup's wellbeing. However, Westley-zi or Master Westley, doesn't have quite the right ring to it so we may want to stick to the Dread Pirate Roberts. After all, the name is the important thing for inspiring *Dao*.

I, Myself, Am Often Surprised at Life's Little Quirks

The Princess Bride is a contemporary means of encouraging you to find your way—to become one with the *Dao*. It demonstrates the value of learning the *wei* and *wu-wei*. Westley is Zhuangzi's butcher in Goldman's clothing, advocating the nurturing of your inherent potential to live well. Luckily for Goldman, it's unlikely that the legal problems brought forth by Shog will be replicated on behalf of Zhuangzi. The important thing is that the *Dao* is taught—not by whom or in what manner.

* * * * *

If you find this interpretation too far from the story you love and adore; if you want to re-simplify the interpretation, to allow the Dao *to flow unacknowledged beyond your conscious awareness, please proceed as you wish.*

Postscript

Upon review by legal representation I was advised to make clear that there is no evidence that Goldman was influenced by, or ever heard of, Eastern Philosophy. Any resemblance in the former to the latter is to be interpreted as entirely coincidental. Additionally, and more alarmingly, it has been revealed that Morgenstern (and any extension therein including but not lim-

ited to: his estate and its legal representation Kermit Shog) is a machination of Goldman's mind; a ruse he had been sustaining for decades. One should read his commentary about Morgenstern and Florin with skepticism. For those of you for whom this is a new revelation, I apologize for being the bearer of bad news. Fortunately, as I pointed out earlier, the value of The Princess Bride *isn't dependent upon the existence of Morgenstern.*

23

Why No One Would Surrender to the Dread Pirate Westley

CLINT JONES

The Princess Bride is a story about a lot of things—fencing, fighting, torture, revenge, giants, monsters, chases, escapes, true love, miracles—but let's look at the swashbuckling exploits of Westley after he moves out of Buttercup's stable and finds himself in the hold of the Dread Pirate Roberts's ship waiting to most likely be killed in the morning.

While Westley is aboard the *Revenge* honing the skills necessary to replace Ryan as Roberts, Florin is inching closer to an identity crisis not unlike the one Westley experiences when he first tries to captain the pirate ship and realizes that no one would surrender to the Dread Pirate Westley. No one, indeed.

The figure of Roberts both as a person and as a persona is the creation of years' worth of cultural capital. Not unlike the terrifying figure of Blackbeard off the coast of Carolina or L'Olonnais off the Spanish Main, Roberts, as a pirate, seems to have a special meaning to the citizens of Florin. It's not just that Roberts is a pirate. It can't be as simple as that.

If all the story needed to get Westley from farm boy to cavalier hero was an unfortunate mid-emigration run-in with pirates, then merely telling Buttercup his ship had been captured by pirates would've been enough. But it's significant that it was *this* pirate and not just because he is famous for his cruelty—most pirates (or the most successful ones anyway) were cruel—but because of his relationship to the country and citizens of Florin. Otherwise, again, any pirate would do, in fact, the Dread Pirate Westley would've been just fine. But Roberts is significant to the story because of his shifting identity; he

represents the mythological underpinnings of Florinese identity which, as we shall see, is also undergoing a major change.

What Kind of Book Is This . . . ?

It's not unusual for mythology to conjure up ideas about the
divine exploits of ancient gods, in ancient civilizations, as stories told by ancient peoples who couldn't explain the happen-
ings of the world they lived in. But, as Roland Champagne
has pointed out, mythologies are more than just tales of
divine hijinks; they encompass the moral, cosmological, and
historical, while intersecting with various contexts ranging
from the political to the sexual, and can integrate the geo-
graphical, economic, sociological, and cultural. However, few
people are comfortable with the idea that mythology plays an
important role in society even today and permeates our entire
cultural identity.

Modern mythologies contribute directly to how we understand who we are and do so with the same relevance Achilles
had to the identity of the average Greek. Mythologies create
common social bonds through shared experiences and provide
a means for understanding the internal impulses of our culturally formed self. According to Jerome Bruner, "by symbolically making internal impulses external we can share
communally in the nature of internal experience and, thus, recognize ourselves and others as connected through a cultural
identity." The Dread Pirate Roberts is just such a connection for
Buttercup and Westley as he is for all the Florinese citizenry
inside and outside of the Thieves Forest.

Mythology doesn't always come shrouded in the misty
remembrances of a foregone time; rather, it often attaches itself
to the very idea of cultural inclusion, our sense of belonging—
who *we* are. A sense of belonging is just as important to us as
it is to Fezzik—who lives a vagabond's life and fears being
abandoned—or even to Goldman who feared being passed over
as the author of *Buttercup's Baby* in favor of Stephen King
(who has Florinese relations). The sequel to *The Princess Bride*
included in the thirtieth anniversary edition of the novel
appears with a substantial preface where Goldman relates the
tale of nearly losing the opportunity to translate Morgenstern's
sequel to Stephen King. How we understand ourselves is con-

nected directly to the cultural mythology we take to be central to the identity we experience individually and collectively.

It has always been the way of multitudes to interpret their own symbolically rendered identity literally, because, according to Joseph Campbell, "such literally read symbolic forms have always been—and still are, in fact—the supports of their civilizations, the supports of their moral orders, their cohesion, vitality, and creative powers." And so, when a particular myth is no longer taken to be central to the cultural identity, it is updated, not merely dismissed out of hand, and this process allows for continuity and cohesion of a cultural identity through time. Joseph Campbell presents a snapshot of this process when he examines how the concept of a flat earth surrounded by a monster-filled cosmic sea slowly fell out of favor in the west and was replaced by notions of a sphere in space.

In the United States, for example, the concept of "rugged individualism" is linked to the mythos of the Frontiersman, then the Cowboy, then the rags-to-riches immigrant street urchin of the early twentieth century and today is bandied about in praise of small business start-ups and the Main Street crowd making their way in a corporate world. The Cowboy is indelibly linked to the American West. As a result, the American West, both our popular conceptions and misconceptions of it, fuel ideas about what it means to be an American. These images can be distilled into particulars, like Billy the Kid, who, over time, cease to be "knowable" historical figures and merely become mythological legend. To say that Billy the Kid isn't knowable is to say that we know the legend of Billy the Kid better than we do the kid who was actually Billy. Scholars and history buffs aren't sure what Billy's real name was, where he came from, how old he was, how many people he killed, and people today still debate whether or not he was gunned down by Pat Garrett.

We can imagine that this is precisely what's happening to the figure of the Dread Pirate Roberts in *The Princess Bride*, where it matters less and less *who* the pirate is than who the people *believe* him to be. Like Billy the Kid, who symbolizes an American cultural concept of the youthful underdog fighting a corrupt system while seeking to mete out righteous vengeance, the Dread Pirate Roberts has a definite symbolic meaning to the Florinese people—what that is, and why, is left largely unexplored in the novel and the movie. But we do pick up some clues about how the idea of Roberts is perpetuated and how the stability of the identity of the Dread Pirate Roberts offers a glimpse into the stability of Florinese identity during the tumultuous times of Prince Humperdinck.

His Ship Was Attacked by the Dread Pirate Roberts

Mythologies in culture can be used to shape our identities at all stages of life. In childhood the boogeyman under the bed or Santa Claus are often used to motivate good behavior. In Goldman's novel, the Fire Swamp is used in just this way, and it clearly shapes Buttercup and Westley. Similarly, the use of the Founding Fathers' revolutionary spirit to ramp up social patriotism has the same trappings as the origin story of Romulus and Remus in Ancient Rome; as David Maclaine notes, regarding Alfred Duggan's novel of the feral twins, it's a "story of how people of varied backgrounds came together to build a city like nothing that had been seen before." Pound for pound, George Washington and company in the American "melting pot" have become an updated version of the traditional origin story.

Though it takes satirical aim at the fairytale genre itself, much like *Shrek* or *Hoodwinked*, what marks *The Princess Bride* as a different sort of divergence is that Goldman plays by the rules, so to speak, achieving his critique via over-the-top representations of certain fairytale characters, imagery, and devices rather than inverting them or otherwise doctoring them to suit his needs. However, regardless of Goldman's intent to destabilize the fairytale as a genre, his social criticisms are effective because they are built around the very ideas mythological stories, fables, and fairytales use to construct a stable social identity, both inside the story and among those who might hear or tell the story.

When we find out that Westley has been captured by pirates we have a set of pre-conceived notions about what that entails—just as Buttercup does, which is why she mourns Westley. Both our and Buttercup's reaction to the news is a product of the same relationship to pirates as figures in our cultural mythology—yet, because it is the Dread Pirate

Roberts and not, say, nondescript Barbary pirates, Buttercup is more distressed than we are because she knows things we don't about Roberts.

When mythological stories achieve cross-cultural status they function in the same way across cultures as they do within cultures. The earliest tales of Old St. Nicklaus have permeated cultures around the world and taken on the trappings of those various cultures while maintaining a recognizable link to the original idea of Santa Claus. As we've already seen, the idea that the Fire Swamp is a place where parents will dump their naughty children is an idea that connects with the reader because of Santa's twice-checked naughty list and the fear of a lump of coal—though somehow being left by your parents in the shadow of R.O.U.S.'s seems far more sinister.

Our concern here, however, is not with misbehaving children so much as it is with pirates—the Dread Pirate Roberts to be exact. We might wonder why pirates are the go-to miscreants chosen to intercept Westley on his voyage to the New World as opposed to, say, brigands prowling the King's Highway. The obvious answer is that he was sailing to the Americas and, sometimes, getting plundered by pirates is what happens on the high seas, but this misses the importance of the antagonistic relationship between Westley and Prince Humperdinck. Prince Humperdinck is the embodiment of the state, he is Hobbes's Leviathan, representative not of any particular person, but of, as Hobbes would have it, mankind—or, in this instance, all Florinese.

Westley, as a simple fortune-seeking traveler, is nothing more than a Florinese immigrant, but Westley as the Dread Pirate Roberts is definitely state-less and as such he embodies the very identity crisis of the New World. This is in direct contradistinction to, say, Robin Hood, who is, whatever else he may be, decidedly and always English. So, having been captured by the Rogue Bandit Roberts would not have had the same meaning in the story. Florin is on the sea coast and unlike Guilder (as far as we know), Florin keeps a standing navy, whereas Guilder has a "frontier" upon which Buttercup's body was to be disposed of by Vizzini and company. The use of a pirate, then, signals that Roberts-as-pirate has significance to the Florinese in a similar way that Blackbeard probably meant more to the people of coastal Carolina than of the Ohio River Valley. But Roberts-as-pirate also signifies the New World, the cosmopolitan opportunity to re-make yourself just as Westley and his predecessors have done when they assumed the role of Roberts.

Who Is the Man in Black?

Though both Florin and Guilder exist in a world that is recognizably our world in a medieval sense (though obviously after the discovery of the New World) the characters in Florin are keenly aware of who the Dread Pirate Roberts is while outsiders are acutely unaware of his reputation. The poor lost circus performers are decidedly ignorant of who they are dealing with during their encounters with the Man in Black: Inigo, before losing his swordfight and being struck unconscious, asks, "Who are you?" Fezzik, in his pre-wresting match banter, inquires, "Why are you wearing a mask?" Vizzini's life or death battle of wits begins with him elucidating what he knows of the Man in Black but—in spite of his worldly knowledge and condescension to Socrates—he never makes the connection between his adversary and the Dread Pirate Roberts.

This is not the case with Buttercup. After being unblindfolded in the wake of Vizzini's death, but before being whisked away by the Man in Black, Buttercup asks, with a small measure of awe, "Who are you?" We can safely surmise that Buttercup having lived a very sheltered life—both in the movie and the novel—is at exactly the same loss as Inigo when he poses the same question. However, unlike her non-Florinese abductors, it does not take Buttercup long before she exclaims with absolute certainty, "I know who you are, your cruelty reveals everything."

Though it's too easy to paint this as a cheap resurrection myth we might pause here to wonder why it is that Buttercup is able to piece together who she is dealing with when Vizzini could not, when they were, for the most part, working with the same information. It seems as though Buttercup has a piece of information that Vizzini is missing, namely, a familiarity with stories of the Dread Pirate Roberts. Of course, we know from Prince Humperdinck's exchange with Buttercup regarding the recall of Westley prior to their nuptials that "the Dread Pirate Roberts is always close to Florin this time of year." So, while Vizzini had the same clues as a blindfolded Buttercup,

Buttercup knew the mythology of Florin that provided the links to draw the conclusion Vizzini could not—it's likely that Vizzini would still be alive if he were from Florin.

We can also assume that the Dread Pirate Roberts is embedded in a Florinese mythological identity because in spite of the fact that the Dread Pirate Roberts has been terrorizing the high seas for twenty years, Inigo, who has traveled the world studying fencing, has no concept of who he is before or during their sword fight. This is made even more apparent when the Man in Black, while climbing the Cliffs of Insanity, refuses Inigo's help for no better reason than he has "known too many Spaniards" to put much trust in Inigo. So, while the Man in Black is all-too-familiar with Spaniards, Inigo is clueless about his opponent. Fezzik is also well traveled, having begun his life in Turkey before traveling extensively on world wrestling circuits with his parents until he is hired by Vizzini in Greenland. Yet, when Fezzik inquires about the mask the Man in Black points out that he thinks everyone will be wearing them soon enough, suggesting that few, if any, people, and, perhaps, especially pirates, are wearing masks.

Here we're given a glimpse into the trademark of the Dread Pirate Roberts and yet Inigo and Fezzik remain ignorant of his identity even as they are preparing to storm the castle. It's not until the planning of the castle break-in that Inigo and Fezzik are made aware of who the Man in Black is, which we learn only because as Fezzik is being wheel-barrowed toward the castle and threatens the guards that there will be no survivors, he identifies himself as the Dread Pirate Roberts. We know that Westley has confided in them to some extent not only because they use the reputation of the Dread Pirate as a ruse, but also because (in the movie) he offers the job to Inigo during their escape from Humperdinck's room. (Inigo repeatedly says that there is no money in the revenge business, but at the end of the movie he's considering a job as captain of the pirate ship *Revenge*.) Nevertheless, when confronted with the Dread Pirate Roberts, the reaction from the guards is immediate and panicked—it's almost as if the giant version of the Dread Pirate Roberts presented by Fezzik is every bit as terrible as their imaginations have led them to believe—setting him ablaze seems wholly unnecessary amid the chaotic retreat of the guards. Surely, a pirate of such renown ought to be immediately recognizable especially as he has been performing feats few people could hope to do even minimally well.

For instance, Vizzini attempts to allay the fears of his two-man crew and reinforce the hopelessness of a captive Buttercup by pointing out that "only Fezzik is strong enough to go up" the Cliffs of Insanity "our way" and yet the Man in Black does the inconceivable. He bests the fencing wizard Inigo at swordplay, the giant Fezzik at strength, and Vizzini at wits and it becomes clear in doing so that in order to step into the role of the Dread Pirate Roberts that Westley inherited, he must become capable of perpetuating the character in word and deed. That is, to put it more mildly, given what we know of the history of the Dread Pirate Roberts, Westley must be able to live up to the reputation of the Dread Pirate Roberts.

This is a two-fold necessity for Westley. First, as he points out to Buttercup, "no one would surrender to the Dread Pirate Westley" as 'Westley' has no reputation upon the seven seas to make commercial captains fearful. Second, if Westley expects to make his fortune—the whole reason he has set out from Buttercup's farmstead to begin with—he cannot allow the reputation of the Dread Pirate Roberts to become anything less than fearsome. Doing so might not only leave him poor and humiliated, if not hung from a European gibbet, but there's good reason to believe that ruining the name of the Dread Pirate Roberts might entail a reckoning with the original Dread Pirate.

Failing at the latter condemns Westley to futility given the former and, being aware that he's in a position to retire from the role, we know that he has at least managed to maintain the reputation of the Dread Pirate Roberts even if he has not contributed to it through his own dealings. Either way, a masked man, clad completely in black, capable of climbing the Cliffs of Insanity, shifting effortlessly to successful swordplay against a recognized Wizard, physically defeating a giant and out-thinking a Sicilian with such a dizzying intellect ought to have been readily identifiable to everyone. Yet, he was not.

People in Masks Cannot Be Trusted

It seems fair to conclude that the Dread Pirate Roberts is to Florinese identity what the Cowboy, in the form of Billy the

Kid, is to American identity. This is no small matter because a stable identity is necessary for social cohesion—as necessary as having recognizable enemies. Jacques Derrida argues, in his *Politics of Friendship*, that our relationships are defined in context with others and that to know our friends is to identify our enemies. At the state level, then, there is greater stability when an enemy is clearly defined in opposition to us as, for instance, the Russians were during the Cold War compared to the post-9/11 world where everyone could be a terrorist; today social identities are less stable as a result of al-Qaeda terrorism precisely because al-Qaeda is state-less. Such an identity crisis easily explains why Prince Humperdinck is planning to use Guilder, as the sworn enemy of Florin, to rally the citizens to him as he ascends the throne—to remind them who they are.

Prince Humperdinck is willing to go to great lengths to start a war with Guilder even relishing the necessary revision to his plan to have Buttercup murdered on their wedding night instead of dumped on the Guilder frontier because it will be a more potent call to arms and solidarity for his Florinese subjects. Whatever else his warmongering intentions may rest upon, Humperdinck is definitely aware that the impending war with Guilder will rally the people to him—that is, sparking a war with Guilder seems a necessity for reinforcing Florinese solidarity as, perhaps, one among many other potentially nefarious reasons. Realistically, after five hundred years, cementing Florinese identity might be a paramount concern in the evolving socio-political landscape of a developing European world expanding into the New World.

The New World means new ideas and opportunities and a re-thinking of the way things are—that is, a re-evaluation of the mythologies that create Florinese identity—so it's no surprise that Prince Humperdinck wants a war. With the loss of stable symbols, says Joseph Campbell, "there follows uncertainty . . . disequilibrium, since life . . . requires life-supporting illusions; and where these have been dispelled, there is nothing secure to hold on to, no moral law, nothing firm." How many others, like Westley, have abandoned their place in Florinese society to journey to the New World seeking greater fortunes? Prince Humperdinck is inheriting a country with an identity crisis.

And, as a result, it seems reasonable enough in such conditions that Prince Humperdinck might be concerned about losing his subjects to an identity crisis. As Andrew Lytle has pointed out, great upheavals in a society can thoroughly destroy a way of life, especially when there is a transition from an older, more traditional way of life and a newer, modern one, even when memory and habit, manners and traditions are slow to die. Humperdinck's reasons seem transparent enough. But, more than that, we might reasonably wonder why Westley, having amassed a fortune (small though it may be after only a few years pirating) and having returned to the arms of his true love, would care at all about passing on the title of the Dread Pirate Roberts.

You'd Make a Great Pirate Roberts

Certainly Westley has a great deal of respect for Inigo and there is no good reason to assume that Inigo, provided he survives his wounds, would not be able to learn, as Westley did, how to inhabit the role of the Dread Pirate Roberts. We know that Westley's concern here is not focused on keeping his crew employed because we know that the transition from one Roberts to the next requires that the crew be disbanded and a new one raised. So, why not just walk away? Why not just retire the Dread Pirate Roberts? Recall that Westley, like Buttercup, is Florinese and, presumably, for them, the Dread Pirate Roberts is not just another pirate; culturally speaking, he is more than that to them, after all, they were born when the original Roberts was hoisting his black flag, so they, in essence, grew up with Roberts. Hence, it would be important to Westley to pass the title on—even to a Spaniard.

We do not know if any of the other instantiations of the Dread Pirate Roberts were non-Florinese persons, but we do know that the original Roberts relocated to Patagonia. Why is this? Perhaps the original Roberts is Patagonian or Patagonia is, generally speaking, just a lovely place to retire, and these are both, certainly, reasonable conclusions. However, it's equally likely, given what we know, that the original Roberts was Florinese himself. Given that he frequently sails in the area the use of a mask would make sense as would his penchant for leaving no survivors—he wouldn't have wanted anyone to recognize him—and it explains why he didn't return to Florin upon his retirement.

We could also easily make the assumption that Westley's captor, Ryan, for whatever other reasons he had, chose Westley as his replacement because he was a *suitable Florinese choice* at the right place at the right time. It was Westley's description of Buttercup that moved Ryan to spare him initially—what more moving motivation does one need to spare a life than to realize a kinship with a guy after hearing him describe a native beauty? We know that Prince Humperdinck is not going to get his war with Guilder, at least not soon, but, of more importance, is that bestowing the title of the Dread Pirate Roberts on a Spaniard could signal the discontinuity of a significant Florinese mythos. Where Westley embodies the state-less defector and Humperdinck the traditional state, Florin under-goes the transition from medieval state to modern country los-ing the Dread Pirate Roberts to a larger, more inclusive, that is, worldly, mythology. This parallels the very transformation that Westley has undergone to become the Dread Pirate.

. . . Is This a Kissing Book?

Where Joseph Campbell begins his analysis of myth by inves-tigating the tensions between shifting mythological ground in the face of new "facts," Karen Armstrong posits that "mythology and science both extend the scope of human beings . . . mythol-ogy, is not about opting out of this world, but about enabling us to live more intensely within it." Myths are not meant to harden into facts, but a myth with no grounding in the experi-ence of those who know it can never manifest in culture as a key for unlocking the insights necessary to understand our complex socio-cultural identity. Whatever else happens between them, Humperdinck is not chasing the Dread Pirate Roberts, he is chasing Westley, even though, during Westley's imprisonment, Humperdinck continues addressing him as the Dread Pirate Roberts in public while he knows the truth.

Hence, whether *The Princess Bride* is a love story or a com-edy or a satirical skewering of the fairytale, it is definitely an opportunity to understand how cultural identity is linked to cultural mythology. In fact, in his skewering of the genre, Goldman has provided a succinct analysis for the dangers inherent in an identity dissolved in a culture saturated by the "known" and not counterbalanced by wonder, imagination, and play. This is made obvious by Prince Humperdinck in his exchange with Westley during the daring rescue of Buttercup on her wedding night. As Westley explains 'to the pain' to a clueless Humperdinck it is clear that the prince thinks he 'knows' what it means. But he doesn't. And, what's more, he lacks the imagination necessary to actually grasp what's at stake because he prefers the traditional 'to the death' and is, unlike Westley, behind the times.

References

Alford, C. Fred. 1997. *What Evil Means to Us*. Cornell University Press.

Aquinas, Thomas. 1999. *Thomas Aquinas: Selected Writings*. Penguin.

Arendt, Hannah. 1973. *The Origins of Totalitarianism*. Harcourt, Brace.

———. 2006 [1963]. *Eichmann in Jerusalem: A Report on the Banality of Evil*. Penguin.

Aristotle. 1999. *Nicomachean Ethics*. Hackett. (Books 8 and 9 on *philia*.)

———. 2001. *The Basic Works of Aristotle*. Modern Library.

———. 2004. *Rhetoric*. Dover.

Armstrong, Karen. 2005. *A Short History of Myth*. Cannongate Press.

Atran, Scott. 2010. *Talking to the Enemy: Faith, Brotherhood, and the (Un)Making of Terrorists*. HarperCollins.

Augustine of Hippo. 1994. *Political Writings*. Hackett.

———. 2003. *City of God*. Penguin.

Bastardi, Anthony, Eric Luis Uhlmann, and Lee Ross. 2011. Wishful Thinking: Belief, Desire, and the Motivated Evaluation of Scientific Evidence. *Psychological Science* 22:6.

Beauchamp, Tom L., and James F. Childress. 2012. *Principles of Biomedical Ethics*. Oxford University Press.

Becker, Ernest. 1975. *Escape from Evil*. Free Press.

Berke, J.H. 1988. *The Tyranny of Malice: Exploring the Dark Side of Character and Culture*. Summit.

Bernstein, Richard. 2005. *The Abuse of Evil: The Corruption of Politics and Religion Since 9/11*. Polity.

Bruner, Jerome. 1959. Myth and Identity. In Henry Murray, ed., *Myth and Mythmaking*. Beacon Press.

Burg, B.R. 1984. *Sodomy and the Pirate Tradition: English Sea Rovers in the Seventeenth-Century Caribbean*. New York University Press.

Campbell, Joseph. 1988. *Myths to Live By*. Bantam.

Champagne, Roland. 1992. *The Structuralists on Myth: An Introduction*, Garland.

Confucius. 2008. *The Analects*. Oxford University Press.

Cooley, Charles Horton. 1902. *Human Nature and the Social Order*. Scribner's.

Davis, Michael. 2008. Justifying Torture as an Act of War. In Larry May and Emily Crookston, eds., *War: Essays in Political Philosophy*. Cambridge University Press.

Davis, W.A. 2006. *Death's Dream Kingdom: The American Psyche Since 9/11*. Pluto.

De Beauvoir, Simone. 2011 [1949]. *The Second Sex*. Vintage.

Derrida, Jacques. 2006. *The Politics of Friendship*. Verso.

Des Pres, Terence. 1976. *The Survivor: An Anatomy of Life in the Death Camps*. Oxford University Press.

Descartes, René. 1993. *Meditations on First Philosophy*. Hackett.

Emerson, Ralph Waldo. 1987. *The Essays of Ralph Waldo Emerson*. Belknap.

Graham, A.C. 1989. *Disputers of the Tao: Philosophical Argument in Ancient China*. Open Court.

Goldberg, Carl. 1997 [1996]. *Speaking with the Devil: Exploring Senseless Acts of Evil*. Penguin.

Goldman, William. 1973. *The Princess Bride: S. Morgenstern's Classic Tale of True Love and High Adventure*. Harvest.

———. 1998. *The Princess Bride: S. Morgenstern's Classic Tale of True Love and High Adventure*. 25th Anniversary Edition. Ballantine.

———. 2000. *Four Screenplays and Essays*. Applause Theatre and Cinema.

Hampton, Jean. 1986). *Hobbes and the Social Contract Tradition*. Cambridge University Press.

———. 1997. *Political Philosophy*. Westview.

Hill, Thomas E., Jr. 1991. *Autonomy and Self-Respect*. Cambridge University Press.

Hobbes, Thomas. 1994. *Leviathan*. Hackett.

Hoffman, Bruce. 2002. A Nasty Business. *Atlantic* (January).

Holstein, James A., and Jaber F. Gubrium. 2000. *The Self We Live By: Narrative Identity in a Postmodern World*. Oxford University Press.

Hume, David. 1988. *An Enquiry concerning Human Understanding*. Open Court

———. 1992. *Writings on Religion*. Open Court.

James, William. 1983. *The Principles of Psychology*. Harvard University Press.

———. 2001 [1892]. *Psychology: The Briefer Course*. Dover.

Joyce, James. 2008 [1922]. *Ulysses*. Penguin.

Johnson, Captain Charles. 2010 [1724]. *A General History of the Robberies and Murders of the Most Notorious Pirates*. Lyons.

Kant, Immanuel. 1996 [1797]. *The Metaphysics of Morals*. Cambridge University Press.

———. 1997 [1793]. *Religion within the Limits of Reason Alone*. Harper.

Kubzansky, Laura D., Rosalind J. Wright, Sheldon Cohen, et al. 2002. Breathing Easy: A Prospective Study of Optimism and Pulmonary Function in the Normative Aging Study. *Annals of Behavioral Medicine* 24.2.

Langer, Susanne K. 1957. *Philosophy in a New Key*. Harvard University Press.

Laozi. 2007. *Daodejing (Laozi): A Complete Translation and Commentary*. Open Court.

Lewis, C.S. 2015. *Miracles*. HarperOne.

Locke, John. 1988 [1689]. *Two Treatise of Government*. Cambridge University Press.

Lytle, Andrew. 1959. The Working Novelist and the Mythmaking Process. In Henry Murray, ed., *Myth and Mythmaking*. Beacon Press.

Machiavelli, Niccolò. 1992. *The Prince*. Dover.

Maclaine, David. Founding Fathers. www.historicalnovels.info/Founding-Fathers.

Mahon, James E. The Definition of Lying and Deception. *The Stanford Encyclopedia of Philosophy*.

Martin, Adrienne. 2011. Hopes and Dreams. *Philosophy and Phenomenological Research* 83:1.

Maruta, Toshiko, Robert C. Colligan, Michael Malinchoc, et al. 2000. Optimists vs Pessimists: Survival Rate Among Medical Patients Over a 30-Year Period. *Mayo Clinic Proceedings* 75.

May, Larry. 2008. The Principle of Just Cause. In May and Crookston 2008.

May, Larry, and Emily Crookston, eds. 2008. *War: Essays in Political Philosophy*. Cambridge University Press.

Mead, George H. 1967. *Mind, Self, and Society from the Standpoint of a Social Behaviorist*. University of Chicago Press.

Moeller, Hans-Georg. 2004. *Daoism Explained: From the Dream of the Butterfly to the Fishnet Allegory*. Open Court.

Moore, M.A. 1997. *Placing Blame: A Theory of Criminal Law*. Oxford University Press.

Moseley, Alexander. 2003. *A Philosophy of War*. Algora.

Nietzsche, Friedrich. 1989 [1885]. *Beyond Good and Evil*. Vintage.

Nisbett, Richard and Cohen, Dov. 1996. *Culture of Honor: The Psychology of Violence in the South*. Westview Press.

Parfit, Derek. 2011. *On What Matters*. Oxford University Press.

Park, Hee Sun, Timothy Levine, Steven A. McCornack, Kelly Morrison, and Merissa Ferrara. 2002. How People Really Detect Lies. *Communication Monographs* 69.

Pattison, James. 2008. Just War Theory and the Privatization of Military Force. *Ethics and International Affairs* 22:2.

———. 2010. Deeper Objections to the Privatisation of Military Force. *Journal of Political Philosophy* 18:4.

———. 2014. *The Morality of Private War: The Challenge of Private Military Security Companies.* Oxford University Press.

Piven Jerry S. 2007. Terror, Sexual Arousal, and Torture: The Question of Obedience or Ecstasy among Perpetrators. *The Discourse of Sociological Practice* 8:1.

Plato. 1977. *Phaedo.* Hackett.

———. 1995. *Phaedrus.* Hackett.

———. 1997. *Complete Works.* Hackett.

Reichberg, Gregory M. 2008. Jus ad Bellum. In May and Crookston 2008.

Royce, Josiah. 1995 [1908]. *The Philosophy of Loyalty.* Vanderbilt University Press.

———. 2009. Football and Ideals. In *Race Questions, Provincialism, and Other American Problems.* Fordham University Press.

———. 2013 [1903]. *Pussycat Blackie's Travels: There's No Place Like Home.* Artemis.

Scanlon, Thomas. 1990. Promises and Practices. *Philosophy and Public Affairs* 19.

———. 2001. Promises and Contracts. In Peter Benson, ed., *The Theory of Contract Law.* Cambridge University Press.

Searle, John R. 1985. *Expression and Meaning: Studies in the Theory of Speech Acts.* Cambridge University Press.

Searle, John R., and D. Vanderveken. 1985. *Foundations of Illocutionary Logic.* Cambridge University Press.

Sommers, Tamler. 2009. The Two Faces of Revenge: Moral Responsibility and the Culture of Honor. *Biology and Philosophy* 24:1.

———. 2012. *Relative Justice: Cultural Diversity, Free Will, and Moral Responsibility.* Princeton University Press.

Stein, Ruth. 2009. *For Love of the Father: A Psychoanalytic Study of Religious Terrorism.* Stanford University Press.

Taylor, A.E. 2011. *Plato: The Man and His Work.* Dover.

Wittgenstein, Ludwig. 2009. *Philosophical Investigations.* Wiley-Blackwell.

Zhuangzi. 2009. *Zhuangzi: The Essential Writings, with Selections from Traditional Commentaries.* Hackett.

Zimbardo, Philip. 2002. *Violence Workers: Police Torturers and Murderers Reconstruct Brazilian Atrocities.* University of California Press.

———. 2007. *The Lucifer Effect: Understanding How Good People Turn Evil.* Random House.

Philosophers of Unusual Smarts

CHELSI BARNARD ARCHIBALD holds a Masters of Arts in English from Weber State University. She works in public relations by day and writes snarky television recaps by night for Socialite Life, a celebrity gossip blog. In her spare time, she practices swordsmanship, revenge, and starting wars with Guilder. Her couch companion is a rodent of unusual size named Fezzik who loves to cuddle while they both dine on shrieking eels.

RANDALL E. AUXIER typed this bio with his left hand, in order to go easy on readers who might disagree with it. He's not left-handed, of course, but he wishes he could swashbuckle that way. He has now switched to typing right-handed, but looking at the keyboard upside down. It isn't easy, but it helps him learn to think outside the . . . . oh what was it? You know, the *thing*. He writes silly articles and teaches philosophy at Southern Illinois University in Carbondale.

ADAM BARKMAN is an associate professor of philosophy and chair of the philosophy department at Redeemer University College. He is the author of five books, most recently *Making Sense of Islamic Art and Architecture* (2015), and the co-editor of four books on popular culture and philosophy, including *The Culture and Philosophy of Ridley Scott* (2013), which he co-edited with his Buttercup, Ashley Barkman, and *Downton Abbey and Philosophy* (2016), which he co-edited with Robert Arp.

DARCI DOLL was unemployed in Greenland when she met a Six-Fingered Man who introduced her to unsettling injustice. As a result she dedicated her life to pursuing philosophy. Having found that a life dedicated to philosophical revenge leaves much to be desired, she now imparts her pirate-based approach to philosophy to students at Delta College in Michigan as the Dread Pirate Doll.

CHARLENE ELSBY is an Assistant Professor at Indiana University–Purdue University Fort Wayne. She has drawn up the first map of the Fire Swamp by interpreting the realism of Aristotle's early work. When she's not battling the pesky ROUS that occasionally sneak into her lectures, Charlene researches the Ancients and integrates their metaphysics with the concept of intentional being.

DON FALLIS is a Professor of Information Resources and Adjunct Professor of Philosophy at the University of Arizona. His philosophical work includes the scholarly articles "What Is Lying?" and "What Is Disinformation?" Given his expertise in deception, you can clearly not choose the wine in front of you. But since he is used to spicy Sonoran food, Don may be counting on his strength to save him. So, clearly you cannot choose the wine in front of him.

JUSTIN FETTERMAN studied philosophy at Ohio Wesleyan University and creative writing at Emerson College. A writer and teacher in Boston, his work has recently appeared in *Midwestern Gothic* and *The Portland Review Online*. His stories and free time are filled with fencing, torture, revenge, giants, monsters, chases, escapes, true love, miracles, and some kissing parts.

TOBIAS T. GIBSON is an associate professor of Political Science and Security Studies at Westminster College, in Fulton, Missouri. While he has long wished he were a Spaniard, he discovered that it was much easier to be a Man in Black.

RICHARD GREENE is a Professor of Philosophy at Weber State University. He also serves as Executive Chair of the Intercollegiate Ethics Bowl. He's co-edited a number of books on pop culture and philosophy including *Girls and Philosophy: This Book Isn't a Metaphor for Anything* (2015), *Boardwalk Empire and Philosophy: Bootleg This Book* (2013), *Dexter and Philosophy: Mind over Spatter* (2011), and *The Sopranos and Philosophy: I Kill Therefore I Am* (2004). Richard keeps using that word. He does not think it means what he thinks it means.

LAURA K. GUIDRY-GRIMES is a Clinical Ethicist at MedStar Washington Hospital Center in Washington, DC. In addition to embarrassing pirates with her fencing skills, Laura consults with clinicians and patients on moral decisions and writes on vulnerability, disability, and modes of being in bioethics. She has contributed articles to *Psych and Philosophy: Some Dark Juju-Magumbo* (2013), *Journal of Clinical Ethics*, and *International Journal of Feminist Approaches to Bioethics*. She spends her free time counseling former damsels in distress on how to take control of their own happiness while still believing in true love.

DANIEL HAAS is an instructor of philosophy at Red Deer College, Red Deer, Canada. He has contributed chapters to *Anime and Philosophy*, *Dexter and Philosophy*, *Game of Thrones and Philosophy*, and *Supernatural and Philosophy*. His general approach to philosophical argument is to put the poison in both glasses whenever he's engaged in a game of wits with a logician.

JOSHUA HETER received his PhD in philosophy from Saint Louis University. Currently, he is an instructor at Iowa Western Community College. His interests include sword making, as well as consuming mutton, lettuce, and tomato sandwiches.

CLINT JONES earned his PhD from the University of Kentucky in 2013. He specializes in social theory and writes regularly on utopias and mythology. He has published numerous books and articles and has recently contributed chapters to *Justified and Philosophy: Shoot First, Think Later* and *The Devil and Philosophy: The Nature of His Game*. He has decided that academia and revenge have one thing in common: there's not much money in it unless you have your own pirate ship.

TIM JONES once read a chapter on *The Princess Bride* with a very similar title to the one with his name below it in this very book. He really liked it, except for all of the boring bits, and so decided to cut them all out so that you guys could get through it without falling asleep halfway. When he's not abusing the work of other writers, he teaches Literature at the University of East Anglia and is also an elected councilman for Norwich City Council.

TRISTAN KÄÄRID is a free-lance philosopher who still fights for true love. While he also believes this has little to do with his somewhat dormant love of professional wrestling, he could still learn a thing or two from Fezzik. One day he hopes to give a nice pile drive to the face of the Prince Humperdincks of the world.

ROB LUZECKY is a lecturer at Indiana University–Purdue University Fort Wayne. When he is not busy avoiding shrieking eels, he spends his free time contemplating whether or not things are inconceivable.

His research interests are aesthetics and realist approaches to miraculous entities like works of art.

JAMES EDWIN MAHON is a Professor of Philosophy and Chair of the Department of Philosophy at CUNY-Lehman College in the Bronx. Born and educated in Ireland, he first saw *The Princess Bride* as an undergraduate when it was screened by a student society at Trinity College Dublin, and takes great pride in the fact that some parts of the movie were shot in Ireland (the Cliffs of Insanity are actually the Cliffs of Moher). In writing this chapter he has fulfilled a lifelong wish to pay homage to this movie, the comedy that should have been Rob Reiner's last (sorry, Rob).

Hello. My name is DANIEL MALLOY. I teach philosophy at Appalachian State University. Prepare to learn. Hello! My name is Daniel Malloy! I teach philosophy at Appalachian State University! Prepare to learn! HELLO! MY NAME IS DANIEL MALLOY! I TEACH PHILOSOPHY AT APPALACHIAN STATE UNIVERITY! PREPARE TO LEARN!

ELIZABETH OLSEN studied economics and English at Oberlin College and received her MBA from the Wharton School. She currently holds a day job in finance, and she writes, travels and tries to hold chaos at bay in her free time. The writing and traveling is going well, the holding chaos at bay . . . not so much. So far, though, she has successfully avoided winding up on the Cliffs of Insanity *and* she has avoided any involvement in land wars in Asia.

JERRY S. PIVEN is steeped in evil, having two hippopotamic cats, a rabidly Reagan-loving relative, and a wife who shrieked "Dear God! What is that thing?" on their wedding night. He actually studied the Capo Ferro and Agrippa fencing styles once upon a time, but now spends his days in his own Zoo of Evil writing about inconceivable subjects and appeasing his true bewoved.

RACHEL ROBISON-GREENE is a PhD Candidate in Philosophy at UMass Amherst. She is co-editor of *The Golden Compass and Philosophy: God Bites the Dust* (2009), *Dexter and Philosophy: Mind over Spatter* (2011), *Girls and Philosophy: This Book Isn't a Metaphor for Anything* (2015), *and Orange Is the New Black and Philosophy: Last Exit from Litchfield* (2015). She has contributed chapters to *Quentin Tarantino and Philosophy*, *The Legend of Zelda and Philosophy*, *Zombies, Vampires, and Philosophy*, and *The Walking Dead and Philosophy*. Rachel is only mostly dead.

BRENDAN SHEA teaches philosophy at Rochester Community and Technical College in Rochester, Minnesota. In recent years, his research has focused on issues in the philosophy of science, applied ethics, and the history of philosophy. This is his tenth contribution to a volume on philosophy and popular culture. A student once told him that his lecturing style was "a bit like Vizzini, but in a good way."

CHARLES TALIAFERRO, Professor of Philosophy and Chair of the Department of Philosophy, St. Olaf College, is the author or editor of over twenty books and is the co-editor of the forthcoming six volume *The History of Evil.* While he has not been dead or only mostly dead, he is grateful to his friends (including co-author Elizabeth and two psychiatrists) who have (from time to time) been like Miracle Max.

JAMIE CARLIN WATSON is Assistant Professor of Philosophy and some-time pirate at Broward College in Ft. Lauderdale. When he is not smuggling iocane powder out of Australia, he writes on the nature of expertise and epistemic authority, especially in the fields of ethics and political philosophy. He has contributed to a number of popular culture and philosophy anthologies, including *Johnny Cash and Philosophy: The Burning Ring of Truth* (2008) and *The Catcher in the Rye and Philosophy: A Book for Bastards, Morons, and Madmen* (2012). He is also co-author of *What's Good on TV? Understanding Ethics through Television* (2011) and *Critical Thinking: An Introduction to Reasoning Well* (2015), both with Robert Arp.

IVAN WOLFE has actually gotten a crowd to part by yelling "Hey, everybody move!" (more than once). He competes (and sometimes wins) in Scottish Highland Games and has a PhD in Rhetoric from the University of Texas—Austin. He currently teaches at Arizona State University and spends summers in his hometown of Homer, Alaska. Despite extensive family history research, he has yet to find any ancestors from Florin or Guilder, but he refuses to give up hope.

WAYNE YUEN is the editor of *The Walking Dead and Philosophy: Zombie Apocalypse Now* (2012) and *The Ultimate Walking Dead and Philosophy* (2016), co-editor of *Neil Gaiman and Philosophy: Gods Gone Wild!* (2012), and contributor to several volumes in the Popular Culture and Philosophy series. He was educated in Florin, teaches at Ohlone College in Fremont, California, lives in San Jose, and vacations in Guilder. He is neither left- nor right-handed, which is not inconceivable but rather just indicates that he's clumsy.

Index

DOCTOR WHO

POLICE PUBLIC BOX

POLICE BOX

POLICE TELEPHONE
FREE
FOR USE OF
PUBLIC
ADVICE AND ASSISTANCE
OBTAINABLE IMMEDIATELY
OFFICERS AND CARS
RESPOND TO
URGENT CALLS
PULL TO OPEN

AND PHILOSOPHY
BIGGER ON THE INSIDE

EDITED BY COURTLAND LEWIS AND PAULA SMITHKA